Mature Students:
Entry to Higher Education

Mature Students:
Entry to Higher Education

A guide for students and advisers

Judith Bell
Shiela Hamilton
Gordon Roderick

Longman
London and New York

Longman Group UK Limited
Longman House, Burnt Mill, Harlow
Essex CM20 2JE, England
Associated companies throughout the world

*Published in the United States of America
by Longman Inc., New York*

© Longman Group UK Limited 1986

First published 1986

British Library Cataloguing in Publication Data
Bell, Judith, 1930–
Mature students: entry to higher education:
a guide for students and advisers.
1. Universities and Colleges——
Great Britain——Admission 2. Adult
education——Great Britain
I. Title   II. Hamilton, Shiela
III. Roderick, Gordon W.
378′.1056′0941   LB2351.4.G7
ISBN 0-582-49719-1

Library of Congress Cataloging in Publication Data
Bell, Judith, 1930–
Mature students, entry to higher education.
Bibliography: p.
Includes index.
1. Continuing education——Great Britain. 2. Adult
education——Great Britain. 3. Universities and colleges
——Great Britain——Admission. 4. Education, Higher——
Great Britain. I. Hamilton, Shiela, 1943–   . II. Roderick,
Gordon Wynne. III. Title.
LC5256.G7B385 1986   374′.973   86–2756
ISBN 0-582-49719-1 (pbk.)

Printed and bound in Great Britain
at The Bath Press, Avon

Contents

CONTENTS

CONTENTS

CONTENTS

Acknowledgements

We have been helped throughout the production of this book by the interest and hard work of colleagues and friends who were mature students themselves, or who have taught mature students over the years. We should like particularly to thank Eira Hughes, Open University tutor counsellor, for her work in connection with Chapter 10; to Sue Falla, Open University graduate and senior lecturer at Wigan College of Technology, for her contributions to Chapter 11; to Patricia Fiske, formerly of the South Manchester Educational Advisory Service, for her assistance with Chapter 6; to Margaret Barrow, another Open University graduate and librarian at the University of Manchester Institute of Science and Technology, for the preparation of the bibliography; to Dorothy Eagleson, president of the National Association of Educational Guidance Services and organiser of the Belfast Educational Guidance Service for Adults for advice about regulations and practices in Northern Ireland; to Ian Sinkinson, of the Student Awards Section of Manchester LEA, who read the draft of Chapter 10 and made a number of helpful suggestions; to members of the Association of Graduate Careers Advisory Services Working Party on the Training and Employment of the Older Graduate, for their generous sharing of information and expertise; to Letitia Opie, of the Manchester Educational Advisory Network, Ann Wood, higher education/adult co-ordinator at the Sheffield Careers Service, Ian McNay, lecturer in education management at the OU and Iris Price, yet another OU graduate and former president of the Open University Students' Association, who commented on the draft outline and suggested additional items; to Her Majesty's Stationery Office for permission to reproduce Inland Revenue leaflet IR47 (Crown copyright); to all the institutions of higher education who provided information relating to the admittance of mature students (presented in Part Two); to colleagues in the north west region of the OU, who provided not only moral, but also practical support – and to the many friends who saw scripts, offered advice, pointed out omissions or errors, checked addresses, references, proofs and facts, our grateful thanks.

Judith Bell
Shiela Hamilton
Gordon Roderick

Introduction

This book concentrates mainly on opportunities for study at degree level for mature students, though information about diploma and certain degree-equivalent courses is also provided. It provides information about what opportunities exist, how to set about applying and preparing for study at degree level and about pitfalls which might be avoided with a little care and perseverance. Addresses of individuals and organisations are provided, from whom further information about various specialist areas may be obtained and a bibliography of materials relating to mature student study and opportunities gives ample scope for further reading and study.

A major problem for any adult wishing to study is not that there are so few opportunities, but that there are so many. Finding out what is available and where, knowing about grants and sponsorship, weighing up alternatives – all require a knowledge of the educational system which few people have.

Adults contemplating a course of higher education need to understand the difference between the numerous courses offered at universities, polytechnics, Scottish central institutions, colleges/institutes of higher education, colleges of education and colleges of technology, and the different functions of these institutions. They need to analyse the advantages and disadvantages of different types of provision, to consider whether there is any likelihood of a job at the end of the course and to explore sources of funding. Even more important is the need to weigh up chances of success. Is there any point in applying to

Cambridge or would it be better to apply . . . somewhere else? Is there really a chance of getting into a medical school, or would it be more realistic to consider another field of study?

Folklore abounds. It is assumed that grants will not be available for older people, that A levels are always required for admission to degree courses, that the older we get the less capable of serious study we become. Well, some of us may become less capable the older we become. Some adults won't get a grant for a whole variety of reasons and some institutions and departments will demand A levels at specified grades. But applicants and advisers need to be sure of the facts before making any decisions.

Mistakes made in choice of course can sometimes have far-reaching effects. Incorrect or incomplete information given to enquirers by receptionists at colleges, Job Centres, local authority offices or by friends and relations can so discourage potential students that they may abandon the idea of studying completely, or, even worse, they may find themselves on an unsuitable course.

Often adults find their way on to a course because they 'just happen' to talk to someone who tells them about a course or training scheme. These chance encounters can play a significant part in many people's lives but committing oneself to a course of study that can last anything from three to eight years requires serious consideration. Such decisions should not have to depend on chance encounters.

Applying for a place in higher education is not merely a matter of filling in a form and hoping for the best. It requires planning and preparation. We trust the following pages will provide sufficient information to enable potential adult students to make reasoned decisions about their educational future and to give themselves the best chance of success; but we also hope it will be equally useful for those people who work in information, careers and educational guidance services, in libraries, in colleges and adult centres, who find themselves in the position of being asked for information and guidance about opportunities for study in higher education.

PART ONE

Mature Students: Introduction to courses, degrees, information, applications and finance

Chapter 1

Mature students and higher education

When is a mature student mature?

There appears to be general agreement that a mature student is someone who has had a significant break from formal study between leaving school and embarking on a new programme of study – but there the agreement ends. Different institutions, organisations and individuals have different views about the age at which we become 'mature'. The Scottish universities and the University of Wales adopt 23 as the age at which a student is deemed to be mature (and so able to take advantage of non-standard entry procedures). In English universities the minimum age ranges from 19–26. The Council for National Academic Awards (CNAA), which validates most degree courses in polytechnics, colleges/institutes of higher education and Scottish central institutions, adopts 21 as the age of maturity. Until recently, the minimum age at which students could be admitted to the Open University was 21 and there is no upper age limit. We shall be discussing the special role of the Open University in Chapter 5 but this chapter concentrates on the 'traditional' institutions which were set up with school leavers in mind.

With the exception of medicine and some professions supplementary to medicine, age is not these days generally regarded as being a major disadvantage and most institutions are at least willing to consider applications from mature students. In fact, as apparent from the encouraging tone of many of the extracts in the 'Access to Higher Education' section in Part II of this book, many institutions positively welcome mature students.

5

There are at present over 20,000 mature students on full-time degree courses and over 92,000 on part-time courses. A third of non-university and approximately 10 per cent of university students are mature. There have always been small numbers of adults who found their way on to degree courses, but demand from adults now, though not comparable with demand from 18-year-olds, is certainly more than the trickle of 20 years ago.

So, what chance do mature applicants have of obtaining a place on a degree course, particularly at a time when demand from 18-year-old students is greater than it has ever been?

Chances of getting a place: the numbers game

At first sight the position is not encouraging. In July 1981, universities suffered on average a 15 per cent cutback (it was as high as 34 per cent in one university) and this was quickly followed by an announcement that there would be a 16 per cent cut in public sector funding. Altogether, some 20,000 places were lost in the universities and some 24,000 in polytechnics and colleges in the two-year period up to 1983/84. At one stage the Department of Education and Science (DES) predicted a fall in demand for higher education of between 14 and 19 per cent by the mid-1990s because of demographic changes (the next 10 years or more will see a steady fall in the 18+ client group for higher education). However, a Royal Statistical Society Working Party has pin-pointed a number of factors as being likely to lead to an increase in demand, namely occupational mobility, information technology, changes in job structure, the need for skilled manpower, female emancipation and most significantly increasing demand from adults.

Whether demand for higher education decreases or increases remains to be seen. If demand does fall, then it might be assumed that opportunities might be made available to new kinds of students, but a recent statement of the Government's Expenditure Plans (Cmnd 9143 II) makes clear that, at least until 1987, the government's policy is to reduce expenditure rather than to increase access. In 1985, Peter Brooke, Under-secretary for Higher Education, argued that it was not acceptable to make up the expected fall in demand for places with 'just any kinds of students'. He identified quality and efficiency as the cornerstone of ministerial judgement. 'The scope for other participation,' he stated, 'would need to be examined in the light of the absolute needs of the country for skilled manpower'.

However those needs are measured, it is a sad fact that at

present the proportion of the 18+ age group in higher education is smaller in the United Kingdom than in most other developed countries. At about 11 per cent, it is much lower than in Germany (19%), Japan (39%) and the USA (42%). Although the chances of getting in to any higher education institution will inevitably deteriorate as a result of these cuts, getting into university is likely to be most difficult of all. In 1977, 1979 and 1981 the numbers of home applicants for undergraduate places were respectively 132,000, 142,000 and 149,000. The numbers of accepted students were 71,000, 77,000 and 74,000 respectively. By 1983 the number of applicants had increased to 157,000 but only 69,000 were accepted. In 1977 there were 1.8 candidates for each place, in 1979 1.84 and in 1981 there were 2.0. By 1983 the position had deteriorated to one where there were 2.3 candidates for each place. Between 1977 and 1983 there were 25,000 additional candidates for 2,000 fewer places.

Applications from conventional age home candidates increased by over 30 per cent between 1975 and 1985 but demand from women and from mature applicants increased at an even faster rate. In this period there was a 39 per cent increase in demand from mature applicants, and whilst the demand from women under 21 grew by 50 per cent, that from mature women applicants increased by 66 per cent. Demand is undoubtedly buoyant, but not all those who apply are accepted.

Thirty-six per cent of mature candidates were accepted in 1983 compared with 45 per cent of young students. (The women mature applicants were generally more successful – 39 per cent of women were accepted compared with 34 per cent of men.) Perhaps surprisingly, the over-30s did better than the under-30s: 42 per cent of this age group were successful in their application. Students over 50 fared less well, but in 1983, of the 5,570 mature students accepted by universities, 1,532 were over the age of 30 and 417 over the age of 40.

Subject choice and chances of acceptance

The eight subjects most in demand among conventional age students in universities in order of popularity are medicine, law, mathematics, English, modern languages, electrical engineering, geography and history, although accountancy, business, management and computer studies have been increasing very rapidly in popularity in recent years. Choices made by mature students generally follow similar lines though sociology replaces modern languages in the first six most popular subjects.

In general as might be expected, the greater the demand from

7

students, the harder it is to get a place. A crude measure of 'chance of acceptance' can be taken to be the number of students accepted for a subject divided by the number applying for a place in that subject. On such a measure medicine comes bottom of the list, closely followed by law, English, electrical engineering, mathematics and accountancy. In 1983, 42 per cent of the conventional age applicants for medicine succeeded in gaining a place, but the proportion for mature applicants was only 15 per cent – and substantial numbers of those who were accepted already had a degree in the biological sciences. In law, the respective figures for conventional and mature students were 43 per cent and 23 per cent.

The best chances of success for conventional students were in metallurgy, chemistry, physics, botany, modern languages, mining and theology, where the majority of qualified applicants succeeded in obtaining a place. Mature applicants appear to have the best chance of being accepted in theology, chemistry, mining, metallurgy and physics in that order, but chances are also good in sociology, philosophy, archaeology and modern languages.

Fashions change of course, but it seems likely that demand will continue to be high for medicine, dentistry, law, electrical engineering, mathematics and English, for the foreseeable future.

On the basis of these figures, students thinking of applying for a place in medicine or dentistry but with doubts as to whether they can achieve the high grades required might well be advised to consider chemistry, physics, botany, zoology or biochemistry as possible alternatives, where the chances of acceptance are very much better. The same kind of considerations which apply in medicine can also be held to apply to other subject areas. Some applicants for English, for instance, might be well advised to apply to read history, geography, archaeology or modern languages. Likewise, some students applying for mathematics might be diverted to chemistry or physics, students of law to government and public administration, and students of civil, mechanical and electrical engineering to mining and metallurgy. The problem is of course that many applicants have a commitment to a subject and/or a career and feel that a second choice will not be good enough. In the end, you have to decide whether to risk applying for a high-demand course or to settle for a different subject.

Qualification and chances of acceptance

Over 90 per cent of conventional age students applying to universities have two or more 'A' levels (or Scottish Highers) compared with only 51 per cent of mature students. The 'A'-level grades demanded by departments depend on the institution, the subject, and the views of individual admissions tutors.

In 1983, over half the accepted candidates had an 'A'-level score of 9+ (calculated on the basis of A = 5 points, B = 4, C = 3, D = 2 and E = 1 point), so a score of 9 would be CCC or AB or BCD or ADD. Of those accepted on the basis of 'A' levels, 31 had a score of 13+ (i.e. at least AAC or ABB), but the 'A'-level grades of accepted students varied markedly from one subject to another. Very few places are available for veterinary science and as a result required grades are high. Of accepted veterinary science students 87.5 per cent had a score of 13+. Of the 3,770 candidates accepted for medicine in 1983, 62 per cent had a score of 13 or over (in 1980 it was 54 per cent – a measure of how things are getting harder).

Medicine and veterinary studies are exceptional but not unique. Departments of classical studies, law and English also attract high fliers. Not all institutions and subjects require such high grades however, and the situation can change from year to year. Generally speaking, the polytechnics and colleges have not in the past required such high entry qualifications, though the position is evening out somewhat now and as can be seen from the extracts in the 'Access to Higher Education' section in Part Two, many institutions will consider mature applicants who do not have the normal 'A'-level requirements. One-in-five mature students enter university and one-in-four enter polytechnics on the basis of having Ordinary or Higher National Certificates/Diplomas, Business and Technician Education Council (BTEC) Certificates/ Diplomas or similar qualifications. Others gain admission by virtue of having nursing, teaching or police qualifications or by means of special schemes for mature applicants.

The picture which emerges from a study of statistics relating to admissions indicates that in spite of cutbacks and increasing applications from conventional age and mature candidates, opportunities are still available and mature applicants are still being offered places on degree courses. Chances of being offered a place are less good in some subjects than others and it is sensible to study the admissions statistics before finally deciding which subject/s to select. Study of statistics alone appears to indicate that mature applicants have a slightly less good chance of acceptance than conventional age candidates, but discussion with admissions tutors indicates that the figures may not reveal the full story. A significant proportion of mature applicants withdraw their application at some stage, possibly because they get a job which seems to offer good prospects, possibly because they find they are unable to get a grant, or for any number of other reasons. Some candidates can provide no evidence of recent study or present their case so badly that they are immediately rejected. 'Serious' mature applicants appear to have a good chance of being offered a place in most areas of study. It is a case of weighing up the position in a realistic way – of balancing hopes against hard facts. To give yourself the best chance of success, it is important to know the sort of grades certain departments demand, to know which type of institution, which subject and which mode of study is likely to be best for you.

Getting a place is the first stage in the process, but it is only the beginning. The aim, of course, is to get a degree, so it is worth giving some thought to your chance of success on the evidence of those mature students who have already completed a degree course. The following chapter discusses some of the evidence relating to the performance of mature students on degree courses.

Chapter 2

The degree performance of mature students

A good many researchers have studied the degree performance of mature students and tried to come to some firm conclusions as to whether mature students perform better or worse than conventional age students in their degree examinations. Results vary and what appears to be proved in one study is sometimes contradicted by another. However, some interesting trends do emerge and the available evidence provides encouraging support to the view that mature students can, and do, perform well on degree courses in most subjects. The success of mature students in arts and social sciences has been noted in a number of studies. Hopper and Osborn (1975) reported a survey of students on degree courses at the London School of Economics and at Reading University. Their evidence suggested that at LSE, adult students did just as well as 18-year-old school leavers and at Reading they did much better.

The University of Sussex pilot scheme designed to admit a number of adults who left school early, but who appeared to be graduate material, demonstrated again that mature students succeeded in arts and social sciences, though they were less successful in science and technology. Other studies report similar findings.

Walker (1975), in his investigation of mature undergraduates at the University of Warwick, discovered that mature students obtained significantly better degrees than non-mature students overall and performed particularly well on arts courses. Interestingly enough, Walker's study revealed that those mature students who had entered university without satisfying the general entrance requirement performed better than those who entered with the normal 'A' level qualifications.

Research carried out by the CNAA found that 'non-traditional' graduates of polytechnics and colleges also performed significantly better than those who entered higher education after 'A' levels. At a conference in 1984, a CNAA assistant registrar reported that 10 per cent of a sample of 3,000 CNAA graduates had 'non-standard' qualifications on entry to their course, 42.5 per cent of whom gained upper seconds or better, compared with 31.9 per cent of standard students.

A study carried out at Lancaster University in 1975 found that 12 per cent of mature students obtained first-class degrees compared with 4 per cent of conventional age students and that 45 per cent obtained upper seconds compared with 30 per cent of school-leaver students. A follow up to this study (Ward and Lucas 1985) confirmed the earlier results and noted that mature students did consistently better than conventional age students in the humanities and social sciences but once again performed worse in sciences, computer studies and mathematics. Even so, over the three years on which the research was based (1978–80) no fewer than 52 per cent of mature students obtained first or upper second class degrees compared to 33 per cent of their younger contemporaries.

Not all studies have produced such encouraging evidence. Nisbet and Welsh (1972) in their study of 177 mature under-graduates at the University of Aberdeen discovered no significant difference between mature and younger students. They con-cluded that the category of 'mature student' was too heterogeneous to draw firm conclusions.

A disturbing aspect of recent studies by Roderick and Bell (1981) and Roderick, Bell and Hamilton (1982) is that a higher proportion of mature students (and particularly those mature students who did not have 'A' levels on entry) dropped out at some stage, generally for non-academic reasons, but occasionally because they were not reaching the required standards. However, a recent study of university statistics carried out by Woodley (1985) indicates that drop-out of mature students was only 4 per cent higher than that of conventional age students. He reports that 83 per cent of mature students who entered universities in 1972, 1973 and 1974 graduated, compared with 87 per cent of conventional age students. Evidence does sometimes conflict, but the main findings in Woodley's (1985) study tend to confirm earlier surveys of British university mature students. Very few systematic studies of mature student performance have been conducted in polytechnics and colleges and so, inevitably, the evidence presented here concentrates on universities. Woodley's analysis suggests that:

1. Mature students are slightly more likely to leave university without a degree, though, as has been indicated above, the difference is small.
2. Mature students are just as likely to gain a first or upper second as conventional age students. Students in the 26–30 age range achieved the best results, though Woodley acknowledges that the relationship between age and performance is not a simple linear one, and performance will inevitably be influenced by sex, subject studied, entry qualifications and, no doubt, numerous other variables.
3. In arts and social sciences, life experience appears to have a positive effect on study, but the reverse appears to be the case in science.
4. Women students gain better degrees than men in all age groups, except the 18-year-olds. Any number of reasons can be offered for this. Woodley suggests 'one possible explanation might be that women returning to study are of a higher academic calibre than men. Boys are nearly twice as likely to enter university on leaving school and therefore there must be proportionately more highly intelligent girls who are excluded at this stage'.

Woodley concludes by saying

In terms of policy-making the present findings would suggest that universities should have few qualms about increasing their mature student intakes. As a group they perform as well as younger students and women and those aged twenty-six to thirty are particularly successful. The only problem area would seem to be in science subjects, where mature students are more likely to fail and less likely to gain a good degree.

Perhaps the problem with science, technology and related subjects lies in the fact that a knowledge base is assumed and mature students may have forgotten a lot of what they learned at school, or have prepared inadequately. The message appears to be clear. Life experience may be a positive factor in arts and social sciences, but not in science where thorough preparation is essential if a mature student is to succeed on a degree course. Though much work needs to be done in studying the relationship between age, subject studied, sex and entry qualifications, it appears that age itself does not constitute a significant barrier to learning.

The situation is complex, but mature applicants to higher education can be encouraged by the research evidence.

Chapter 3

What's in a name?
Types of degree course

Assumptions are often made in prospectuses and careers publications, and terms are used which may not always be familiar to readers. Before we begin to discuss courses and institutions, it will be worth spending some time on definitions and explanations of certain terms and expressions.

This book is concerned mainly with first degrees – called bachelors' degrees – most of which last for three or four years full time or considerably longer part time. Students on these first degree courses are called **undergraduates**. When undergraduates have passed all their examinations, they become **graduates**, and a very small proportion of all graduates continue to **postgraduate** study and aim for higher degrees at masters' or doctoral level.

First degrees are either honours or ordinary (sometimes called pass or general) and in England, Wales and Northern Ireland are usually either bachelor of arts (BA), or bachelor of science (BSc), but there are a number of variations. Architects can graduate with a BArch, some engineers will leave with a BSc, others with a BEng or BTech. Law students are awarded bachelor of laws (LLB) degrees in some universities, and some music students end with a BMus. Oxford, Cambridge and the Scottish universities are out of step with the others and with each other, to the extent that all first degrees at Oxford and Cambridge are BAs and many Scottish first degrees are MAs. To be fair though, Oxford, Cambridge and the older Scottish universities were the first on the scene – by several centuries in fact – so it could be said that it is the newer universities that are out of step, rather than the other way round.

If you are thinking of becoming a teacher, you may probably be aware of the fact that at one time it was possible to become a qualified teacher by obtaining a certificate of education. Certificate courses have now been phased out, and since 1980 student teachers have been required to take a degree – either a bachelor of education (BEd) degree, or a degree in the subject or subjects of their choice followed by a postgraduate certificate of education (PGCE).

Whatever the name, a first degree serves much the same purpose, and requires much the same amount of time and effort. External examiners, and the validating bodies for the polytechnics, central institutions and colleges, do their best to ensure that equivalent standards are achieved across the higher education sector, and although there are inevitably differences in content and structure, a bachelor's degree from any United Kingdom institution of higher education will generally be acceptable for admission to courses of postgraduate training, provided the required degree classification has been achieved.

Degree structure

There are many different types of bachelors' degrees which can be structured in a number of different ways. For *single honours*, the main subject is studied throughout the course, although subsidiary subjects are often also required. In a *joint honours* course two subjects are studied in depth throughout the course, although students are not normally expected to do twice as much work as would be required in a single honours degree. *General* (sometimes called pass) degrees usually involve study of several subjects in less depth than would be required for honours.

The structure and form of degrees varies greatly. Courses may be classified as *multidisciplinary, interdisciplinary, combined modular,* or *sandwich. Multidisciplinary, interdisciplinary* or *combined* courses can and often do cross the usual faculty and discipline boundaries, but the quality of such courses does vary. At best, they provide students with an educationally coherent and stimulating course, but at worst they can have the appearance of a mixed bag of unrelated subjects.

Some degree courses start with a *foundation year*, in which students are given a chance to sample a variety of subjects before having to narrow down their studies later on in the course. Some institutions have broad foundation years for all first year students, which allow students to defer a decision about an honours subject; others have a few terms during which the number of subjects studied is fairly large, but related to each other and to the final area of specialisation.

Combined degrees and degrees which delay the choice of

15

specialisation have the advantage that students can gain experience of different disciplines before committing themselves to a final choice. However, what is gained in breadth of study must be at the expense of depth and students with a deep interest in a particular subject may find this approach unacceptable. Sometimes, subjects offered under a combined degree are taught in isolation from each other. This may be a deliberate plan, but it may also be the result of a lack of planning and collaboration between the departments responsible for mounting the course.

A different approach again is the *modular* structure. The usual pattern for modular courses is one of a foundation year followed by study of many different course 'modules' within several subject areas. Modular courses have a flexibility about them which enables students to put together subjects or parts of subjects in various combinations to reflect their developing interests, abilities and experiences. This system has been used very successfully by the Open University. One criticism of modular schemes is that students can end up with a hotch-potch degree of unrelated subjects that is of little use on the job market. The 'supermarket approach', where students lift courses off the academic shelves on impulse, is easy to criticise, but in practice few students have such varied interests and so little thought for the end product that they end up with a useless degree, and all institutions will offer guidance about suitable groupings of subjects. The advantage of modular schemes is that all students are not obliged to follow the same course, and the element of choice is likely to provide courses which will suit the individual student's abilities and interests.

The most unusual form of modular course is the *Independent Study* format pioneered by the North East London Polytechnic (NELP). Here the students have a considerable degree of choice and flexibility in designing their own course, with guidance from academic staff. This approach is usually more attractive to adult students who sometimes find the constraints of a highly structured course restrictive. The NELP Independent Study students are recruited on to a *Diploma in Higher Education* course, which is a qualification in its own right, but which is in practice generally used as the first half of a degree course. At one time it seemed as though the DipHE would become a common way of starting degree study, but its popularity has waned in recent years, possibly because the universities were not generally very interested in building DipHEs into their degree provision. The NELP Independent Study initiative registers students for a two-year DipHE and most of those who succeed on the diploma continue with their degree. One major problem is that the DipHE is a two-year course, and although institutions offering the course will usually make arrangements for their students to continue to final degree courses, other institutions generally require two further years of study at least, so that students who could have graduated in three years have to take four or even five years to complete the degree course. Even so, some of the courses are interesting and innovative, and as long as you are aware of possible problems of transfer and degree completion, they are certainly worth considering.

Sandwich courses take a variety of forms, but the essential common element is that a part of the course will be devoted to work/practical experience which is directly related to the discipline being studied. As a result, sandwich degree courses take longer to complete but students have the advantage of first-hand industrial or business experience which should stand them in good stead when they look for jobs. They are usually four years in length (five in Scotland), and the way in which the academic part of the course is combined with the work experience falls into two main patterns. In **thick sandwich** courses you will usually spend two academic years at college followed by a full calendar year of supervised work experience with a final academic year back at college. A **thin sandwich** has shorter periods of work experience alternating with periods of study.

There are different types of arrangement for sandwich courses, and if a course of this kind is of interest, you should consult the college of your choice, to see what is on offer and what qualifications would be required. Some students are sponsored by firms and receive a small salary for the period of the course. The best of these schemes provide first-rate work experience, with a good chance of a permanent job at the end of the course. The disadvantage is that holidays are much shorter than full-time undergraduates would enjoy, but sponsored places are keenly contested and successful applicants appear to be perfectly willing to return to work at the end of the university or polytechnic term rather than to go home, or find a job elsewhere. See Chapter 10 for more information about sponsorship.

Degree classification

General degrees are not normally classified: you either pass or fail. However, all honours degrees, whatever the structure and length, have a final classification which varies slightly from institution to institution but which is generally graded as first class, second class (often divided into upper second (or II i) and lower second (or II ii), third class, or pass. Oxford differs from most universities by having first, second, third and fourth class degrees.

Degree classifications are important, as they are invariably taken

17

into account in applications for postgraduate courses and can even make the difference between being offered an interview for a job or not.

Scotland

First degrees in Scotland are sufficiently different from the rest of the UK to merit a separate section. The major difference arises because they are designed to cater for school leavers who hold Scottish Certificate of Education (SCE) qualifications. These are normally obtained at the age of 17+ and though many students remain at school for a further year, there is nothing to stop them beginning their university career a year earlier than would be general elsewhere in the UK. That means that teaching begins at a point which assumes knowledge to SCE higher grade only and English 'A'-level holders may find themselves marking time in their first year. On the other hand, this extra year can serve as a very useful period of consolidation and many 'A'-level candidates have welcomed the opportunity to broaden their reading.

Scottish honours degrees last four years (compared with three years for many other UK degrees), mainly to take account of the 17+ entry. In the Universities of Aberdeen, Edinburgh, Glasgow, St Andrews and Dundee, students are admitted on a faculty rather than a departmental basis and in most cases this means that students can sample a range of subjects before finally deciding where to specialise, in much the same way as students on foundation courses in the Open University and certain other non-Scottish universities.

All institutions will have their own special requirements and peculiarities of course and the only way to find out exactly what is on offer is to obtain the prospectus and to check with the department or faculty of your choice.

The validation and award of degrees

All universities are empowered to award their own degrees under the terms of their Charter. The staff of the university set and mark the examination papers and standards are maintained and controls established by means of a comprehensive system of external examiners and assessors.

Polytechnics and colleges and institutes of higher education do not at present grant their own degrees, though discussions are taking place which may lead to changes in methods of validation. Their degree courses are validated in some cases by nearby universities but in the great majority of cases, by the Council for National Academic Awards, and degrees are awarded by that body. The CNAA, founded by Royal Charter in 1964, is the largest single degree-awarding body in the United Kingdom. CNAA degrees are comparable in standard to those awarded in universities and are recognised as such by employers, professional institutes and by the universities themselves for purposes of entry to professional membership or to higher degrees.

If degrees awarded in different institutions are comparable in standard, then decisions about where to study will centre around the type of course, the subject, location, the mode of study and, of course, the type of institution that seems to be best suited to your purposes.

Chapter 4

Where to take a degree: who provides what?

Degree courses are provided in institutions of higher education – that is, universities, polytechnics, colleges/institutes of higher education, some colleges of education, Scottish central institutions and a few colleges of technology (which are also sometimes called institutes of technology or technical colleges). It is even possible to study for a degree entirely by correspondence, though this route is lengthy and arduous and only the most committed students succeed.

The universities are said to belong to the independent sector and most of the remainder of higher education institutions to the public sector. Most receive the majority of their income from central government in one form or another, though funding is complex and there are many variations. With the exception of the University of Buckingham, which is self financing, and the Open University, which receives its grant direct from the DES, universities in the United Kingdom receive their funding via the University Grants Committee, though many have additional income from investments, endowments and from research and other contracts. Local education authorities control most public sector institutions in England and Wales and allocate resources from funds supplied by central government and from the local rates. Methods of allocating resources vary in different parts of the country. Eleven of the fourteen Scottish central institutions are financed directly by the Scottish Education Department (SED) and the Department of Education in Northern Ireland (DENI) takes responsibility for funding the colleges of education in Northern

Ireland. The churches retain a significant financial involvement in the various denominational colleges and increasingly, all institutions of higher education are looking to outside bodies for additional income. Higher education is costly and institutions are becoming more and more cost conscious as grants are cut and increasing numbers apply for the available places.

Universities

There are forty-nine universities in the United Kingdom from which to choose, each one having a character and ethos of its own. Oxford and Cambridge have been in existence for several centuries and have the longest and possibly the most firmly held traditions. They are both based on some twenty or so individual colleges whose students are for the most part in residence. The majority of these colleges are now mixed, though a handful of single-sex colleges remain.

Most universities have between 5,000 and 10,000 students. London, which by British standards is very large (40,000 or so students), is an early-nineteenth-century creation and is a loose federation of many colleges among which University College, King's College and Imperial College are the largest. Then there are the civic colleges or so-called redbrick universities of the late nineteenth century set in industrial towns and cities, like Manchester, Liverpool, Leeds, Birmingham and Sheffield. Universities which began life as university colleges in the late nineteenth and early twentieth century but which did not receive university charters until later in the twentieth century include Nottingham, Leicester and Southampton. Then there are the mainly post-war institutions which were either established as new universities, usually in rural areas, as is the case with Keele, Sussex and Kent, or the universities which began life as technical institutions, became colleges of advanced technology and finally acquired university status – like Salford, Aston and Brunel.

Scotland has eight universities – the four ancient foundations of Aberdeen, Edinburgh, Glasgow and St Andrews, and the four newer institutions of Dundee, Heriot-Watt, Strathclyde and Stirling. Wales has a single university comprising a number of federated colleges – Aberystwyth, Bangor, Cardiff, Swansea, the University of Wales Institute of Science and Technology (UWIST) and Lampeter. Northern Ireland has two – Queen's College, Belfast, and the University of Ulster (newly established from the New University of Ulster at Coleraine and Ulster Polytechnic).

Universities, which were the first in the degree-awarding field, have always laid stress on the development of the mind and the broadening of intellectual horizons. They have traditionally embraced a philosophy of 'liberal education' which can loosely be defined as learning a subject for its own sake regardless of any material or vocational advantage or gain to the learner. In modern languages, for instance, the emphasis has traditionally been on the literatures rather than on the languages themselves, though some of the new universities have broken away from this tradition and established courses more relevant to commercial and industrial life and established courses in which a language is linked with business studies or with economics. Likewise, in the social sciences and pure sciences. In practice, universities have for centuries been in the business of training people – for law, medicine and more recently for engineering and modern technologies. Nevertheless, they still claim they are as concerned to develop and broaden the minds of students as they are to train them in vocational and technical skills related to jobs and careers. The older and more traditional the university the stronger is this philosophy held, but to an extent this spirit pervades the whole higher education system.

Universities vary widely in their traditions and attitudes, but all offer a great variety of courses, most of which fall within well-established faculty groups – arts and humanities, social sciences, pure sciences, engineering and technology, law, architecture, medicine, dentistry and veterinary studies. (Some 70 per cent of students currently studying at United Kingdom universities are found in the first three groups.)

Each has a character of its own – traditional and collegiate, like Oxford, Cambridge and Durham, or a federated college structure like London. Some are in urban surroundings, others are rural. Some are in a campus setting with extensive grounds, others part of the town in which they are located. Whatever the environment and character, all universities have a Students' Union, medical services, a careers and appointments service, good facilities for study and recreation, a good supply of halls of residence and generally excellent libraries.

The Open University (OU) is the only university which does not quite fit into this pattern. Devised from the outset for mature students, it conforms to the academic standards of other similar institutions, but is structured on very different lines. There is more about the OU in Chapter 5.

Polytechnics

The thirty polytechnics in the United Kingdom came into being in the 1970s, though most were established from existing technological institutions or amalgamations of various colleges, some of which had been in existence for many years. They provide full-time, sandwich and part-time courses at degree and sub-degree levels in a wide range of subjects. Originally, it was anticipated that the polytechnics would provide courses that were more related to the needs of industry and commerce than was the case with the universities. They have certainly provided many vocationally relevant courses, but have also developed what might be called traditional university-type courses in the arts and humanities. In all thirty polytechnics, the range of courses offered is very wide.

Subjects range from accountancy to visual communication and, in addition to the conventional subject groupings, include more unusual areas of study such as creative and performing arts, European studies, dietetics, fashion, graphic design, home economics, information science, jewellery, knitwear design, land administration, media studies, naval architecture, occupational hygiene, polymer science and technology, quantity surveying, speech therapy, theatre design and urban and estate surveying. Narrow and broad, cultural and vocational: the list is endless.

Courses at polytechnics are generally organised on a faculty basis, just as they are at universities. At Sheffield City Polytechnic, for instance, there are faculties of art and design (comprising communication arts, painting and paintmaking, sculpture, design and history of art); business and management studies (comprising accountancy and company administration, economics and business studies, hotel and catering studies, professional studies, physical education and human movement studies, education management, in-service education and education services); engineering (building, civil engineering, electrical and electronic engineering, mechanical and production engineering); humanities (communication studies, English, history, modern languages, music); and science (applied physics, biological sciences, chemistry, computer science).

The content of polytechnic courses is individual to the polytechnic, as is the case with the universities, so you will need to send for the latest prospectus to be sure of what is on offer. Many polytechnic courses are designed to suit the needs of industry, commerce and the professions, and in some instances professional bodies recognise courses as being of a standard sufficient to afford exemption from the relevant professional examinations. If you are interested in professional exemptions (for example for accountancy, social work or engineering), you should enquire from the appropriate department before you commit yourself.

Because of their commitment to the needs of industry and commerce, polytechnics not only offer more vocationally-oriented degrees, they also offer more part-time degrees. If you are an adult and

23

are confined geographically to the area in which you now live either for domestic or work reasons you may well find that your local polytechnic provides a degree in a subject relevant to your interests.

Polytechnics generally provide the same range of student services as are found in universities – halls of residence, a health service, a careers and appointments service, Students' Union and sporting facilities, but although there has been extensive building in recent years, in some polytechnics facilities are not quite as good as in universities, probably because in most cases the universities have been in existence longer and so have a head start, and also because until recently the universities had more generous funding from central government. If sporting facilities are important to you, or if you feel it is imperative you should live in a hall of residence, then you should ask what the position is – if possible, before you make a formal application. If that is not possible, make sure you have a good look round when you attend for interview, and ask students for their opinions. The consumer view will usually give you a realistic picture of life as it is as opposed to life as presented in a glossy prospectus.

If you think you might be interested in studying at a polytechnic, start reading about what is available. The Committee of Directors of Polytechnics have produced two excellent guides: *Polytechnic Courses Handbook*, and a free leaflet *The Polytechnics*, obtainable from The Secretary, Committee of Directors of Polytechnics, 309 Regent Street, London W1R 7PE.

The CNAA produce an excellent *Directory of First Degree Courses* and, of particular interest to mature students, a leaflet entitled *Opportunities in Higher Education for Mature Students* – both free of charge from CNAA, 344–354 Gray's Inn Road, London WC1X

Colleges and institutes of higher education

There are over sixty colleges or institutes of higher education, most of which were originally colleges of education specialising in teacher training, or amalgamations of colleges of education and other institutions. They tend to be smaller than polytechnics and universities, though the range is very wide – from the Charlotte Mason College of Education in Ambleside, which has only 300 students and only one degree, namely a BEd, to colleges like the Chelmer Institute of Higher Education in Essex, which has 1,250 full-time and 6,300 part-time students and a range of BEd, BA and BSc courses.

The larger colleges provide degree courses, diplomas, professional courses of various kinds and in some cases a range of short, non-examination courses, but a major role in most cases continues to be in the area of teacher training, in spite of recent severe reductions in the number of teacher-training places available. The degree courses not specifically geared to education tend to be in areas like creative arts, combined studies, social studies, humanities and environmental studies. One advantage of the colleges and institutes for students unable or unwilling to leave home is that there are more of them than universities and polytechnics, so there is a better chance of finding one within travelling distance of home. One problem is that they tend to concentrate on the arts and social sciences, so if you are interested in science or technology you may have to look elsewhere. However, there is a great variety on offer, from history of art to law. As in the case of the universities and polytechnics, the only way to find out what a college/institute is offering at any particular time is to write for a prospectus.

Most colleges and institutes pride themselves on their level of concern for the individual student, and for the emphasis on pastoral care. This probably stems from the fact that they often began as small teacher-training colleges which had almost all students in residence. The fact that many were built in rural areas, away from the distractions of city life, added to the sense of community. Many colleges have pleasant surroundings and comfortable living accommodation, and if that is important to you, you should almost certainly investigate facilities in the colleges and institutes of higher education. It is of course only one dimension, but an important one.

Detailed information about courses in colleges and institutes of higher education is provided in *The Colleges and Institutes of Higher Education Guide*, produced by the Standing Conference of Principals and Directors of Colleges and Institutes of Higher Education, and in the *Handbook of Degree and Advanced Courses in Institutes/Colleges of Higher Education, Colleges of Education, Polytechnic Departments of Education, University Departments of Education*.

Scottish central institutions

The fourteen central institutions (CI) provide most of the advanced full-time courses in Scotland outside the universities and colleges of education. They were designated in 1901 'in the hope that they might develop into Institutions worthy to rank in quality and advancement of work with the best of their kind in any other country'. In recent years, the number of degree courses offered by the CIs has increased greatly, to the extent that there are now more than 15,000 undergraduate students in the CIs. Most degrees are validated by the CNAA, and the main feature which distinguishes them from the university courses is that most are vocationally orientated and generally aim to prepare students for a career. The fourteen institutions vary greatly in size, character and in the subjects offered and if you think you might be interested in a CI degree course, it would be wise to study the information in the Scottish Central Institutions Handbook (obtainable from the Assistant Registrar, Paisley College of Technology, High Street, Paisley PA1 2BE) and then to contact the institution of your choice for further information.

Colleges of technology and technical colleges

A few colleges of technology and technical colleges still provide degree courses. This is mainly because a college has established a specialist expertise in some area, is located a very long distance from any other degree-awarding institution, or historically has established a reputation as a centre for certain types of course. Courses are usually validated now by the CNAA, and can be full time, part time or sandwich, in the same way as polytechnic courses. They tend to be in the areas of science and technology, and the only way of finding out which courses are available in any one year is to ask the college. **Do not trust prospectuses entirely**: they are no more than a guide to what the college expects to be able to offer, but sometimes course approval is not obtained in time, or approval for courses is withdrawn at short notice, or funding is not available, and courses have to be withdrawn.

There are sometimes criticisms that libraries are not as well stocked as universities, for example, and there is generally very little in the way of residential accommodation for students. However, the CNAA will need to be satisfied that library stocks are adequate, teaching staff well qualified and accommodation and specialist facilities up to standard so there is no need to fear that a degree obtained from a college of technology would be in any way inferior.

Correspondence colleges

The Open University has already been mentioned as a possible means of obtaining a degree by part-time, distance study, but if the Open University does not appeal, or if it does not offer the subjects you want, you may wish to look elsewhere. It will pay to take a little time to check credentials of correspondence colleges. The Council for the Accreditation of Correspondence Colleges (CACC), which is an independent organisation set up to inspect colleges which ask for accreditation, has a full list of accredited colleges and information about what each one does.

You can study for a degree by correspondence but the going is hard and it is easy to underestimate the time needed to keep up to date. Some colleges have a student adviser who will answer your queries, so try to find out as much as you can before you pay. Ask yourself:

1. Is the college helpful to the intending student? (For example, does it answer enquiries swiftly and well?)
2. Does the college provide full information about its courses and staff?
3. What are the terms of reference for the tutors? Do they, for instance, merely provide model answers or do they also provide individual comments and advice?
4. Above all, does the college worry about students who fall behind and make every attempt to ensure that they continue with their studies?

The greatest problem with private study by correspondence is self-discipline and self-motivation. There is no support from members of a group all pursuing the same course of study, and no personal contact with a tutor (though in a few cases correspondence colleges do offer week-end courses, or co-operate with local colleges of further education and adult centres in providing classes). On the other hand, a correspondence course does not commit you to three or four years of full-time study, nor does it use up your one chance of an LEA grant.

The courses are not cheap, so you need to be sure you have selected the right course, and have the time and determination to succeed. Fees, which can usually be paid by instalments, vary from college to college and from course to course.

The National Extension College (NEC)

The NEC is different from most other correspondence colleges in that it is a non-profit-making body governed by an Educational Trust. It was established in 1963 to provide high quality home study courses for adults and now provides courses for well over 12,500 students. These cover a wide range of 'O' and 'A' levels, courses in learning skills, languages, English, mathematics, science, social studies and professional courses at a variety of levels. They also have a significant number of students who are

27

studying as external students of the University of London. The University of London continues to offer degrees for private external candidates who are able to satisfy the general entrance requirements of the university (information about entrance requirements is provided in Regulations Relating to University Entrance Requirements, obtainable from The Secretary, University Entrance Requirements Department, University of London, Senate House, Malet Street, London WC1 7HU). Students are prepared for a wide range of subjects leading to the degrees of BA (Hons), BSc (Econ), LLB and BD. Full information about studying for a degree with the National Extension College is provided in their *Degree and Professional Booklet*, obtainable from the NEC at 18 Brooklands Avenue, Cambridge CB2 2HN.

Studying by correspondence is usually the only way of acquiring qualifications for people who are housebound, or who work shifts or who live somewhere far removed from the nearest educational institution, but it is very hard. Some people like to study alone, but for many it is impossible to study for a long period of time without personal, face-to-face feedback from fellow students and/or tutors. If you wish to take a degree part time then, as we have said before, you would be well advised to enquire whether the Open University has courses to suit you. They probably will, as they have over 100 courses in the faculties of arts, social sciences, education, science, technology and mathematics. The Open University does not cover all subject areas, however (for example, it is not possible to take a law degree), so if you have your heart set on a degree that is not covered by the Open University, send for prospectuses from those correspondence colleges that offer degree courses, and which are on the CACC list, work out how much it will cost, how many hours a week will be needed and how long it will take to graduate.

Full information about correspondence colleges can be obtained from the Council for the Accreditation of Correspondence Colleges: *CACC*, 27 Marylebone Road, London NW1 5JS (Tel: 01 935 5391).

How to choose

Deciding whether to study by correspondence, or to apply to a university, polytechnic, college/institute of higher education or a college of technology will depend on what you want to study, your preferred mode of study, your geographical mobility, your views about living accommodation and a great deal more. You will have your own requirements and priorities. If you have young children, nursery facilities may be more important for you than the quality of

28

the library. If you are unable to leave home, you will have to investigate facilities and institutions within travelling distance of home. If you are physically handicapped, you may decide to attend an institution which has a sympathetic attitude towards handicapped students. Life is not as simple for a mature student as for an 18-year-old and it may be that non-academic factors have to be considered first.

The only way to find out what facilities are available is to go to see for yourself. You would not buy a house without seeing it. You will be living and working in the college for three years at least, so make sure it has what you want before you decide.

Each type of institution has its own character and ethos. You will need to decide what is likely to suit you best. Whether you graduate with a degree from the Open University, with a London external degree studied by correspondence, with a degree awarded by a polytechnic, college/institute of higher education, a college of technology, or university, you will have a degree which has national currency. If it is good enough, your degree will give you access to study at higher degree level and entry to a range of professions.

Just one word of warning. Prospectuses can be very beguiling. No institution is going to point out to you that the catering facilities are terrible, that there is not a blade of grass for miles and that the teaching accommodation is substandard. All institutions, even if they are overwhelmed with applications, will present their best face to the world in their prospectus. Use prospectuses as a guide but then check. Some modules or options may be offered alternate years. If the one specialist in Arabic leaves after the prospectus has been printed, it may be that Arabic will not be available after all. Some departments have been obliged to re-duce the number of options, as an economy measure and some institutions are themselves under threat of closure. There are certain disadvantages to studying in an institution which has a limited life, so if you apply for a college or institute you should do your best to find out what the position is. Making a decision about where and what to study is not as straightforward as it at first seems, so make sure you leave yourself sufficient time to study, to see and to check.

Chapter 5

Degree-awarding institutions catering for mature students

The majority of mature candidates will find their way to the Open University or to one of the established degree courses in a university, polytechnic or college of higher education and will attend the same courses as conventional age students. However, there are several institutions which cater for mature students, three of which deserve special mention here, namely Birkbeck College, which is a constituent college of the University of London, the Open University and Lucy Cavendish College, Cambridge.

Birkbeck College

Birkbeck College has for many years been in the business of providing degree level teaching and research facilities primarily for students who are 'engaged in earning their livelihood during the daytime' – though that requirement appears to be liberally interpreted to include those whose domestic circumstances are such as to prevent their pursuing full-time study. Students are classified as internal students of the University of London and so have access to the same facilities as students in other colleges of the university. The main difference between Birkbeck and the other colleges is that all essential formal teaching takes place in the evening. The first degree courses normally consist of four years of part-time study, though students may complete the requirements for the degree by following a one-year course of full-time study.

Qualifications for entrance are fixed centrally by the University of London for all its member colleges, and are quite tough. As is the case in applications to all institutions of higher education (with the exception of the Open University), the general entrance requirements and the course requirements have to be met. We shall be discussing entrance requirements more fully in the next chapter, but the sort of qualifications that are considered to satisfy the general requirements are GCE 'A' levels, a three-year teacher's certificate, certain professional qualifications, Scottish Highers, Dip HE, certain foreign matriculation qualifications and certain Extra-mural Certificates or Diplomas of the University of London.

Alternative qualifications are considered by the university's Special Entrance Sub-Committee, if the appropriate admissions tutor is willing to recommend the student. All this sounds rather daunting, but there is another route for students who are at least 23 years old. The Birkbeck prospectus outlines the procedures:

> Mature students who lack the conventional educational qualifications may also be considered by the Sub-Committee if they are recommended by the College authorities. If you wish to apply as a mature student, you must be at least 23 years old and be able to show a record of mature-age study, i.e. study pursued successfully after the age of 23. This can be in the form of an Extra-Mural award, a GCE Advanced level pass, an Open University Credit, publication of written work, or successful completion of a Birkbeck Preparatory course.
>
> Mature students who cannot prove a record of mature-age study which satisfies the Sub-Committee, but whose work at their entrance test and interview convinces our Admissions Tutors of their ability to follow a degree course, may (subject to the approval of the Head of Department) be offered admission to the first year of a BA or BSc programme on a provisional basis. Such students complete the normal first-year course work and examination, but their progress into the second year of the course and the completion of their formal registration with the University depends on the Sub-Committee's approval.

The general entrance requirements are one step in the process of gaining entrance to a degree course. The next step is to satisfy the course requirements stipulated by the department. Different subjects have different requirements and the only way to find out what is needed for the subject of your choice is to write to Birkbeck for advice. Not unnaturally, the college wishes to be sure applicants are sufficiently well prepared to cope with the demands of the course, and it is in your interests also to be ready for study at this level. Some departments will admit students for preparatory studies leading to a first degree course and there are many other ways to prepare and update yourself for a rigorous course of study.

The majority of Birkbeck students are of mature age and the majority have jobs, so they have to face up to the problems that always face part-time students. They attend classes after completing a day's work, have to reach the same standards as any other student of the University of London and have to cope with the demands of home, family, work and study. It is a hard path to tread, but many have trodden it over the years and have succeeded. Birkbeck staff are well experienced in teaching mature students and the success of many hundreds of students over the years is evidence of their expertise.

The Open University

The Open University is a very different type of institution organisationally, though in academic matters it is exactly the same as any other university in that it has its own charter, awards its own degrees, has similar aims and maintains the same rigorous academic standards. Studying with the Open University is certainly not a soft option, as the 70,000 graduates will be able to testify.

Until recently, students had to be over the age of 21 when they began their course. 18-year-olds can now register, though some OU staff feel that the distance teaching methods which form the backbone of the system are not well suited to younger people. Be that as it may, students aged 18 are now admitted. There is no upper age limit. There have already been several graduates over the age of 80 and students in the 60–65 age range have shown themselves to be among the most successful in the university.

An important difference between the OU and other institutions of higher education is that no entry qualifications are required. Students are admitted on a first-come-first-served basis. Having said that, even the foundation courses are difficult, and if you have done no studying for many years, it would be unwise to apply for an Open University course without some thought and preparation. The enquiry service of your regional office will give you advice if you are doubtful about how best to prepare yourself.

The enquiry service will also give information about facilities if you are disabled in any way. The OU has a disabled students' office (and a large number of disabled students and graduates) and really goes out of its way to welcome and support handicapped students. If you declare the nature and extent of your handicap, a member of the university staff will contact you to discuss ways in which you can be helped. If you are offered a place and cannot attend a study centre, arrangements may be made for you to have some tutorials at home, if necessary, and throughout your course efforts will be made to provide the sort of conditions that will enable you to get the most out of your studies. Tapes are provided for blind students, and transcripts of radio and TV programmes are sent to deaf students.

Most OU courses have a compulsory summer school. If you are very severely handicapped and feel it would be impossible to cope away from home for a week, then it is usually possible to be excused, but a good many severely handicapped students have managed to attend and have enjoyed the experience. The OU allows you to take a helper, and pays for his/her bed and board. If you do not have a helper, in most cases a volunteer helper can be provided who will help you domestically and escort you to classes and meals if necessary.

The educational standards required are, of course, the same as for able-bodied students. What the university does is to try to provide the sort of support that will enable you to reach those standards.

One feature which sets the Open University apart from traditional universities is that, as in the case of Birkbeck College, the undergraduate courses are intended for part-time study. Some students do in fact take two full credits a year, and so complete a general degree in three years, but the vast majority are fully employed elsewhere and so study with the Open University in their spare time. Courses are organised on a modular system, each course leading to the award of a credit or a half-credit, students accumulating credits until they have enough for a degree (six for a general degree and eight for an honours degree). Some students study without a break until they have completed all six or eight credits. Others take a year or more off and then return to study when they have the time or the motivation.

There are still more differences. Most educational institutions start their academic year in September or October. The Open University term begins in February, and students then have three months to decide whether they wish to continue. They pay an initial tuition fee before they start the course, and the final fee in April.

In some circumstances the Open University will give credit for full-time study successfully completed in other institutions of higher education. For example, if you took the first year or two years of a full-time degree course in a university, college or polytechnic, passed the examinations but then decided to leave,

33

you might be able to count those successes towards a degree with the Open University and complete your degree part time as an Open University student. So, if you start a degree course somewhere, but disaster strikes and you have to leave, or if you decide you have made a great mistake and do not wish to continue with your course, all is not lost.

A number of institititutions of higher education now have reciprocal arrangements with the Open University and will give exemptions to holders of OU credits. Information about credit transfer is provided on one of the university's recognition information leaflets and your nearest regional office will be able to tell you which institutions have agreed to reciprocal transfers.

The final, but possibly the most significant, difference between the Open University and other institutions is the way in which teaching materials are prepared.

Radio and television programmes form part of every course. Written course material is sent through the post and students are expected to study the material (usually presented in 'units') and to submit assignments to locally-based tutors. Tutorials are provided in local study centres (often colleges of further education or polytechnics) and telephone tutorials are often arranged for students who are unable to attend the study centre, but the units, broadcasts, home experiment kits (where appropriate) and various other teaching materials are complete in themselves and if you are not able or do not wish to attend tutorials, you will be able to complete the course perfectly satisfactorily. Although there are distinct advantages in attending tutorials, many students, such as merchant seamen and students in remote parts of the country, are never able to attend, and such students have in the past maintained high academic standards.

All foundation courses and many second and third level courses have one-week summer schools. Although the university regards these summer schools as being compulsory, in exceptional cases excusal can be granted. Women with children, students with dependent relatives, and those who are seriously ill or handicapped, or whose employers refuse to release them will all generally be excused from the commitment to attend summer school.

Study with the Open University is rigorous and courses should not be undertaken lightly. It is estimated that you will need to spend at least ten hours a week on a full-credit course, but some students report that at times they have to spend twice that amount. You need to decide whether you can spare this time and (probably more important) whether you can stick it for a whole year. If you have not done any study for a long time it may be advisable to wait a while before applying for a place and to invest some time in a return-to-study course or an 'O' or 'A' level. The university takes students on a *first-come-first-served* basis, so they will not turn you down because you are educationally under-prepared. They might advise you in your own interested to take a preparatory course but in the end the decision will be yours: if you apply in time you will be offered a place. Looking ahead sufficiently far to give yourself time to prepare will pay off, and it is better to wait a year than to flounder with your first foundation course.

A major disadvantage of the Open University is the re-lentlessness of it. Six years for a general degree and eight for an honours (assuming you get no credit exemptions and take only one credit a year) is an eternity. Few households can avoid illness or personal crisis some time or another but whatever disaster strikes those units come through the letter box and deadlines have to be met. It needs a lot of thought before you decide to take the plunge. If you are interested, but you cannot make up your mind whether to apply, telephone your regional office and ask to speak to a senior counsellor or to the regional enquiry service. They will give you a realistic idea of what will be involved. Remember that the university academic year starts in February, but demand for places is still so high that you need to have your application in a year ahead.

Addresses of the Open University regional offices are in Appendix 1.2.

Lucy Cavendish College, Cambridge

By British standards, the Open University is enormous. It has approximately 75,000 students who live in all parts of the United Kingdom, some of whom work in remote parts of the world. If a student's work takes him to the Antarctic, he can in most cases take his units with him and continue his studies. Examinations have been arranged in strange locations to accommodate such students!

Lucy Cavendish College at Cambridge could hardly be more different. It is one of the youngest of the Cambridge colleges, having been recognised by the university as an Approved Society in 1965 and granted Foundation Status in 1984. Up to a total of fifty women undergraduates are admitted, the condition being that they should be either mature (that is, over 25 years of age) or affiliated students (that is, graduates of other universities). In most other ways it follows the traditional Cambridge pattern. Lectures, practical classes and seminars are organised by the university and are attended by students from all colleges. In addition, Lucy

35

Cavendish provides personal teaching (supervision) for its members. An important condition for mature women is that Cambridge is a residential university and students are required to live in, or near, Cambridge during university terms. All this seems a far cry from the rigours of part-time study whilst coping with work and family commitments, but for those women who are able to live in or near Cambridge and who can give three years to full-time study, it presents interesting possibilities. The staff of the college have experience of the special needs of mature students and any woman contemplating the possibility of study at Cambridge might well consider applying to this college. Of course, entrance requirements for any Cambridge college are likely to be exacting and the Lucy Cavendish publicity material suggests that intending applicants might wish to take advantage of the college's willingness to offer advice about preparation. Throughout this book, we stress the importance of planning and if you hope to apply to this college, ask for an appointment to discuss preparation in good time.

Lucy Cavendish is not the only Cambridge college willing to admit mature students of course. St Edmund's House and Wolfson College admit some mature men and women as undergraduates and men and women over 25 who are unable to matriculate can take advantage of a special procedure in applying to any college. This involves preparation of a curriculum vitae and applicants are then asked to state which course they wish to take, how that fits in with their future plans and how they intend to finance themselves. Finally, applicants are asked to give the names of two referees who will be willing to give an opinion about their academic potential.

We have no information about the numbers of mature candidates who gain admission by means of this process and the likelihood is that very few are successful. However, the special scheme does exist and if you can convince the admissions tutor of the college of your choice that you are capable of succeeding on a Cambridge honours degree, you may be lucky and find that you have a place. Convincing the admissions tutor will not be easy. You may be asked to take certain papers of the Cambridge Colleges' Examination, or to prove your worth in other ways. As always, it is important to be well prepared and to give yourself the best chance of succeeding.

It would be wrong to imply that Birkbeck College, the Open University and Lucy Cavendish College are the only institutions of higher education which have a major commitment to mature students. Most institutions now admit mature students and many make a special point of welcoming mature applicants, as you will

36

see when you read the institutional entries in Part II of this book. Every year there are new developments, new courses, new ideas designed to help mature students to take advantage of degree level study. Part-time degrees are available in many institutions and external degrees of the University of London are still provided by the faculties of theology, arts, law, music and economics, though the university now provides no teaching for the external degrees. Students who wish to prepare for a London external degree need to take advantage of courses provided by correspondence colleges, or to obtain tutorial assistance in other ways. Demand for the London external degrees has fallen in recent years, but there are still substantial numbers of mature students who graduate by this route.

The part-time route to a degree is not second best, to be followed only if a full-time course is not possible. It is an alternative, and presents different challenges and different demands. It is by no means easy and no one should embark on a part-time course of study without weighing up carefully how much time, effort and money it is likely to require. If it is to be 'spare time' study, then there is unlikely to be any time for social activities, gardening, house painting or family outings, and this may be too high a price to pay. Before committing yourself, you should talk to admission tutors, or to the regional enquiry service if you are applying to the Open University, to find out how much time will be needed. You will be studying for several years, so invest time at the beginning to make quite sure you are doing the right thing. The same applies of course whether you are planning to study full time or part time.

In spite of increased competition for places on degree courses and a reduction of student places in some institutions, indications are that mature students are still able to obtain places and in many institutions are welcomed. You will need to do quite a lot of work to find out which is likely to be the best course for you – and then even more work to prepare yourself as fully as possible. The opportunities are there, but you will need to make sure you make the most of them.

Chapter 6

Where to go for information
and advice

A major problem for any mature student hoping to return to study
is not that there are so few opportunities, but that there are so
many. The problem is how to select a course and an institution
that will be right for you, how to know which programmes of study
will adequately prepare you for the next stage, or which courses
will qualify you for your chosen profession. Before you commit
yourself, you will need to read widely, consult prospectuses and
reference books, consider the implications of different approaches
and then, to cross check each piece of information that you are
given. However, publications may not tell you all you need to know
and you may have questions after having read all the available
materials. There comes a time when you may need to discuss
options – not so that you can be told what to do, but so that you
can make a more informed decision about what to do.

There are a number of organisations and agencies that might
be able to help and as part of your planning and preparation you
may wish to contact one or more of them to discuss your future
plans.

Educational Guidance Services for Adults

You may be fortunate enough to live in an area where an
educational guidance service for adults is well established. If so,
start there. A list of EGSAs that were in existence when this book
went to press is provided in Appendix 14, though, as many of
them are dependent on short-term funding, and may close if

funding ends, you will need to check that they are still fully operational. The longest established EGSA is in Belfast. Since its inception in 1967, thousands of enquiries have been dealt with, and interviews given. The service operates independently of any educational institution, sees a wide range of enquirers from those who need help with reading and writing to those who are looking for postgraduate courses and funding. EGSAs come in various forms. Some, like Belfast, are entirely independent organisations; others are funded by LEAs and form part of LEA educational provision. They are often located in a college or a community education centre, sometimes in a Job Centre or a library, and occasionally, they have their own premises in shopping areas.

Regardless of who pays for their upkeep, all have the aim of providing a client-centred service of information (usually with guidance and counselling as well) for adults who wish to make choices about learning. They are not, or should not be, recruiting agencies for the educational establishments in which they happen to be located.

EGSAs vary in how much information they have on the premises, but all have a wide range of useful local and national contacts to whom they can refer any enquiries which they cannot answer themselves. They often produce their own fact sheets on local provision, and invariably have built up links with local libraries, Job Centres, adult education centres, further education colleges and higher education establishments.

Some of the EGSAs are staffed by paid full-time staff who over the years have built up an extensive knowledge of educational opportunities for adults. Others are staffed by 'professional volunteers' – that is, people who may be employed in another capacity, but who have a wealth of experience in education. Some EGSAs have a small central staff supported by a network of experts from different organisations, agencies and institutions. Whatever the organisation, you can be confident that EGSA staff will do their best to provide you with full information about options open to you and many will also provide educational counselling.

Not all parts of the country have EGSAs, but if you are within travelling distance of one of the services listed in Appendix 14, write or telephone for an appointment, or to ask what services they offer.

Libraries

It is easy to overlook the obvious. Most of you will be members of a library but it may not have occurred to you to look to libraries for educational information. Librarians have vast resources at their disposal and if you tell them what your general area of interest is, they will look out materials and point you in the right direction to find more. Ask at the information desk whether anyone on the library staff has made a particular study of educational opportunities for adults. You may be lucky and find someone who has specialist knowledge of the field.

Every branch library will have information about local colleges and their courses and the larger, central libraries will have details about colleges of higher education, polytechnics and universities. Many libraries also have helpful books giving information about career choice, qualifications needed for entry to courses, prospectuses, directories and handbooks. Some librarians now participate in EGSA networks and have become very knowledgeable about courses and requirements. Sometimes, EGSAs hold regular sessions in libraries and some libraries have hosted an 'Education Week', when representatives of all the local providers join together to provide an opportunity for the public to ask questions and browse through literature.

Not all libraries will offer these facilities but even small branch libraries will have a range of materials, and library staff will be able to tell you which libraries have larger stocks. In most areas, if you have a library ticket for a small branch library, that will give you access to all libraries in the same local authority. That means that you can go direct to the main library in your area if you wish, and that you are not restricted to the sometimes limited resources of your own branch library.

Citizen's Advice Bureaux (CABs)

The Citizen's Advice Bureaux exist to give advice on almost any subject or problem which is brought to their attention. Generally, they do not find themselves dealing with many educational queries, though they do have an Educational File which is regularly updated as part of their information system. If you want friendly and competent advice, your local CAB would be a good starting point, and if the staff are unable to help they will certainly be able to refer you to a more appropriate point. The staff are very experienced in giving information about topics related to education, such as grants, housing, and general advice on how to live on very little money.

If you are disabled, the CABs have addresses of all the voluntary bodies for specific handicaps, and will advise you on your rights. They will quite often agree to visit you in your own home if you cannot get to them, though they will do their best to give information over the telephone, if you are unable to call.

40

CABs are listed in telephone directories, so consult your local directory to see where the nearest bureau is.

LEA careers services

If there is no EGSA in your area (or even if there is), you may find help from your LEA careers service (the former Youth Employment Service). Their responsibilities centre mainly on the needs of those who are in full-time education or who have recently left, together with anyone who takes a part-time course with a view to career change. This includes students in further and higher education, many of whom will be in their twenties. The 1973 Employment and Training Act empowers LEA career services to see other groups, and that would include adults who are looking for information and guidance about educational opportunities. The problem is that few have been given additional resources to cope with this potentially large client group and so they tend not to advertise their services because they fear the response would be overwhelming. They are probably right. It is undoubtedly true that careers services, like all other local authority departments, are under financial pressure and a good many officers feel that they are understaffed for their existing case load of school leavers, without the additional burden of an adult clientele. However, in spite of problems of staffing and overwork generally, many careers services now acknowledge and accept responsibility for the educational and vocational guidance of adults. Some, like Birmingham, Coventry, Knowsley, Renfrew and Sheffield, actually advertise the services they offer to adults. Others offer a service but merely respond to demand. A few are unwilling to see any adults. So, the only way you can find out what is on offer is to ask at your local careers office. Look in the telephone directory under 'Careers Service' or' . . . Education Committee – Careers Service' and start from there. If you have difficulty in finding the careers office, ask at your local LEA office (see appendix 11 for the addresses). Telephone and ask whether there is a careers officer who specialises in educational and vocational guidance for adults, and if so, ask for an appointment. If not, try to find out which careers office in your area might offer such a service.

The careers services in major cities will probably offer the best chance of success. They will have a large staff and therefore a greater spread of expertise. A few services will actually have full-time officers who are real experts in the educational guidance of adults, and who are engaged full time on work with adults. Sheffield Careers Service, for example, has an Educational and

Vocational Advisory Service for Adults, staffed by a team of full-time specialist officers. Not all local authorities can achieve this level of provision, but most of the larger services will now offer some service for adults.

Try them. If you draw a blank with your first approach, try another office. The help you get will depend on the knowledge, expertise and availability of the careers officer you see, and the money that has been spent on reference material. It would be unrealistic to suppose that all officers are equally knowledgeable, helpful and patient. If you are unlucky at the first attempt, try somewhere else.

In the best services, you will probably be given a preliminary interview of up to an hour, and will have opportunities to explore various possibilities. The best services will have extensive information about courses, careers, grants and training opportunities, and will have prospectuses for just about every college and university in the country. You will have the opportunity to consult their stock of pamphlets and books. That interview may be the first of several; the careers officer may wish to see you again, or may refer you to other agencies or individuals. The important thing is that you will be able to talk through your plans at an early stage.

One major advantage of discussing your educational plans with a careers officer is that there may well be eventual employment implications that should be considered at an early stage. In fact it is almost impossible to separate educational from vocational plans. Most adults will need a job of some kind when they finish their course, and likely openings, problems, limited employment prospects, salary levels or possible age restrictions should be discussed at an early stage. It would be tragic to spend several years on a course, expecting to gain professional recognition for example, only to discover that you are too old, should have taken a different course or could have obtained recognition on the qualifications you had originally. Such things have happened, so a discussion of the vocational implications of your educational plans is very necessary.

If you are solely interested in one particular subject, for which you know there are no job prospects, then good luck to you. The desire to study a subject in depth for its own sake is good enough reason for taking a course – as long as you do not assume that jobs will be available in your specialised area when your course ends.

Manpower Services Commission

Like most government departments, the MSC is reorganised periodically. Schemes, personnel and policies change and government initiatives can result in changed services and training programmes. At the time of going to press, the MSC was in the process of extensive reorganisation and a certain amount of emphasis was being given to training adults for changed occupations. If this policy continues, it may be slightly easier for adults to receive training allowances to enable them to move into different areas of work, though under present legislation it is unlikely grants will be given to enable you to study for a first degree, 'A' levels or similar courses of general education.

Your best source of information about MSC services is likely to be your local Job Centre or Employment Office. Look in the telephone directory under 'Employment Service' to find your nearest office. Job Centres hold a wide range of information on occupational and employment-related subjects. This includes advice on job hunting, training (for adults and young people), entry and training and requirements for different types of jobs and MSC special schemes. The information is available from leaflets and booklets which are generally on display, though Job Centre staff will be on hand if you are unable to find the particular information you need.

The larger Job Centres will employ a Disabled Resettlement Officer. The main task of the DROs is to try to place disabled people in suitable employment; but many have become very knowledgeable in the course of their work and may have information about special grants and courses. If you are handicapped in any way, try your DRO. You may find he or she has information that does not appear in the reference books or prospectuses.

A major part of the MSCs work is concerned with training and retraining for employment and, over the years, several thousand adults have taken MSC funded Training Opportunities (TOPS) courses in colleges or training centres. Job Centres will give you details of what is available, though much less is on offer under this scheme now than previously. As you might expect, most courses lead to a qualification for a job, but there are a small number of sponsored places available on certain postgraduate courses (see Ch 10).

Though a Job Training Scheme course will not prepare you for entry to higher education, it may be possible to find a course that will give you training for a job and which will also get you back into the habit of studying. It will at any rate be worth enquiring at your local Job Centre what the current position is over training grants.

There is another good reason for paying a visit to your Job Centre. As we said earlier, you will no doubt need to get a job after you graduate and though the employment market can change radically over a three- or four-year period, it would be sensible to consider what job prospects might be for graduates in your subjects.

At present, the MSC is still offering a Professional and Executive

43

Recruitment (PER) service. Your Job Centre will have a copy of *Executive Post*, which is the executive job hunter's newspaper, published weekly. If you would like a copy sent (free) to your home, you can register with PER through your Job Centre. You will then also be eligible to attend one of their half- day job hunting seminars held in various parts of the country. The Executive Post has details of these seminars and also of current Job Training Scheme courses.

Universities, polytechnics and colleges of higher education

Most universities, many polytechnics and some colleges of higher education have a special department which arranges courses for adults. This department is known as a department of extramural studies, department of adult or continuing education, department of external studies – or something similar. A few of these departments offer a special advisory service for adults who are interested in taking a degree course in their own or another institution. Even where there is no formal advisory service, many departments are these days willing to give advice to would-be mature students. It is a good idea to ask in good time for advice about the best way to prepare from the department of your choice. The department may prefer you to get a good grade in one 'A' level rather than poor grades in three, and you need to know about that before you embark on a quite lengthy course of pre- degree study.

The Open University is rather different. Departments do not as a rule give advisory interviews, but the regional offices offer an enquiry service which in many cases covers far more than information about OU courses, though their main responsibility is to provide information and guidance about the OU. The staff have a good deal of knowledge and expertise about educational opportunities generally and will often be prepared to discuss alternatives with you. There are regional offices in Belfast, Birmingham, Bristol, Cambridge, Cardiff, East Grinstead, Edinburgh, Leeds, London, Manchester, Newcastle upon Tyne, Nottingham and Oxford. Some of the larger offices have an extensive range of reference books and copies of Open University texts that can be consulted – usually by appointment. Telephone your nearest OU office and ask for the regional enquiry service. The staff there will do their best to help.

Colleges of further education, adult and community centres

Colleges of further education (sometimes known as technical colleges or colleges of technology) and adult centres usually do a good job in providing information about their own courses. A few establishments offer a first-class advisory service that goes well beyond mere information-giving. However, the existence of these services often depends on the goodwill and interest of individuals who are on the teaching staff, and may vary from year to year. It is fairly common to find that teachers who were themselves mature students take on the unofficial and unpaid role of adviser to mature students. If you can find someone like this, you will be in luck.

Check with your LEA for addresses and telephone numbers of colleges of further education and adult/community centres or look in the yellow pages under 'Schools and Colleges'. Some LEAs may offer an advisory service themselves. It is worth asking about.

University, polytechnic and college of higher education careers services

Once you are registered as a student in a higher education institution, you will have the services of that institution's careers and appointments service. You may be fortunate and find someone who is willing to talk to you about the chances of employment even before you become a registered student, but, like the LEA careers service, they are hard pressed, generally short staffed and overworked, and they might not have the time to give you an interview. They are generally very helpful people, but their first responsibility is to registered students of the institution. However, most will have a well stocked information room or library and if you need to find out some specific piece of information about career requirements, you may be given permission to consult the generally large stock of books, pamphlets and information from employers. Write to the careers service of your local institution of higher education to see what the position is. You have no absolute right to use the facilities, but if you say why you would like to refer to some of the items in the information room or library, you may be given permission.

One valuable source of information which will be available for consultation in the careers libraries is the series of careers information booklets prepared by the Association of Graduate Careers Advisory Services (AGCAS) and published by the Central Services Unit for Careers and Appointments Services (CSU), which is based at Crawford House, Precinct Centre, Manchester M13 9EP. These booklets (on sale from CSU, if you are unable to consult copies in a careers service library) cover a wide range of careers, including regulations for professional membership, qualifications, etc. Many have a section relating to mature entrants to professions.

The Open University has no careers service as such, but it does have a selection of occupational information leaflets, which are written specifically for OU (and therefore mature) students. They are

45

not generally available on demand, but the regional enquiry service of your nearest OU office will tell you whether they are available for consultation in the regional office. Registered OU students are entitled to receive copies of the occupational information leaflets and the AGCAS leaflets.

Sources of information for handicapped students

These days, most institutions of higher education are willing to consider handicapped students in principle, but you need to find out exactly what is going to be involved, what support you can expect to receive and what you will be entitled to get in terms of allowances at an early stage. Information about grants and allowances is given in Chapter 10, but even before you begin to enquire about finance, you need to enquire about facilities and, if necessary, special provision for students with your particular handicap.

The main source of information and advice for handicapped students and applicants to higher education is the National Bureau for Handicapped Students, which is based at the Thomas Coram Foundation, 40 Brunswick Square, London WC1N 1AZ (Tel. 01–278 3459). It produces a variety of leaflets and if you are considering higher education, you might like to send for *Applying to Higher Education – some notes for disabled students* (price 50p at present). This publication is not concerned primarily with mature students, but it is full of useful information and advice and is well worth obtaining.

Other groups and organisations have also provided information which may be helpful. The Royal Association for Disability and Rehabilitation (RADAR), 25 Mortimer Street, London W1N 8AB (Tel. 01–637 5400) has published a report entitled *Access to University and Polytechnic Buildings*, and some institutions and Students' Unions now produce their own handbooks or information sheets which give guidance to mature applicants. The Office for Students with Disabilities of the Open University, based at Walton Hall, Milton Keynes MK7 6AA (Tel. 0908 74066) produces information sheets about facilities, and the regional enquiry services will also have information. Don't forget your local library. They may have useful books such as the *Directory for the Disabled* and *Disability Rights Handbook* and leaflets produced by the national bodies for specific handicaps. If they do not have the leaflets, they (and the Citizen's Advice Bureaux) will be able to give the address to which to write.

Books

In the bibliography at the end of this book you will find a list of books which give information about courses, institutions, grants, careers and a great deal more. You will not be able to consult them all. If you did, you would have no time to study! However, a brief account of what the books contain is provided so that you will be able to judge which of them is likely to provide you with the information you need. Not all libraries will stock all of them and even those which do may keep them in the reference section or at the counter. You will have the best chance of finding a selection at major libraries, but you might also try your local secondary school. Schools sometimes have good careers sections in their libraries so if you have a contact with a school, either as a parent or as a former pupil, it might be worth exploring this avenue.

The Educational Counselling and Credit Transfer Information Service (ECCTIS)

The ECCTIS development, which was initially funded by the Department of Education and Science, and undertaken by the Open University, provides information to enquirers about (1) post-graduate taught courses, first degree courses and higher national diploma and certificate courses available throughout the UK and (2) non-advanced further education courses (e.g. City and Guilds, RSA, etc.) in South-West England.
The following information is provided:

Course title.
Duration.
Mode of study (e.g. full or part time).
Any associated professional qualification awarded on successful completion of the course.
Normal entry requirements.
Name, address and telephone number of the educational institution.

ECCTIS is also developing credit transfer information to help adult applicants find out where they might obtain credit for previously gained experience and partial or completed qualifications.
Information about courses is stored on a computer and can be given to enquirers by telephone, by letter, through Prestel or on microfiche. Telephone Milton Keynes (0908) 368921 (5 lines) for the ECCTIS Information Centre (enquiries may be sent to the Centre through the response frame on Prestel 21161) or write to

Subject

Please write in what you want to study:

Reply

a single subject, please specify as precisely as possible

OR

two subjects at the same level, or as 'major' and 'minor' subjects, please specify both

OR

several subjects in a modular course, please specify them and underline your main interests

OR

for a teaching qualification, please specify whether for primary/secondary/further education, and intended teaching subject

Level of Study

Please tick in the level(s) at which you want to study:

- Postgraduate ☐
- First degree ☐
- Higher national diploma or certificate ☐
- non-advanced further education ☐
  (e.g. City & Guilds, Royal Society of Arts, etc.)
  ECCTIS information at this level is at present only available for courses in South-West England

If your interest is in postgraduate or first degree level study, please write in whether you want information about Universities and/or Polytechnics and/or Colleges and Institutes of Higher Education and/or Scottish Central Institutions

Place of Study

Please write in where you want to study,
e.g. anywhere in the UK, or in specified regions, or in or near specified towns. Please name these specified places.

Mode of Study

Please write in how you want to study, i.e. full-time or part-time.

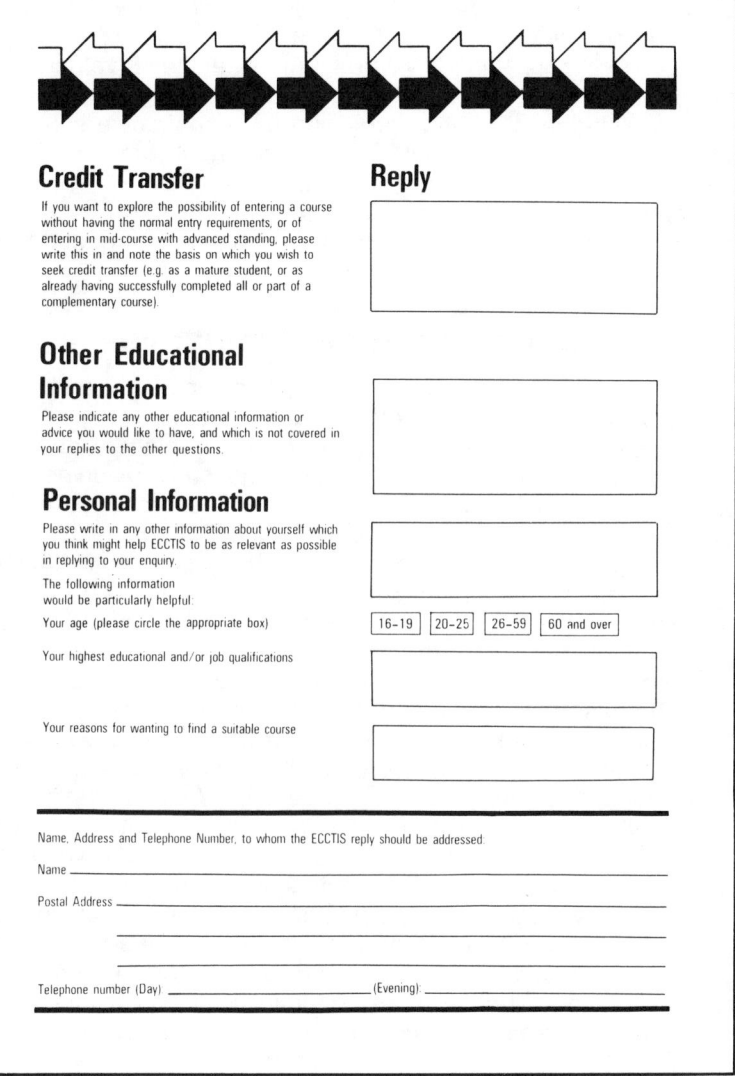

Credit Transfer

If you want to explore the possibility of entering a course without having the normal entry requirements, or of entering in mid-course with advanced standing, please write this in and note the basis on which you wish to seek credit transfer (e.g. as a mature student, or as already having successfully completed all or part of a complementary course).

Reply

Other Educational Information

Please indicate any other educational information or advice you would like to have, and which is not covered in your replies to the other questions.

Personal Information

Please write in any other information about yourself which you think might help ECCTIS to be as relevant as possible in replying to your enquiry.

The following information would be particularly helpful:

Your age (please circle the appropriate box) | 16-19 | 20-25 | 26-59 | 60 and over |

Your highest educational and/or job qualifications

Your reasons for wanting to find a suitable course

Name, Address and Telephone Number, to whom the ECCTIS reply should be addressed:

Name _____

Postal Address _____

_____

_____

Telephone number (Day) _____ (Evening) _____

49

ECCTIS, Freepost, Walton Hall, Milton Keynes MK7 6DD for further information.

At present, this service is free but once the developmental stage is over it is intended that it should operate as an independent self-financing body providing an authoritative source of up-to-date information about courses and credit transfer.

If you wish to ask for information from ECCTIS, it will help if you are precise in stating your requirements. The form shown on pages 48–9 indicates the sort of information that is needed to be able to provide you with a complete reply.

Local and national initiatives

Even if we knew of them all, it would be an impossible task to list all the local agencies and organisations that might give information and/or guidance about opportunities in higher education. One example of the sort of local initiative that can provide help to a special group is the Special Education Resource Information Service (SERIS) based at Anson Road, Manchester (Tel. 061–225 8319). This is an educational information service funded by Manchester Education Committee, though it is used far more widely than within the city boundaries, for all handicapped people, their relatives and their advisers.

There are many similar initiatives and the only way to find out what there is in your area is to ask at your local library, at CABs and information centres and to keep an eye on local newspapers.

One example of an organisation which has a national remit is the National Advisory Centre on Careers for Women. They are not specifically concerned with access to higher education, but they do give advice about careers for women of all ages so you might wish to call on their services at some stage. Their policy is to help women to see the whole range of career possibilities open to them and to encourage colleges and employers to make flexible and practical arrangements to encourage people to train for a new range of careers. They have a substantial collection of information about careers, education and training and they produce literature for sale and a termly bulletin for members. There is a membership subscription. Further details from NACCW at Drayton House, 30 Gordon Street, London WC1H 0AX, Tel. 01–380 0117.

Conclusion

If you think you would like to take a degree as a mature student, you will need information and you may need guidance before you commit yourself to one course in one institution. Read widely, consult prospectuses and reference books. Then try to find someone who has a wide range of information about all sorts of opportunities for mature students (entry qualifications, special schemes, funding, career implications, etc.) *and* the experience and background to be able to offer guidance about alternative routes, implications of certain courses of action and possible problem areas. Make sure you have canvassed all shades of opinion. Be prepared to persist. If people are unhelpful, do not give up. Try somewhere else. Only when you have obtained all the available information, balanced one possibility against another can you make an informed decision. Only then can you make up your own mind exactly what it is you want to do, and where and how you want to do it.

Chapter 7

Applying for a place

As we said in the introduction to this book, applying for a place on a degree course is not just a matter of completing a form of application and hoping for the best. Particularly for a mature candidate, who may have to give up a job and suffer loss of income for several years, the decision needs to be considered and preparation carefully planned. Applying for a place comes at the end of the planning and preparation process, but knowledge of admissions requirements may help you to decide how to prepare – whether to take 'A' levels, to register for a New Horizons course, to take an Open University foundation course, or to consider other methods. Success in some preparatory courses may disqualify you from applying for a place under a special scheme for mature candidates. As you will discover when you read Chapter 10, if you take certain types of course you may disqualify yourself from receiving a mandatory grant. So it is advisable to know what the requirements and options are, *before* you decide on the best way to prepare.

The information and advice given in this chapter is based on the assumption that you have carefully considered the choice of subject, course and institution and have tried to make a realistic assessment of your chances of being accepted. You may have started from the position of wanting to go to a university, polytechnic or college and chosen your subject and course accordingly, or you may have started from the position of selecting your subject, such as medicine (which is only available in universities) or a subject which is only available in a polytechnic.

Whatever your final decision, it is hoped you will have reached it only after studying all the available information and considering all the choices open to you.

Information about subjects, courses, degrees and 'A' level grades demanded by departments is available in a number of reference books (see the bibliography), but two of the most useful are The *Student Book* by Klaus Boehm and Nick Wellings and *Degree Course Offers* (updated annually) by Brian Heap. Neither is written specifically for mature students, but both include the sort of information that will help you to make up your mind about what to do. *The Student Book* covers degree courses in all institutions of higher education and provides thumb-nail sketches of study areas from accountancy to zoology. *Degree Course Offers* gives useful guidance about institutions and courses, but also provides information about offers made by departments.

Useful though these publications are, no book can provide the sort of detailed information that is included in prospectuses, so when you have drawn up your long short list, consult the appropriate prospectuses. If you are unable to find a copy in your local library, send a postcard to the registrar of the institutions you have selected, requesting a prospectus. You should state quite clearly which course interests you, as most institutions have different prospectuses for different faculties. NEVER depend on an out-of-date copy. Courses change rapidly and you should not run the risk of accepting a place on a course, only to discover, after you have started, that the options you particularly want are not available any more.

You might also enquire whether an alternative prospectus is produced by the Students' Union. If so, this will tell you what the institution is like from the students' point of view. These alternative prospectuses are variable in quality, but the best can be informative, helpful publications. Some institutions now have a Mature Students' Union, so enquire whether the institution of your choice has such an organisation, and what they do. There is now a national Mature Students' Union. The address changes according to who is president or chairman, but you should be able to get the current address from any Students' Union.

General entrance and course requirements

Before you can be admitted, institutions will require you to satisfy the general entrance requirements in one way or another. These will vary slightly from institution to institution and you will need to check in the prospectus of your selected institution exactly what the general entrance requirements are. Generally, they are on the following lines.

- Grade C or better in English Language 'O' level (or a pass in an approved test in English)
  AND
- Passes in five GCE subjects, two of which must be 'A' level
  OR
  Passes in four GCE subjects, three of which must be at 'A' level.
  OR
- Passes in five subjects in the Scottish Certificate of Education, three of which are at the higher grade
  OR
- Passes in four subjects, all at the higher grade
  OR
- Ordinary National Certificate or Diploma (usually with a 60% pass mark in three specified subjects)
  OR
- An appropriate BTEC certificate, or diploma. Specific subjects and 'passes with merit' will generally be required
  OR
- The Leaving Certificate of the Department of Education, Republic of Ireland, gained after 1 January 1952, provided that at one sitting the candidate passed at Grade C or better in five approved subjects at the Higher level, such subjects to include English.
- The army Special Certificate of Education.
- The International Baccalaureate.
- The European Baccalaureate.
- Three-year full-time Certificate of Education.

Satisfying the general entrance requirement is one step along the path to success, but all departments will also stipulate a *course requirement*, and it is likely to be the course rather than the general requirement that causes the problem. You may satisfy the general requirement with a few 'O' levels and two 'A' level passes at grade E, but it is unlikely you will be offered a place in any of the popular institutions. The department can ask for whatever grades it likes. Naturally it will wish to fill all available places, so will not wish to frighten off all applicants. On the other hand, once a firm place has been offered, it will be obliged to honour the offer so it does not want to fix the offers so low that too many students have to be found places. Admissions tutors and departments have to trust their judgement, and no doubt each year hope they have got it right so that just the required number of students get the grades, and all the places are comfortably filled.

It is difficult to give any firm guidelines about course

54

requirements. As demand for places increases, it is inevitable that higher qualifications will be needed to get a place on a degree course. The only way to know for certain what a department will require in any particular year is to ask the admissions tutor.

As we indicated in Chapter 2, some subjects are in such great demand that departments can (and do) ask for very high entry qualifications. Occasionally, restrictions are imposed on entrants and departments or professional bodies draw up their own sets of rules about a candidate's suitability.

The BMA, in a recent statement on mature or graduate entry into medical schools, makes the point that competition for medical school places is generally very keen and that 'deans usually give priority to school leavers who are embarking on their first university course and will have the greatest length of service to offer the profession. Consequently, very few places are available to mature students'.

Individual medical schools do vary in their selection policy but, as the statement points out, 'most seem to put the age limit at 30, others restrict their intake to candidates in their mid-twenties. Applicants are therefore advised to make direct enquiries to the medical schools in which they are interested, to ensure they are eligible to apply'. Depressing reading for any older candidate who feels committed to a career in medicine. Applicants over the age of 30 have been admitted in the past, but they have generally been exceptionally well qualified and/or experienced and, in some cases, exceptionally persistent.

Mature entry schemes

Most mature applicants do in fact apply through the normal 'A' level route, or on the strength of a professional qualification which is considered to be the equivalent of (or above the level of) 'A' levels but all is certainly not lost if you cannot satisfy the general entrance requirements. If you think you are sufficiently well prepared to embark on the course of your choice, you will need to enquire about special arrangements. If you consult the Access to Higher Education section in Part Two of this book, you will see that most institutions are now willing in principle to consider 'unqualified' mature candidates. Whether the principle extends to practice is dependent on many factors, but you can judge the extent to which institutions are prepared to consider mature candidates by studying the individual replies from institutions in Part Two.

Most institutions have the power to admit mature applicants

who do not satisfy the general entrance requirements and many will do so, provided applicants can satisfy the institution concerned that they have the potential ability and necessary skills to cope with the course. So, you have a choice. Either you can take one of the examinations listed above, and take your chance along with all the 18-year-old applicants, or you can seek entry through a mature entry scheme, if one exists. If you have 'A' level passes (even poor ones taken many years ago), you will normally be excluded from mature entry schemes, so be careful. It takes a great deal of time and effort to achieve good 'A' level passes by part-time study and you should check well ahead whether 'A' levels are absolutely necessary. If you decide you want to test yourself and to take an 'A' level course, departments may possibly be more impressed with one pass with an A or B grade than with three with grades D and E. You must find out what the position is.

Some institutions state in their prospectuses that 'mature students are welcome', or 'mature students can be admitted in certain circumstances'. This usually means that normal entry requirements can be waived, though no matter what the regulations say, the final decision rests with individual departments. A university prospectus may indicate that 'A' level passes are not always required, but if you wish to read mathematics say, and the department of mathematics insists that you have 'A' level passes in mathematics, physics and chemistry, then that is that. Either you take 'A' levels, or you try somewhere else. Some institutions, and some departments within institutions will refuse to have anything to do with mature entry schemes, and will tell applicants so. As we said in Chapter 1, faculties of medicine are very reluctant to consider 'unqualified' mature applicants. They have many more applicants than places available, the course is demanding and a certain amount of background knowledge is assumed before students begin. A few adults have gained admission without the normal 'A' level passes, but not many.

The Joint Matriculation Board special entry scheme for mature students

Some institutions have long-standing and well-tried arrangements for admitting mature students. The universities of Birmingham, Leeds, Liverpool, Manchester and Sheffield, for example, have operated a special scheme since 1919 which is administered by the Joint Matriculation Board (JMB). The JMB produce a leaflet entitled *21+ – Returning to Learning*, obtainable free of charge from the Joint Matriculation Board, Manchester M15 6EU, which gives full information about the scheme and instructions about how to apply.

If you ask for consideration under the JMB special scheme, you will need to complete the Universities Central Council on Admissions (UCCA) form in the usual way (more about UCCA later in this chapter) and also a special form of application which the JMB will forward to the university of your choice.

Take care to complete your form of application well. Make sure you have answered all questions accurately. Provide any additional information you think might help the admissions tutor to decide whether you are worth interviewing. First impressions can be important. All this sounds very obvious, but experience has shown that some applicants submit forms which are almost illegible, which omit vital information and which appear to have been completed in haste and without reference to the instructions provided.

The five universities have a considerable degree of discretion as to how they admit 'unqualified' applicants. Practice varies. Some universities interview every student who applies through the JMB special scheme, though it remains to be seen whether this practice will continue if the number of mature applicants increases dramatically. The intention is that even if an applicant is rejected at the interview stage, the interviews will at any rate be able to provide helpful advice which may enable him or her to look for education or training opportunities elsewhere. Other universities attempt some sort of preliminary selection from the application forms, and so the way the forms are completed and the nature of supporting evidence sent with the forms is important.

Exceptionally, applicants may be offered a place at the first interview, though this rarely happens. The more usual course is that examinations are devised to test specific knowledge or skills. Most JMB candidates will be asked to take a Use of English examination, and then papers in the specialist subject or subjects. The form of the examination is decided by the department concerned, sometimes in consultation with the applicant; it can be a formal, specially devised written examination; it can be a combination of a written examination and interview; it can take the form of essays which the applicant completes over a period of time. The intention is that a form of test will be devised which is suitable for the candidate and for the subject.

Many other universities, polytechnics and colleges of higher education will have their own scheme. Policies may change from year to year and the only advice we can give is that you should write to institutions that have courses that interest you, to ask if they have a special scheme for mature applicants. Some institutions (see Part Two of this book) have pamphlets which give useful information for prospective mature students, so when you make your initial approach, ask if any such publication is available.

Interviews

A word about your interview. When you are asked to attend for interview, whether it is a preliminary advisory interview given at your request, or a formal interview in connection with a special entry scheme for mature students, it is important to be well prepared. Interviews can be worrying, particularly if you do not know what to expect. You may not know whether you have been invited to have a friendly chat with one member of staff, or to be given a rigorous oral examination by a panel of academics. Either can be nerve-racking. Somehow or other, you have to convince the interviewers that you are a suitable candidate and that you have thought through all the implications of becoming a student, living on a grant, moving house, caring for children and so on. It may seem that such matters are nothing to do with anybody but you and your family, but occasionally questions are asked, and it is as well to be ready for them.

You are almost certain to be asked what you have read in your chosen subject area. If you can think of nothing, the interview is likely to be short. If you think you may well forget what you have read in the stress of the interview, make a list and refer to it if necessary. You may be asked for your opinions about a book, so it is dangerous to claim knowledge you do not have. An interviewer is unlikely to be impressed to hear that you have read a hundred books, but cannot remember anything about any of them, but an informed opinion about four of them would no doubt be well received.

Departments will be looking for evidence of recent study, of commitment to study and some knowledge of the subject area. They will not expect you to know everything, but they will expect you to know something. Say what you have read and studied, and if you are asked about a topic that you know nothing about, say so honestly.

Put yourself in their position. They are being asked to decide whether you have a chance of coping with degree-level study, and as you have no 'A' level passes, they have little to go on. Interviews can be something of an ordeal, but most interviewers will be genuinely trying to find out what you know, not trying to trip you up. Give them all the help you can. Take some written work with you, in case they would like to have some evidence of your ability to write. The interviewers may not wish to see it at this stage – but they may. Go as well prepared as you possibly can. Keep thinking of questions, and then try to answer them.

Trying to obtain a place on a degree course through a special mature scheme is certainly not an easy option, but it is a possibility for a certain number of adults who because of their professional background and the studying they have done since leaving school, are perfectly capable of starting degree-level study. For them, it would be a waste of time to spend several years on 'A' level courses.

The application process

There are different procedures for applying to universities, polytechnics or colleges and it is important to follow the instructions which are issued by the admissions bodies. Read the documentation carefully, write out your answers in rough form and check carefully before you complete the required forms of application.

Applying to universities

There is a central admissions system for universities, and whether you are applying through a special scheme or not, you will need to conform to the procedures laid down by the Universities Central Council on Admissions (UCCA). The UCCA system was introduced to simplify procedures (though it doesn't always seem that way to candidates struggling to complete the forms) and to prevent the chaos of students applying to many universities and possibly accepting all places. It is a system that does work, enables applicants to know where they stand, and enables institutions to make realistic plans about student numbers. With the exception of the University of Buckingham and The Open University, to whom applications should be sent direct, all applications for *full-time first degree courses* have to be made through the UCCA scheme. The University of Buckingham is the only independent, privately funded university in the country, and does not participate in the UCCA scheme, and the Open University courses are designed to be part time and so are also outside the scheme. All applications for part-time degree courses should be made direct to the institution concerned. Remember that the Open University academic year begins in February. Demand is generally so great that you will need to apply approximately a year ahead. Regional offices, or the admissions office at the OU headquarters at Walton Hall, Milton Keynes MK7 6AA will give you details.

If you are applying to universities in the UCCA scheme as an unqualified mature candidate, you need to contact the admissions officer of the department of your choice *before* you submit your UCCA form, and then to insert a note (in section 6 of the form) indicating that you are a mature candidate.

You will need to check the regulations with the current edition of

How to Apply for Admission to a University (often referred to as the UCCA handbook). If you are attending a course at a college, the college should have a copy, but if not, you can obtain your own copy and form of application from the Universities Central Council on Admissions at PO Box 28, Cheltenham, Gloucestershire. GL50 1HY. The handbook is extremely helpful, clearly written and absolutely necessary because you cannot complete the application form without it.

The Compendium of University Entrance Requirements for first degree courses in the United Kingdom should also be compulsory reading before you complete the application form. The Scottish universities publish the *Scottish Universities Entrance Guide* and there are various other publications which serve as a guide to applicants for law and medicine (see the bibliography).

Five choices

You are allowed to choose five different universities. You may choose fewer of course, but you cannot add any to your list later on. Because of this restriction, it is very important that you do not waste any of your five by applying for a course which is unlikely to consider you. Early contact with departments, and a careful study of Brian Heap's *Degree Course Offers* should provide you with sufficient guidance to enable you to judge where you stand a chance and where not.

Timetable

If your choices do not include either Oxford or Cambridge, the closing date is mid-December, though it is wise to get your application in as soon as you can. Some universities will start to interview and to make offers well before the closing date. It is possible to submit a late application, but the later you are the less chance you have of being offered a place. Incidentally, it may be possible to 'book' a place for a year later. Departments have different policies about deferred entry but if you would like to be sure of your place before working or studying for a further year, it is worth enquiring about.

Oxford and Cambridge

Although applications to Oxford and Cambridge also have to be made through UCCA, the procedures are rather different. At present, both universities are in the process of changing their admissions procedures, though these changes will mainly affect sixth formers who wish to take the Oxford or Cambridge entrance examinations. However, if you are aiming for Oxford or

Cambridge, you will need to check exactly what the regulations are at the time you apply. The individual procedures are explained in the UCCA handbook. It is possible to put both Oxford and Cambridge on your UCCA form as two of your five choices – possible, but unwise. They have so many applications that the chances of being considered by your second choice are so remote as to be not worth considering.

We have already discussed the Lucy Cavendish College at Cambridge in Chapter 5 and St Edmund's House and Wolfson College, which are mainly for graduate and affiliated students, also admit a few undergraduate mature students. However, you will (or may) be considered by all colleges, if you can convince the admissions tutor that you deserve a place.

Applications to Oxford and Cambridge (and incidentally, also to Durham and London, which operate similar collegiate systems) have to be made to the college and not to the university. The Cambridge Admissions Prospectus gives details of the admissions procedure at Cambridge (obtainable from the Cambridge Intercollegiate Applications Office, Kellet Lodge, Tennis Court Road, Cambridge CB2 1QJ or from any college) and the Oxford University prospectus gives information about Oxford (obtainable from the Oxford Colleges Admissions Office, University Offices, Wellington Square, Oxford OX1 2JD).

UCCA forms for Oxford and Cambridge have to be returned between 1 September and 15 October and, in addition, a preliminary application form, naming the college of first preference, has to be forwarded direct to a college.

The UCCA form

The UCCA handbook explains very clearly how you should fill in the form, so read the instructions carefully and make sure you provide all the information asked for. You are asking a university department to consider you on the basis of your UCCA application, so make it good. You will need a referee, who will be asked to provide a statement about your abilities and suitability for degree level study. Take a little care over whom you ask to provide you with this statement. School pupils will be able to ask the head of their school to provide a reference, but it may be some years since you have had contact with an educational institution. If you know no one who can provide a full and honest account of your abilities and potential, it may be better just to ask someone to provide a character reference and to explain why you are unable to present an academic reference. You should receive a printed acknowledgement approximately one month after your form reaches UCCA, and this will give you your UCCA serial number and the universities/colleges to which UCCA has sent your form.

Interviews and offers

When your UCCA form has been completed and you have a serial number, you wait for offers. The procedures are different if you are applying through a special scheme for mature students, but if you apply through the normal route you will be considered in much the same way as the conventional applicants.

Some universities will offer you an individual interview, which is a two-way process. The department will wish to see you to decide whether, in their opinion, you are sufficiently able and motivated to succeed, and you will wish to find out what the course is all about, and to decide whether you want to spend three or four years there. Other universities will offer group interviews, or will say that applicants may come and have a look round, if they wish. Some will make *conditional offers* (with or without an interview). A conditional offer is subject to certain grades being achieved in acceptable examinations. If you already have 'A' levels or equivalent, you may be made an unconditional offer.

In our opinion, you should always seek an interview or, if your department refuses to see you, you should certainly find time to visit the university and to ask if you can speak to one of the students. It is important that you try to get as clear an idea as possible about what will be involved before you make your final decision. The main problems are likely to be time and cost. The interviews take place at a time when you may be working for 'A' levels and have little time to spare. You may have to find travel costs and expenses do mount up. If your interview is short, you may feel it has hardly been worth your while, but do your best to make it worth the effort. If you are not offered a tour of the department and the campus, try to have a look round anyway. Think of all the things you want to know, write them down, and when the interviewer has finished his or her questions, ask yours. There is not much point in thinking of all the things you would have liked to have asked on the train home, so prepare yourself before you set out for the interview.

Take the same care with these interviews as you would with the interviews held in connection with special entry procedures. Prepare well and try to anticipate the way the interview might go. You never know. You might so impress the admissions tutor that he or she will make you an offer well below the going rate.

You may only accept one firm and one conditional offer. 'A' level results are published in the middle of August and then universities will make final decisions about conditional offers.

The continuing application procedure (CAP) and clearing scheme

If you receive no offers at all, then the continuing application procedure comes into operation. This starts in January and enables a candidate who has received no offer to make an additional application as soon as the last rejection slip has been received.

If you happen to be in this position, UCCA will automatically send you information about the CAP scheme. You will be able to name four further course choices. UCCA will send your application to one of these universities provided those universities have told UCCA in confidence that they will consider more applications for the courses you have named. If not, UCCA will choose another university on your behalf and send your forms on their way. The object is to try to give more hope to some candidates and to reduce the number for whom nothing can be done until *clearing*, which takes place in late August/early September. Clearing enables unplaced candidates to have another opportunity at entrance to universities other than those to which original applications were sent. Details are sent to candidates not holding an offer in June/July, and to candidates holding a conditional offer in August/September. So, if you don't achieve the 'A' level grades necessary or haven't had any offer during the year, the clearing scheme may find something for you. UCCA will provide all the details about the operation of the scheme.

However, you do not *have* to leave it all to UCCA. You can, and in our opinion should, take action yourself. If you have received no offers by the time your 'A' level results come out, or do not achieve the grades required by your provisional offers, there is nothing to stop you telephoning admissions tutors in other universities to enquire:

1. whether they have any vacancies; and
2. whether they might consider your 'A' level grades.

At this time of year, admissions tutors have a hard time. The telephone never stops ringing and they are inundated with letters asking for special cases to be made. However, you have no time to waste sympathising with admissions tutors. You need answers to those two questions, and speed is important, so **get organised**. In case you need them, get the telephone numbers of the universities you might be telephoning **before you get your results**, so that you can start work immediately. If you find departments that might be willing to consider you, ask if you can go for inter-

63

view immediately. If the department agrees to accept you, then you have to have the place confirmed through UCCA, but from your point of view, a verbal offer will be enough. You are in!

Applying to polytechnics

Polytechnics now operate a similar system to UCCA, called the Polytechnics Central Admissions System (PCAS) and much of what has been said above about the university system applies equally well to PCAS. PCAS operates the application process for all full-time and sandwich first degree and Diploma of Higher Education courses in polytechnics, other than those leading to qualifications in Art and Design or initial teacher training (more about these courses later in this chapter). Until 1985, students could apply to as many polytechnics as they wished and, if their conscience allowed them to do so, accept provisionally places in all of them. As might be imagined, this created great problems for polytechnics and for individuals and so the new system should improve matters.

PCAS offers a continuing application procedure and a clearing system, in much the same way as UCCA. There are minor differences in matters of detail, but these are explained fully in the PCAS leaflet entitled *The Polytechnics Central Admissions System*, obtainable free of charge from PCAS, PO Box 67, Cheltenham, Gloucestershire, GL50 3AP. Though the UCCA and PCAS systems are compatible, they operate entirely independently. You may apply for a university place through UCCA, and for a polytechnic place through PCAS – and hold two offers from each. There is no cross referencing between the two systems.

Colleges and institutes of higher education

At present, there is no clearing system for applications to colleges of higher education, nor to colleges of technology. It is hoped that if the PCAS system works well, that the colleges might be incorporated into the scheme. However, it may take a year or two for that to happen and in the meantime you will need to make individual applications to the colleges/institutes of your choice. Most will have a form of application and most will be willing to consider applications from mature applicants in exactly the same way as the universities and the polytechnics. Each institution will have its own procedures for considering mature candidates – qualified and unqualified and you will need to find out what these are, preferably before you make a firm application.

The advanced further education information service

This service, set up by the Department of Education and Science and administered and organised by LEA careers services all over the country, operates for a two- or three-week period after the 'A' level results are published. The officers have up-to-date information about polytechnic and college (not university) vacancies on full-time and sandwich degree courses, DipHEs and BTEC higher diploma courses. Most are also willing to provide information about day release and part-time courses, student grants, entry requirements and enrolment procedures. This is a free service and if you find yourself without a place in mid-August/September, you would be well advised to call in at your careers office to see where there are still vacancies in your subject. Every year, around 30,000 people make use of this advanced further education information service. Most are young people, but the service is not limited to school leavers. The officers manning the service will give you information, and they may also be willing to contact departments on your behalf and to arrange interviews.

Remember that the service only operates for a short period each year, so, unfortunately, you will not be able to take advantage of the information and guidance offered at other times of the year. However, keep the dates in mind in case you need help.

Courses of teacher training

Polytechnics and colleges/institutes of higher education may offer courses of initial teacher training, and although many colleges have now diversified their provision and offer a variety of non-teaching degrees, many of their courses are still BEds designed to prepare students for a career in teaching. There is a central admissions scheme for all teacher-training courses and for a number of other degree courses in colleges. Prospectuses will explain which courses are part of the scheme. Application forms and information about how to apply are obtainable from the Central Register and Clearing House (CRCH), at 3 Crawford Place, London W1H 2BN. Courses using the scheme are also listed in the *Handbook of Degree and Advanced Courses in Institutes/Colleges of Higher Education, Polytechnics and University Departments of Education*.

The procedure for applying is as follows:

1. Write to the institutions of your choice.
2. They will send you a prospectus and a clearing-house registration form (called an MW card).
3. Send the MW card to CRCH.

4. CRCH send you an instruction booklet and a clearing-house application form. Study the booklet carefully before you complete the form. Mistakes can cost you your place.
5. You are allowed up to *six* institutions on the clearing-house forms.
6. Send the completed forms and the registration fee to your first choice (accompanied by the institution's own application form).
7. You may be accepted. If you refuse or if you are rejected your forms are sent on to your second choice and so on down the line.

There is a late application system, so if you make up your mind very late in the year (even after your 'A' level results) you may still be lucky – but don't count on it. If you think there is a chance you may wish to apply for a college or institute course, it would be as well to send for prospectuses and forms very early, so that you can decide your order of priorities and take immediate action when you need to. **Be prepared for all eventualities**.

If you want to teach but do not wish to take a BEd, then the usual procedure is to take a first degree, followed by a post-graduate certificate in education (PGCE), which is a one-year course offered by polytechnics, colleges of higher education and university departments of education. The procedure for applying for a PGCE course is slightly different. The Graduate Teacher Training Registry, also based at 3 Crawford Place, London W1H 2BN, deals with PGCE applications. Applications have to be sent to GTTR some time after 1 September of the year preceding entry. There is no closing date (apart from Cambridge for which you should preferably apply by mid November) but obviously the earlier you apply, the better the chance of being offered a place. As always, institutions vary in the way in which they conduct their admissions procedures, but generally most would ask for references, call selected candidates for interview and give a place to students who appeared to be qualified academically and personally.

These days, everyone who wishes to teach in a state school has to be qualified either through the BEd or the PGCE route. Moreover, entrants to teacher training now have to have passes at GCE 'O' level (or equivalent) in English language and mathematics. It is not at present a requirement that teachers in independent schools should be teacher trained and teachers in institutions of further and higher education are similarly exempt. Many are trained of course and an increasing number of further education teachers have taken certificate of education courses in one of the four colleges of education (technical) at Bolton and Garnett Colleges or Huddersfield and Wolverhampton polytechnics. The further education certificate in education is outside the GTTR scheme, so applications should be made direct to the institutions (addresses in Appendix 4). The courses at these four colleges do not automatically confer qualified teacher status, which is necessary if you want to teach in a maintained primary or secondary school, though the LEA employing you may request the Department of Education and Science to give qualified teacher status. Requests of this kind are rarely turned down.

The Scottish system is rather different and altogether more formal than in other parts of the UK. In Scotland, all teachers employed in education authority and grant-aided schools have to be professionally qualified *and* to be registered as qualified teachers with the General Training Council (GTC) for Scotland.

Qualified status may be achieved by following several routes, namely:

1. A three-year diploma taken at a college of education (for primary teachers only).
2. A four-year course, normally provided jointly by a college of education and a university and leading to a BEd (for primary and secondary).
3. A one-year postgraduate course provided by a college of education (for primary and secondary).
4. A three- or four-year combined course of technical and professional training in subjects such as music or technical education (for secondary).

Information about entry requirements are contained in the Memorandum on Entry Requirements for Admission to Courses of Teacher Training in Scotland, obtainable from HMSO, 13A Castle Street, Edinburgh EH2 3AR or from the registrar of the General Teaching Council for Scotland, 5 Royal Terrace, Edinburgh EH7 5AF.

Degree courses in art

There are two main types of degree course in art. One is an academic degree like any other, and covers areas such as fine art and art history. For those courses, application has to be made in the usual way through UCCA (for universities), through PCAS (for polytechnics) or direct to colleges of higher education. Candidates have to satisfy the same general and course requirements as are required for other degree courses.

There is a different procedure for those art and design courses which developed from the Diploma in Art and which have a strong practical content. Applicants will normally be required to take a foundation course before starting the degree course, and application for the degree has to be made through the Art and Design Admissions Registry, Imperial Chambers, 24 Widemarsh Street, Hereford HR4 9EP. Applications are made in January/ February of the year in which admission is sought, which gives the colleges running the foundation courses time to make an assessment of the students' artistic ability. Full information will be provided by the polytechnic and college departments of art, and guidance given about how to apply.

The Art and Design Admissions Registry receives and processes applications for courses leading to the award of a CNAA first degree in Art and Design and from that point of view fulfils a similar role to UCCA and PCAS. There are differences in the system though. Requests for forms of application can only be made to the Registry in January of the year of entry to the course. Applicants may only state two colleges and colleges will start to select first choice applicants from 1st April onwards. This cycle is much later than for other degree courses. However, the principle is much the same.

Conclusion

Applying for a degree course is not really difficult as long as you read the instructions provided by the institutions and the clearing systems and do what they ask. Make sure you do your homework before you submit a formal application. Ask the department/s in which you are interested if they will give you an advisory interview. That way, you can test the water and find out what the department's attitude to mature students is, and what they are likely to want in the way of entry qualifications. If you can manage it, try to arrange to meet any mature students who are already on the course. You need to have a sound idea of the amount of studying that is necessary, the background required, the good and bad aspects of the course, the institution and the locality. Students who are part of the way through their course will usually be able to give you a reliable idea of what is involved. Listen to what admissions tutors and students tell you about preparation. All this will take time, but it will ensure that the institutions and courses you put on your form of application will be those you really want and for which you stand a reasonable chance of being considered.

A final word of warning

The responsibility for your application is yours. If you waste one of your UCCA or PCAS slots by including an institution which requires qualifications you do not have, or if you do not provide the information that has been requested, then you have reduced your chances of success. It is up to you to check all entries, to do your homework before you complete the form, to prepare yourself thoroughly for interview and to work hard at making yourself lucky.

Chapter 8

Preparing for admission: making sure you are ready

Even if a department is willing to accept you on a degree course, you do yourself no service to apply for a place before you are ready. You may be able to prepare on your own but maintaining concentration and studying systematically over a period of time is difficult, and however determined you are you may find that the company of fellow students and the discipline of having to produce written work on time becomes important.

There are a great many ways of preparing. If you have asked the admissions tutor in the department of your choice how best to prepare, you will have some idea of what is likely to be required when you make your application. If the tutor says that mathematics forms a significant part of your course and that in the past mature students have had most difficulty with mathematics, then obviously you should concentrate on that subject. If, as may well be the case, you are merely told to read as much as you can about X or Y, then you have to decide how best to organise yourself.

If you decide to take a course, you will find there is a great deal to choose from, ranging from a full-time one- or two-year course in a residential adult college to a short study skills course in a local college or adult centre. What you eventually decide to do will depend on how much time you have, what exactly you need to study, your strengths and weaknesses and what you can afford.

Long-term residential adult colleges

If you are able to invest one or two years of full-time study, you might consider a course offered at one of the eight long-term residential colleges. These are Coleg Harlech in Wales, the Co-operative College in Loughborough, Fircroft College in Birmingham, Hillcroft College in Surbiton, Newbattle Abbey in Dalkeith, Midlothian, Northern College in Barnsley, Plater College (formerly the Catholic Workers' College) in Oxford and Ruskin College in Oxford.

Each college has its own ethos and its own programme of studies. Ruskin (founded in 1899) is the oldest, and Northern College (founded in 1978) the newest. What is common to all colleges is that they offer residential study opportunities for adults in a range of areas. The original idea of the residential colleges was that working men, and later on women, should have the opportunity to enjoy a period of liberal higher education, but that when the course ended they should return to their own community. The notion of helping individuals to play a responsible part in the community figures in most of the college prospectuses. Many students do take an active part in community activities, in local politics and in trade unions; some go on to seek election to parliament, but many others use the course as a basis for further study or to move into different areas of work.

The range of courses offered is very wide but all maintain a commitment to liberal and general studies in some form or another. Coleg Harlech offers a two-year University of Wales Diploma in General Studies which is advertised as being accepted by UK universities and polytechnics as satisfying entry requirements. As we have said in the last chapter, the course requirements may be different from the general requirements, but a two-year course of study successfully completed should count for a great deal in any application.

Ruskin College offers college diplomas in such subjects as labour studies, development studies, history, literature and social studies, and though it is quite independent of the university has an arrangement whereby Ruskin students are able to take the Oxford University Special Diploma in Social Studies.

Not all courses last one or two years. Most colleges are now offering short courses which cover a wide range of subjects, and Ruskin is now collaborating in a scheme with the Open University and the Workers' Educational Association to devise what is called the Preparatory Educational Project designed to help adults who lack any formal educational qualifications to break through the barriers created by any lack of confidence, skills and knowledge.

The project will take place in Berkshire, Buckinghamshire and Oxfordshire, so if you live in that part of the country you might enquire about possibilities. The local branches of the WEA and the Oxford office of the Open University should be able to provide you with further information.

Hillcroft College, which admits women only, offers traditional one- and two-year courses but is also actively involved in providing short (two- and five-day) courses designed for students without formal qualifications who wish to restart work, change career or return to education. If you cannot afford the time to take a one-or two-year course, you might enquire about one of the shorter courses on offer.

The long-term residential colleges are grant aided by the Department of Education and Science and accepted students may be eligible for grants under a state bursaries scheme. The colleges will give you full information about these bursaries (more about them in Ch. 10). An important point to note is that if you are awarded a bursary, this will not disqualify you from applying for a grant to take a full-time degree at a later stage.

If you think you might be interested in one of these courses, write to the colleges for further information (addresses in Appendix 7).

General Certificate of Education courses

If you decide to take 'O' and/or 'A' levels, there are a number of ways in which you can prepare. Thousands of adults have studied by correspondence, and if you think you have the discipline to study alone then this may be a good way for you. The addresses of accredited colleges are in Appendix 8. The advice given in Chapter 3 concerning the selection of a correspondence college for degree level study applies equally if you plan to take GCE courses by correspondence. Get all prospectuses and study them carefully before you decide where to register.

Most colleges of further education and many adult centres will also offer GCE courses, full time or part time. Some colleges offer GCE courses for mature students which have been running for many years. The staff of those colleges have long experience of teaching adults and of helping them to prepare for admission to higher education. If you enquire at your local college, ask whether such a course exists. If not, ask whether many mature students attend the classes that you wish to attend and how many take (and pass) the examinations. There can sometimes be problems with evening classes in certain subjects. LEAs generally require colleges and adult centres to recruit a minimum number of students before a class can start. Once recruited, some LEAs will accept that they have a responsibility to keep the class going, even though numbers may drop below the minimum number. However, others have been known to close classes part of the way through the year, and if this happens you can find yourself high and dry. So it pays to ask what the position is likely to be. The college cannot be sure what will happen in any year, but what has happened in previous years may give you some idea.

Open learning and flexistudy

One way of getting the best of both worlds – study by correspondence and tutor support – is sometimes possible in the now wide range of open learning systems being offered in many parts of the country. Systems do vary, but the general idea is that you pay for a set of materials produced by a local college or by a correspondence college, you study the materials but have the benefit of tutorial assistance from a college tutor. The National Extension College collaborates with a number of colleges of further education in providing materials for 'flexistudy' pro-grammes. Watch out for them in your area, because this method is often the answer for adults who want to take a formal course of study, often leading to an examination such as GCE 'O' or 'A' level, but who are unable to commit themselves to regular evening attendance. Flexistudy overcomes the problems of isolation, pro-vides a local contact and yet gives you the benefit of well-produced, tried and tested written materials for home study.

Collaborative access/preparatory ventures

Some institutions of higher education are now collaborating with colleges of further education by producing preparatory courses which are designed to lead directly into degree courses. One such initiative is a 'feeder' course offered at Stocksbridge college in Sheffield linked to Salford University's part-time BA in politics and contemporary history. The feeder course is designed as an introduction to the first level of the BA programme and students completing the course who wish to continue to the degree course are interviewed and considered for admission. No absolute guarantee of admission can be given, but the assumption is that students who satisfactorily complete the feeder course will be very likely to gain admission.

There are many other similar initiatives in different parts of the country. A booklet entitled Access/Preparatory Courses, pro-duced by the Council for National Academic Awards (and available from them free of charge), lists ninety colleges which offer access/preparatory courses which have a direct link to degree courses. Many more linked courses no doubt exist with universities (which do not appear on the CNAA list) and so you will be unlucky not to find one in your area.

Open college systems are also increasing in number. 'Open college' can mean different things to different people, but the system as pioneered at the Nelson and Colne College in Lancashire offers mature students an alternative to 'A'-level study in the form of a series of study units, some of which (the 'B' units) are accepted as alternatives to 'A' level by most institutions of higher education in the North West of England. In 1985, the Open College of the North West moved a stage further when an agreement was reached between Lancashire Polytechnic (formerly Preston Polytechnic) and six local colleges of further education which enables the six colleges to offer the first section of the polytechnic's part-time combined studies degree course. This Lancashire Integrated Colleges Scheme (LINCS) enables students to study near to home for the first part of their degree and provides close links between the participating colleges of further education and the polytechnic. Watch your local newspapers for any similar developments in your area.

A rather special access initiative was launched in 1978 when the Department of Education and Science invited seven LEAs to develop special courses to prepare mature students for entry to higher education. The courses were to be 'aimed at students who have valuable experience but lack the qualifications required and who have special needs which cannot be met by existing educational arrangements', including those 'from ethnic minority groups'.

This experiment was evaluated between 1979 and 1983 and the results were encouraging. The majority of the 1,200 students who attended in this period successfully completed their access course and over 90 per cent of those who completed went on to higher education. Numbers of the early students have now completed their degrees. Some LEAs gave grants to enable students to take these courses full time, but others did not and the availability of grants has had a marked effect on whether courses ran or not. It remains to be seen whether these courses will continue, but the evidence of the pilot scheme points to the fact that there is still a large pool of talent and significant numbers of people who, given the chance to prove themselves, are capable of degree level study.

Fresh horizons, new opportunities, return to study courses

If there are now large numbers of linked access/open college programmes of study, there are even more which are not directly linked with an institution of higher education. Starting on a linked course is all very well if you know exactly what you want to do at the end of the course, but if you are not sure, then you would probably be better to look for a course which incorporates some educational counselling and which will give you opportunities to consider a number of different routes.

New colleges, adult centres and institutions of higher education offer such courses. One of the earliest, the New Opportunities for Women course at Hatfield Polytechnic, was designed 'to be a comprehensive guide to the mature woman who may wish to return to active working life but is unsure or unaware of how best to do so'.

The Fresh Horizons courses started in 1966 by Enid Hutchinson and her colleagues at the City Literary Institute in London had similar aims, though the format of the course was different. The course was described in the prospectus as

> A refresher course in general studies for those in mature life who may be thinking of training for teaching, social work or similar professions and who want to test their ability to tackle regular study or to restore their general educational background. . . . It will also be of value to people who feel they need a disciplined course of study, suited to their needs as adults, for their personal development, or to enable them to meet new circumstances in their lives with more confidence.

This description sums up very well the aim of most Fresh Horizons/Fresh Start/New Opportunities courses: disciplined study combined with confidence boosting and the opportunity to reappraise and think about future plans.

In the space available, it is not possible to do more than touch on a few of the many opportunities for adults wishing to return to study and to prepare for higher education. You will need to check what is available in your own locality, to decide exactly what type of preparation you need to undertake and how best to tackle it. Bear in mind always what is likely to be required by the department of your choice. Look at the course content and if, for example, statistics form a key element in the course and you have no statistical background, you may feel that your efforts should go in that direction. If you decide to take 'A' levels, make sure that you know what the department will require. Remember that if you can satisfy the general entrance requirements you are not normally able to apply through a special scheme for mature entrants, so decide which route you wish to follow.

If you are offered a place on the strength of your existing qualifications, perhaps obtained some years ago, you will still be wise to get yourself into the habit of studying again. You might consider a course offered by a university or polytechnic extramural department or by the Workers' Educational Association (WEA). You might decide to take an Open University course in a related area, or to work out a reading programme for yourself. The advantage of joining others is that you can discuss, question and measure yourself against others. However, the choice is yours. There are plenty of opportunities but you may have to look around to find the study opportunities that are right for you.

Chapter 9

Alternative routes to graduate or professional status

Achieving graduate status by what might be considered to be 'normal' routes – that is, completing a degree course in an institution of higher education by either part-time or full-time study – is not the only way. In some subjects it is possible to follow an alternative route which brings you to the same point. One example is in the field of modern languages. The Institute of Linguists has been offering examinations from beginners' level to advanced for many years, and the extent and difficulty of their membership examination has now been recognised and accepted by the Burnham Committee as degree equivalent.

A number of other qualifications will similarly confer graduate status and you may wish to consider alternative routes before you commit yourself finally to taking a degree. Full information about graduate equivalence, membership of professional bodies and registration is provided in *British Qualifications*, which should be available for consultation in most reasonably sized libraries.

A degree is often the first step on the way to achieving professional status, but not always, and if you have some particular career in mind you should check what the position is before you embark on a degree course. You may find you would do better to start professional training immediately and to abandon the idea of taking a degree altogether.

There are many ways of achieving professional membership without a degree, but we give just two examples here. The first concerns qualification for social work and the second relates to registration as a chartered engineer.

Social Work

If you want to become a social worker, you will need to take the Certificate of Qualification in Social Work (CQSW) to become professionally qualified. Some people take the CQSW course after they graduate, some take a degree course which incorporates professional training, but others embark on the course without having taken a degree. In fact mature applicants who demonstrate that they have appropriate experience and personal qualities and the ability to cope with the academic content of the course may, exceptionally, gain admission with few academic qualifications. You may possibly have better career prospects if you take a degree, but you have a choice and before you commit yourself to a degree course lasting three or four years, followed by a one- or two-year CQSW course (depending on the subject of your degree), you should probably consider the alternative.

CQSW courses are offered in a good many polytechnic and university departments and CQSW admissions tutors will generally be willing to talk to you about the advantages and disadvantages of the different routes. Before you ask for an interview, you might like to study the leaflet produced by the Central Council for Education and Training in Social Work (CCETSW) entitled *Professional Training for Social Work*, obtainable from the Information Service, CCETSW at the following addresses:

England	Derbyshire House, St Chad's St, London WC1H 8AD (Tel: 01–278 2455)
Wales	West Wing, St David's House, Wood St, Cardiff CF1 1ES (Tel: 0222 26257)
Scotland	9 South St, David Street, Edinburgh EH2 2BW (Tel: 031–556 2953)
Northern Ireland	14 Malone Road, Belfast BT9 5BN (Tel: 0232–665 390)

Applications for CQSW courses have to be made through the Central Council for Education and Training in Social Work (CCETSW) Clearing House at 4th Floor, Myson House, Rugby, Warwicks CV21 3HT.

Engineering

The designation 'C.Eng.' (chartered engineer) is the goal of most professional engineers and confers a highly-valued status to holders. The Engineering Council now has responsibility for maintaining the register of chartered engineers and for setting the

78

standards of education, training and experience considered appropriate to this designation.

Many engineers achieve chartered status by taking a degree in engineering or a related subject, followed by a period of experience at an appropriate level. However, a degree is not the only route to registration. These days, most students following the non-graduate route will take higher certificates or diplomas of the Business and Technician Education Council, followed by examinations of the Engineering Council. The member institutions of the Engineering Council (see *British Qualifications* for details of chartered engineering institutions) will provide enquirers with full information about the different routes to chartered status.

The non-graduate route to technical and professional qualification is a well trodden path and many thousands have achieved their goal by this strenuous route. The new regulations of the Engineering Council have certainly not made the route any easier, but they have brought a degree of standardisation into what was (and still is to an extent) a very complicated and, to outsiders, bafflingly diverse system.

Students of any age can take the Engineering Council examinations, but there is a further route to registration that has been devised to take account of the small number of experienced practising engineers who have not passed all the required examinations but who may nevertheless be worthy of chartered status. The mature candidate scheme was designed to provide a route to registration for

> exceptional candidates, who, although they do not have formal academic qualifications at the right level, are able to demonstrate that in later life they have achieved a standard of technical competence comparable to that of their contemporaries who became Chartered Engineers by a normal route. The Engineering Council regards due recognition of engineering talent, at whatever stage it can be identified, as an important contribution to the profession and to the nation, and is anxious that individuals who achieve a high standard of professional competence in the course of their careers should not be handicapped by lack of early educational opportunities.

Demonstrating such professional competence is by no means easy. A technical paper (or papers) at the appropriate level is required, and if that is passed at what is considered to be a sufficiently high standard by the appointed assessors, then the candidate will be given an oral examination 'on the submission and any other matters they (that is the assessors) may consider relevant'.

Preparation of the technical paper and the ensuing oral examination are only part of the mature candidate scheme. Candidates have to be at least 40 years old, have had experience in posts of increasing responsibility in a relevant branch of engineering over a period of at least fifteen years and have attained a position demonstrating a level of competence 'that would have admitted them to Corporate Membership had they satisfied the normal academic requirements'. Enough to make any applicant take a degree after all! Perhaps not surprisingly, few apply and even fewer succeed. Nevertheless, the alternative route does exist and the documentation provided by the Engineering Council gives useful guidance about how to prepare.

The point of discussing these non-graduate routes to professional qualification is merely to draw your attention to the fact that a degree need not be the only, or even the best, way to prepare for a profession. It would be impossible to give any worthwhile indication here of which professions have a non-graduate and which a special mature entry scheme. There are many, and if you have a career in mind you would be wise to contact the professional organisation concerned to find out exactly what their requirements are. It would be dispiriting, to say the least, to come to the end of your degree course, only to find that you have not taken the required options or, worse still, that you already had a qualification that was accepted as the equivalent of a degree. Check first. Do not rely on hearsay, but ask for information from the professional body before you decide which degree course to take, which options will be necessary for your purposes and, most important, whether to take a degree at all.

Chapter 10

Finding the money

For many adults who wish to take up some form of education and/or
training the availability of financial help is likely to be a central, if not a
deciding, factor in whether or not they are eventually able to follow a
course or training programme.

There are a good many publications on the market which provide
very helpful information about grants, sponsorship and scholarships
(see the Bibliography) but sorting out the regulations is a time-
consuming and complicated job, and there are a number of general
points that are worth bearing in mind before you start considering the
detail.

The information in this chapter was accurate at the time of going to
press, but grant regulations can change, so you should always check
with the grant-awarding body to make sure the information you have
is up to date.

The main providers of finance for undergraduate study are

* Local education authorities (in England and Wales)
* Education and Library Boards (in Northern Ireland)
* Education Authorities of the Regional and Islands Councils (in
  Scotland)
* The Department of Education and Science (DES)
* The Department of Education in Northern Ireland (DENI)
* The Department of Economic Development in Northern Ireland
  (DED)
* The Scottish Education Department (SED)
* Employers and professional bodies

- The Manpower Services Commission (MSC)
- The Department of Health and Social Security (DHSS)
- Various educational charities

Grants to students

The majority of what follows in relation to local education authorities applies equally in all parts of the country, but there are certain differences in the way grants are awarded and administered in England and Wales, Northern Ireland and Scotland. In England and Wales, the majority of funding for undergraduate study is provided by the local education authorities. The Education and Library Boards in Northern Ireland and the Scottish Education Department assume similar responsibilities in their own areas. Where the differences are marginal (for example, where the amount of grant varies by a few pounds), they are ignored. Attention is only drawn to those aspects of the regulations which are fundamentally different in some way.

Local education authorities

Local education authorities pay two kinds of grant: *mandatory* (which means that in most circumstances they have a statutory duty to pay an award), and *discretionary* (which means that the LEA may give you a grant if they wish, but they do not have to). Each LEA makes its own policy about discretionary grants, so you may be lucky or unlucky, depending on where you live.

Mandatory grants

Mandatory grants are paid for what are called 'designated courses'. With few exceptions, these are all full-time courses of higher education lasting at least two years, such as:

- First degree courses (and full-time or sandwich courses which are comparable to first degree courses).
- Diploma of Higher Education (DipHE).
- Higher Diploma of the Business and Technician Education Council (BTEC).
- Initial and postgraduate teacher training courses, including Art Teachers' Certificate or Diploma, and some part-time courses.
- Other courses specifically prescribed as being comparable to first degree courses.
- Certain degree level courses provided jointly by a UK and an overseas establishment.

An up-to-date list of the last two categories is obtainable from your LEA, or from the Department of Education and Science, Room 4/50, Elizabeth House, York Road, London SE1 7PH.

Eligibility

In order to qualify for a grant, you have to have been 'ordinarily resident' in the UK for three years immediately before the beginning of the academic year in which the course begins. Special regulations apply for people who are not 'ordinarily resident' in the UK, and local education authorities will advise about that. Absence due to temporary employment abroad by you, your spouse or parents may not make you ineligible. Check with your LEA. Subject to certain conditions, residents of the EEC do not need to be ordinarily resident in the UK, but must be resident in the EEC for three years prior to the start of the course. Mature students who have refugee status (recognised as such under the UN Convention) are also exempt from the three-year resident rule. In the case of other overseas students, periods spent studying in the UK do not count towards the three years' residence.

Possible problem areas

Even though you have the offer of a place on a designated course, and even though you may never have had a grant before, a grant is NOT AUTOMATICALLY PAYABLE if you:

- Have previously attended for more than one term a full-time course of advanced further education (usually considered to be of above 'A' level standard) of more than two academic years' length (excluding sandwich course experience periods) OR successfully completed a part-time course of such education of equivalent length. This applies whether or not you had a grant for the previous course.
- Have previously attended one of the courses designated as mandatory. Previous attendance at one of the long-term residential colleges (see Ch. 4) will not disqualify you. A period of up to one term's attendance on a designated course will be disregarded, but if you have attended more than one course at some stage in your career, that could make you ineligible for a mandatory grant. This regulation can make difficulties for some students who have studied part-time for several years and then decided they would like to transfer to a full-time course. They may have spent the equivalent of two years'

full-time on part-time study and obtained an advanced qualification. Even though they paid their own way, their previous study may make them ineligible for a mandatory grant.

So, try to plan ahead. If you are thinking of taking a full-time degree course after a period of part-time study, you would be well advised to check regulations before you get too far in your part-time course, to make quite sure you are not disqualifying yourself.

Discretionary grants

Discretionary grants can be given (though LEAs do not have to give them) in the following cases:

- To a student who has a place on a designated course, but for some reason does not qualify for a mandatory award. In a case like this, once a grant is given, it will almost always be at the same rate as for mandatory awards.
- To a student who has a place on an advanced course which is not designated (e.g. Certificates of Qualification in Social Work (CQSW)).
- To students taking non-advanced courses such as GCE 'O' or 'A' levels. As LEAs face more and more cutbacks it becomes harder to get grants for non-advanced courses. Where they are given, they take the form of minor awards – that is, fees and sometimes a small maintenance grant.
- To students taking part-time courses, advanced or non-advanced (though at present practically no grants are given for part-time study, with the exception of certain housebound students taking correspondence courses and some support for Open University students).

This difference between full-time degree courses (which attract mandatory awards) and part-time degree courses (which attract discretionary awards) is particularly unfortunate for people who are unable to take a full-time course because of domestic or other commitments. Open University students are all classified as part time and so are particularly affected by this regulation.

Fortunately, many LEAs do support OU students, even in these hard times, but applicants can be lucky or unlucky, depending on where they live.

Policy over discretionary grants varies from LEA to LEA, so the only way you can know what your LEA's policy is is by writing to ask them. At present, a good many LEAs are giving no discretionary awards at all, but it is still worth enquiring. You just may be lucky.

84

The means test

All students applying for an LEA award for their first degree or equivalent will be means tested to assess the award.

There are three possible means tests.

1. *By reference to your own income.* This is applied in every case. If you have any unearned income, you will find that the residual value after assessment is deducted £ for £ from the grant. Until 1985/1986, if students earned £400 or more during term time, their grant was affected but that no longer applies. You will also be allowed to keep;
   (a) the first £790 of trust income where no parent is living;
   (b) up to £1,200 for payments from employers or scholarships (£1,500 in the case of National Engineering Scholarships);
   (c) vacation earnings (though these earnings may make you liable for income tax);
   (d) child benefit and other DHSS benefits;
   (e) disability pensions not subject to income tax;
   (f) payments made under covenant by parents (providing that the parent paying is still a member of the family);
   (g) earnings from periods of industrial experience by sandwich course students.
2. *By reference to parental income.* In the case of students who do not have independent status, though this clause will not affect many mature students. This test is based on parents' residual income (that is the gross income less certain allowances). For 1985/1986, parents were expected to pay £1 in every £7 if their residual income was below £10,300, £1 in every £5 in the £10,300 to £15,000 category and £1 in every £4 for those over £15,000.
3. *By reference to spouse's income.* In the case of independent married students. A similar scale to that in operation for parents applies for married students normally living with their spouse.

Covenants

Parents may feel that if their offspring wish to return to full-time study in their maturity, they should fend for themselves! However, some parents may be willing to help, particularly if a mandatory award is not granted, and if that is the case, they might be persuaded to take out a deed of covenant. A deed of covenant is a legally binding document in which one person promises to pay another so much over a period of time. Some people make a contribution to charities by means of a deed of covenant, the advantage being that the recipient of the contributions is then able to claim tax relief. Parents are able to make covenant payments to their student 'child' in the same way, though it only works if parents are paying tax and the student 'child' is not. There are certain conditions that have to be fulfilled. For example, the 'child' must be at least 18 (or married), the parents must not get any benefit from the transaction, and the agreement must be taken out for a period of seven years (though if the course does not last seven years – and very few do – the period can be shortened). The Inland Revenue produces a leaflet (IR47) which explains the system, and gives deed of covenant forms for England, Wales and Northern Ireland and for Scotland. The idea is that each payment made is a transfer of income from parent to 'child' which reduces the parent's income, and becomes (for tax purposes) the income of the student. So, when the payments are made, the parent is entitled to deduct income tax at the basic rate. For example, if the payment is to be £100.00 and the basic rate of income tax is 30 per cent, then the parent will:

1. Deduct tax of £30.00.
2. Pay £70.00 to his student child.
3. Give his child a certificate on form R185 (AP) (obtainable from the Inland Revenue) showing the gross amount of £100.00, less tax deducted of £30.00, and the net payment of £70.00.

Once the deed form has been completed, the parent will need to give it to the student child, who sends it immediately to the tax office nearest to his/her home. The tax office will return the deed in due course and explain to the student what has to be done to claim the refund of tax deducted from the payments.

The covenant can as a rule be cancelled at any time by mutual agreement (usually at the end of the course – but remember that it is a legally binding document, so both parties have to agree). There is no problem about drawing up the covenant yourself, as long as you follow the rules outlined in the Inland Revenue leaflet IR47, but if you have any doubt, check with the Inland Revenue. You want to be sure there are no arguments when the refund is applied for. One point to watch is that the deed of covenant has to be signed, sealed and delivered. To seal a deed, you need to stick a red disc in the appropriate place (this can be a home-made disc of red paper, or a disc made with red crayon or wax). The following is an example of a deed of covenant for England, Wales and Northern Ireland. (Crown copyright. Reproduced by kind permission of the Controller, Her Majesty's Stationery Office.)

To be completed by a covenantor (parent) resident in England, Wales or Northern Ireland.

DEED OF COVENANT

I . . . .
  name of person making covenant

of . . . .
  address of person making covenant

. . . .

covenant to pay my son/daughter . . . .
  full name of child

of . . . .
  address of child

. . . .

the sum of £ . . . . (gross) on

. . . . in each year
  state date or dates

for the period of seven years, or for the period of our joint lives, or until he/she ceases to be receiving full-time education at any university, college, school or other educational establishment (whichever is the shortest period), the first payment to be made on

. . . .   Dated . . . .
Signed, sealed and delivered by

. . . .
  signature of person making covenant

in the presence of . . . .
  witness's signature and address

. . . .

Person making the Covenant

Please state below the Tax District (and reference number) which deals with your tax affairs

District . . . .   Reference . . . .

Parents resident in Scotland have to complete a slightly different version. The deed is the same apart from the fact that it does not have to be signed, sealed and delivered. Instead, the person making the covenant is asked to write 'Adopted as holograph', in his/her own handwriting, and then to sign and date.

How much are you likely to get?

The mandatory grant consists of tuition fees in full and a basic grant. The basic grant is awarded up to a maximum value fixed for each year, and can be reduced by means tests. So the basic grant, which is likely to change most years, will vary according to the type of accommodation used during term time. The maximum rates of basic grant for 1985/1986 for England, Wales and Northern Ireland, were £2,165 for students living in lodgings in London, £1,830 for students living in lodgings elsewhere, and £1,480 for students living at home. Scottish students received slightly less.

However, the basic grant is only part of the story. Additional grants may be available for a whole range of special circumstances, such as the following.

1. *Travel* – the main grant contains a flat rate sum to cover the cost of travel (In 1985 that was £160 for students living at home and £100 for others), but additional travel costs will be reimbursed where
   (a) costs are incurred by attending courses overseas or away from the main place of study,
   (b) costs are incurred by students with a disability as a result of that disability.
2. *Special equipment* – expenditure on essential equipment can be reimbursed for certain courses.
3. *Extra weeks* – additional maintenance is available for each week (or part of a week) in excess of 30 weeks and 3 days (25 weeks and 3 days at Oxford and Cambridge).
4. *Vacation study* – a daily rate is available from the LEA if you attend an institution not wholly maintained out of public funds. For other institutions, the institution itself is the awarding body.
5. *Two homes grant* – if you have to maintain two homes while studying you may qualify for an additional 'two homes' allowance.
6. *Mature students' grant* – if you are aged 26 or over at the start of the course, and have worked full time for a total of three years during the six years before the start of the course, an additional grant could be available.
7. *Dependants' grants* – if you were married before the first year of your course and have the care of dependants, additional grants may be paid, subject to the income of the dependants. If you do not qualify under the main mandatory award scheme, but are attending a designated course, you can claim under the dependants' allowance hardship scheme, which is administered by the DHSS Students' Unit, Government Buildings, Warbeck Hill, Blackpool, Lancs FY2 0XW. Allowances are means tested on family income and on capital. They are only paid for weeks of term time (except for single parents when they are payable for 52 weeks). The hardship scheme does not apply in Northern Ireland.

88

Northern Ireland

Much of what has gone before applies equally in Northern Ireland but there are certain differences. The Education and Library Boards assume a similar role to the LEAs in England and Wales and enquiries concerning grants for study at any level should be addressed to the appropriate Education and Library Board (addresses in Appendix 13) with the exception of teacher education awards and postgraduate bursaries and scholarships, which are dealt with by the Department of Education in Northern Ireland (DENI) at Rathgael House, Balloo Road, Bangor, Co. Down. Grant regulations follow similar lines to those in England and Wales, the important exception being that teacher education awards for courses outside Northern Ireland are only available if there is no equivalent local course.

Scotland

Scotland again adopts many of the procedures and practices described above, though there are a number of differences. The Scottish Education Department (SED) is responsible for the administration of students' allowances for degree and equivalent level courses. Allowances for other full-time courses of further and higher education are in most cases the responsibility of the Education Authorities of the Regional and Islands Councils though this will depend on the content and entry requirements of the course.

Guidance about the Scottish students' allowances scheme, information about eligibility, how to apply, conditions of awards and the main features of the scheme, are provided in the SED pamphlet *Guide to Students' Allowances*. Copies of the Guide and the application form (Form AB1) are obtainable from the SED, from education authority offices, universities, colleges of education, central institutions and further education colleges.

How to apply for a grant

Application forms are obtainable from the LEA or Education and Library Board in whose area you are or were ordinarily resident on the 30 June preceding the start of your course (31 October or 28 February for courses which start in spring or summer). In Scotland, application forms are available from the Awards Branch of the Scottish Education Department at Haymarket House, Clifton Terrace, Edinburgh EH12 5DT (Tel. 031–337 2477).

You should make an application, in writing, as early as possible so that you can get some idea as to whether you can afford to accept the offer of a place. If you apply after the end of the first term of the course, you may not be eligible for a grant. Some grant-awarding bodies will not accept a firm application from you until you have at least a provisional offer of a place but most awards officers will be willing to give you some idea of whether you qualify for a grant, and if so, approximately how much you might expect to receive.

Awards officers say that mature students sometimes start courses before they have checked how much their grant will be – or even whether they are eligible for a grant – and can then find themselves in difficulties. Occasionally, students get into debt and then ask to be 'bailed out', which can rarely be done. So, as we have been saying throughout this book, check carefully and in good time to see what the position is, before you commit yourself.

Most grant-awarding bodies produce booklets which give information about eligibility, and any special regulations which apply so ask about that when you make your preliminary enquiries. REMEMBER that staff of awards offices will be particularly busy from June to October, to ensure that students starting their courses in October have their grant cheques at the beginning of term, so try not to ask for an interview around that time.

Appeals

If your application for a grant is turned down and you feel you have a good case (or additional circumstances which should be considered), you may wish to appeal against the decision. Most LEAs will have an appeals procedure but, whether they do or not, if you feel you have a grievance you should ask for your case to be reconsidered. Prepare your appeal carefully, try to enlist the support of the institution to which you are applying, and make sure you supply *all* the relevant information. You may feel it is none of the LEA's business that you have been declared redundant and there is no money coming in to the house, but if you do not tell them what your position is, they will not be able to help.

Your best chance of getting enough money to enable you to live for the three, four or five years that it will take to graduate is by applying for a mandatory grant, but if you are not eligible for an award of this kind, there are a number of other avenues that you might explore. You might, for example, investigate the possibility of sponsorship.

Sponsorships

A number of industrial and professional organisations regularly sponsor students who wish to study at degree or higher diploma level

– mainly, though not exclusively, in vocational subjects such as engineering, science, mathematics or business studies.

The Careers and Occupational Information Centre of the Manpower Services Commission at Moorfoot, Sheffield S1 4PQ publish a booklet every year, entitled *Sponsorships*, which lists organisations which are willing to sponsor students through their course. In 1985, eighty-nine firms were listed, though in fact many more offer sponsorship schemes and if you are looking for a sponsor, you should write to firms that are likely to employ people in your field of interest.

These awards may be given in addition to a local education authority or SED grant, and most are well worth having. Several of the schemes are limited to students under 20, but not all. Even where an age limit is stipulated, it may still be worth enquiring.

Obtaining sponsorship does not mean you are guaranteed a place on a degree course, though some firms do have special links with certain institutions and departments. In most cases, you would have to find your own place and apply through UCCA in the usual way. There are slightly different procedures for industry-sponsored candidates who are applying for a sandwich or full-time degree course in certain UK universities. UCCA produce a special leaflet (free) entitled *Industrial awards and the universities' central admissions scheme* which explains all the details.

The Manpower Services Commission (MSC) Job Training Scheme

At present, the MSC fund Job Training Schemes which sponsor adults for certain full-time training and retraining courses for a maximum of fifty-two weeks. They will pay you while you learn, but courses are strictly vocational, and unfortunately, GCE and Return to Study courses are not included in the Job Training Scheme. To be eligible for a Job Training course, you have to be at least 18 years old, have been away from full-time education for more than two years, and have to be available to take up training, so that means you have to be unemployed, or else be able to give up your job at short notice.

You must not have been on a government training course lasting one year during the past three years, and you need to prove you are suited to the course, so you will probably have to take some sort of an aptitude test. Conditions of eligibility for disabled people are sometimes different. For example, the MSC on occasion provide financial assistance for disabled people who want to train for a professional career such as law or accountancy, but only if the LEA has refused to help.

The MSC has never provided financial support for undergraduate study but has occasionally funded postgraduate study. Only courses lasting twelve months or less are eligible for funding under the Job Training Scheme and support is mainly, though not exclusively, reserved for new technology subjects.

Full information about Job Training Schemes and other MSC funding is obtainable at all Job Centres.

There is no MSC in Northern Ireland, but the Department of Economic Development can sometimes help in a similar way.

Department of Health and Social Security (DHSS)

The DHSS will award bursaries for certain courses classified as 'auxiliary medical work', most of which are below degree level. These awards are discretionary, but are paid normally at the same rates as awards made by the LEA for first degree students. The courses covered are:

- Occupational therapists
- Dental therapists
- Dental hygienists
- Physiotherapists
- Orthoptists
- Radiographers

The finance for all these groups, except for occupational therapists, comes from the Regional Health Authority, but the distribution of awards is administrated by the DHSS.

Applications are made through the school/department which offers you a place and the school will give you full information about conditions and requirements.

In Scotland, these grants are administered by the Scottish Education Department, and in Northern Ireland by the Department of Health and Social Security.

Trade unions

Trade unions and the Trades Union Congress (TUC) run various special education and training programmes for their members. Many are run for trade union representatives (full-time officers, shop stewards, safety representatives, etc.), by public educational bodies, on a day-release basis with the TUC paying course fees and the employer continuing to pay wages. In addition the TUC education service runs correspondence courses which are open to members. Enquiries should be made to shop stewards, full-time officers, union branch secretaries or to TUC Regional Education Offices.

Educational charities

There are literally hundreds of educational charities, most of which offer small sums of money (in the region of £50 to £200) to students who fulfil usually very specific requirements (for example, there is one charity which is only open to the children of deceased artists).

Charitable assistance, even for students who are lucky enough to be able to secure aid from several different charities, rarely amounts to an LEA grant or research council award. Trusts will often only help in emergencies and/or in the later stages of a course, and tend to give low priority to people wishing to take further qualifications (especially if the bias is academic rather than vocational) and to part-time students. Furthermore, many charities have a cut-off age limit of 25, which excludes a large number of mature students. A very few charities make loans to particular groups/categories, such as women, single mothers after divorce or bereavement, occasionally young people from deprived backgrounds, refugees and immigrants (although charities sometimes expect the latter to complete the three-year residence requirement required by LEAs), disabled people (generally for gaining initial qualifications) or overseas students (students from the Commonwealth probably fare slightly better). Charities also have a soft spot for medical students who already have a first degree, usually in a relevant subject and need funding for the pre-clinical stages, where they are not eligible for LEA support, though the sums involved are usually small.

Letters of application to Trusts, etc., should cover basic details such as age, college, when the course begins and the expected length of study. Reasons for the application should be given as clearly as possible and it is usually helpful to indicate the amount of assistance needed. It is rarely possible to obtain assistance at very short notice.

Many Trusts meet at infrequent intervals and have to give careful consideration to each application, so some delay between submitting the application and hearing the result can be expected.

The only way to find out if one of the charities would be suitable is to search through the published information. Consult the books recommended in the bibliography at the end of this book, and check what is in stock at your local library.

Scholarships, exhibitions and hardship funds

Institutions may have their own sources or an arrangement with a charitable body to support their students, although such support serves mainly to supplement other funding since the introduction of the mandatory awards scheme. As with the educational charities, many scholarships and exhibitions are limited to students from particular backgrounds, places or taking particular subjects.

In addition, some institutions have hardship funds to help students in financial difficulties. The Open University in particular has fairly extensive funds to assist students who have been unable to get financial assistance elsewhere and students who are unemployed. (Details from The Open University, Walton Hall, Milton Keynes MK7 6AA or any regional office of the Open University.)

If you feel you have explored all avenues with little or no success, you could consult the Educational Grants Advisory Service (EGAS) to see if they can help.

The Educational Grants Advisory Service (EGAS)

This service was established in 1962 by the Family Welfare Association. Subsequently it was administered by the National Council for Voluntary Organisations but, in 1980, the Family Welfare Association resumed responsibility for its management. It endeavours to put students in touch with sources of charitable and other help, taking account of the particular circumstances of each case. Where required and possible, it also advises students when points of difficulty or doubt arise in their negotiations with local education authorities and other official bodies. A leaflet explaining the main features of the scheme can be obtained by sending a 9 × 4 inch stamped addressed envelope to EGAS, The Family Welfare Association, 501–505 Kingsland Road, London E8 4 AU.

They have a small staff and prefer enquiries by letter rather than telephone. Before you contact them, you should make quite sure that all statutory sources have been approached. EGAS will check this with you, so you will save their time if you have copies of applications made to LEAs or other bodies. It is always a wise precaution in any case to keep copies of applications in case forms go astray.

Supplementary benefit

In certain exceptional circumstances some students may qualify for supplementary benefit. As might be expected, the rules relating to entitlement are complicated and applications are dealt with on an individual basis. In order to get supplementary benefit, you have to sign on as being available for work – unless you come into a special category, such as having child care responsibilities, or being disabled. Entitlement will also depend on whether you are considered to be a full-time or part-time student, and the rules relating to this classification are equally complicated.

A recent social security review makes it clear that the government feels strongly that students should not make use of the social security system while receiving grants, so it remains to be seen whether regulations will change to make it more difficult to claim benefit while studying.

All that we can say here is that it may be possible for certain students to obtain supplementary benefits while studying certain courses. Not very helpful but the DHSS Students' Unit at Room 311, Government Buildings, Warbreck Hill, Blackpool, Lancs FY2 0XW will have up-to-date information and should be able to give you advice about your particular situation. They publish helpful notes about hardship allowances, available from your LEA, SED or the DHSS Students' Unit. At a more local level, try the Citizen's Advice Bureau, who are often very well informed about benefits. Needless to say, if there is an Educational Guidance Service in your area, they may also have information.

Postgraduate awards

This book is not specifically concerned with study at postgraduate level, but it is likely that a proportion of mature graduates will wish to take a postgraduate course of one kind or another, and so sources of information are given in the bibliography. Very few postgraduate courses attract mandatory grants. The postgraduate certificate in education is one exception, and all students who are accepted on to a PGCE course will be entitled to a mandatory grant on the same conditions as apply for undergraduate study.

Finance for most postgraduate study is generally the responsibility of various research councils (see the Useful Addresses section of this book) and government departments, but, inevitably, there are many exceptions and if you are contemplating postgraduate study, you will need to investigate sources very carefully. Being accepted on a postgraduate course does not necessarily guarantee a grant. The department to which you are applying should be able to give you full information about finance, but it is as well to make your own enquiries also.

Two very useful booklets, produced by the Central Services Unit (CSU), give information about sources of finance and basic facts about postgraduate study. They are: *Postgraduate Research and Training*; and *Awards for Postgraduate Study*.

These booklets explain the different conditions for residents in England and Wales, Scotland, Northern Ireland, the Isle of Man and the Channel Isles, and give addresses of research councils and conditions of awards.

If you are already a student in a university, polytechnic or institute/college of higher education, the booklets should be available for consultation in your careers service. If not, then copies are available from CSU at Crawford House, Precinct Centre, Manchester M13 9EP.

Conclusion

If this chapter has given you the impression that searching for enough money to enable you to return to study as a mature student is something of an obstacle course, well, that is probably not too far from the truth. Regulations are complicated and it takes time to explore all avenues. For most of you who decide to take a degree, the mandatory grant will provide the main, and possibly the only, source of income. The grant-awarding body will give you an idea of how much you are likely to get, and when you reach the stage of making a firm application will tell you exactly how much you *will* get.

However, as you have seen, there are other sources that might also be tapped. You might consider a sponsorship, you may, possibly, qualify for supplementary benefit and you may find that a charity or special fund will add to your grant. Consult the reference books which are listed in the bibliography (they should be available in most major libraries), and ask at the institution which has offered you a place if there are any special scholarships or funds for which you might qualify. You will almost certainly have to live on a reduced income if you become a full-time student, so every little will help. It all takes time, but all avenues should be explored.

If you are fortunate enough to live in an area which has an established Educational Guidance Service for Adults, consult them. They may know of sources of finance that do not appear in the reference books and should in any case be able to tell you where to go for further advice. The Educational Guidance Service for Adults in Belfast (address in Appendix 14) is now regarded as the central point for information on all aspects of adult/continuing education (including finance) in Northern Ireland, so if you live within travelling distance of Belfast, it will be worth your while to pay them a visit.

As we said at the beginning of this chapter, you should always check what the position is with the grant-awarding body, to make sure there have been no recent changes in legislation. We have only been able to scratch the surface of this very complicated area and the experts in the grant-awarding bodies will fill in the detail and advise you about your own particular circumstances. It would have been impossible to cover all aspects in a book of this kind. One LEA awards officer told us that his training manual ran to 100 pages and needed constant updating. Even so, we think it is advisable for any mature applicant to higher education to have some understanding of sources of finance, about eligibility and entitlement, in good time. By that, we mean before embarking on a lengthy course of preparation and before submitting an application for a grant. Knowledge of the system may help you to take advantage of what is available and to make quite sure that you do not disqualify yourself from entitlement to a mandatory grant.

Chapter 11

After graduation.
Will it all have been worth while?

A degree does not itself qualify you for a job in many cases and you need to be aware of the fact that in order to obtain professional qualification you may face another year of training. Studying for a higher degree may also be a possibility (see Appendix 10 for the addresses of research councils). This will depend on the class and type of degree you obtain and the availability of grants, but even though money for research has been cut back there are still opportunities to study for masters and doctoral degrees in some subjects. However, it is early to be considering postgraduate study before you have begun your undergraduate course, and in any case most undergraduates will be looking for a job as soon as they have graduated. So, after all your hard work and sacrifice, what are your chances of getting a good job?

One problem is that over a three- or four-year period, the job market can change radically and no one can know for sure what will happen. As everyone must know, unemployment has remained at a distressingly high level for a number of years and from time to time we read accounts of unemployed doctors, teachers and other professionally qualified men and women. However, bad though the situation is, graduates still emerge as being more likely to obtain suitable employment than other groups.

The 1985 press statement issued by the Association of Graduate Careers Advisory Services, the Central Services Unit for Careers and Appointments Services and the Standing Con-

ference of Employers of Graduates began with the following encouraging statement:

Employment prospects for graduates in 1985 are even better
than expected at the beginning of the year. Demand for
graduates is markedly higher than in 1984. About 20 per cent
of the available vacancies are still unfilled, the highest proportion of these being in industry.

That statement referred to *all* those who graduated in 1985, and
there is no indication in the available statistics as to whether the
mature graduates fared better or worse than the 21-to-22-year-
olds. We said earlier that, with the exception of medicine, few
institutions of higher education now impose an upper age limit.
However, some employers do, often for what appears to be quite
arbitrary reasons.

Once you are a registered student of an institution of higher
education, you will automatically be entitled to make use of the
services of the institution's careers advisory service. The staff of
the service are well experienced in placing graduates of all ages
and will be able to advise you about any likely areas of difficulty.

If demand for graduates overall is increasing, are the matures
likely to fare as well as the young graduates? Research carried
out over a three-year period by Sue Falla as part of a project at
Salford University reveals some interesting facts. She examined
data on mature graduates on full-time degree courses in British
universities and discovered that over this period, though there
was a rise in the unemployment of all graduates, there was little
difference between mature and young graduates (from 7–10 per
cent for matures and 8–12 per cent for the young group).

Further investigation revealed other interesting features. She
discovered that the 25–29 year age group had more success in
finding suitable employment than any other group, including those
who graduated at the more usual age of 21/22, and that until the
age of 40 or so there was practically no difference in employment
patterns. This applied equally well for men and for women. However, after the age of 40 it appeared to become more difficult and
the few students who were age 50 or over had to wait quite a time
before they found anything suitable.

The mature graduates in Sue Falla's survey sought
employment in a wide variety of professions and approximately a
quarter continued with their education – either going on to take a
higher degree or to take some form of professional training. Again,
the proportions were similar for the younger group.

Generally, there was a fairly consistent trend in job placement
over the three-year period. Jobs in social welfare showed a

99

dramatic rise in importance (from seventh to second place in popularity), compensated for by a reduction in jobs in the scientific, technological and environmental areas. This is no doubt a reflection of the economic recession and resulting shortage of jobs in certain types of industry generally rather than a reluctance on the part of employers to employ mature graduates.

Since 1981, though the employment situation nationally has not improved, opportunities for graduates have, and the careers advisory services of institutions of higher education are optimistic about the job prospects of their students.

Conclusion

Will it all be worth while? Impossible to say. Whether you answer 'yes' or 'no' at the end of your course will depend on what you hoped to get out of it and whether your expectations were fulfilled. For some people, it is enough to have studied for three years, to have broadened horizons, read wisely and enjoyed the company of fellow students. For others, the course will have been a complete waste of time if it does not lead to a better job and a more interesting life. All we can say is that prospects of employment are quite good, even in the still depressed stage of the economy and that many mature students have found studying to degree level a rewarding personal experience.

But let Sue Falla's students speak for themselves. She wrote to students who took part in her research three years after graduation and asked them, Was it worth while? 91 per cent said 'Yes', it certainly was and 74 per cent said the degree had improved their future prospects.

They were asked if they had any comments to make that might be helpful to prospective mature students and the following are just a few of the many responses.

'Be clear about motivation and aims (if any), choosing courses accordingly. I feel that mature graduates must have complete mobility in order to compete in the job market.'
'Degree definitely enhances promotion prospects, but is not any guarantee.'
'Don't be put off by prospective employers' attitudes about age. "Mature" people are always wanted.'
'Age is no barrier in the modern job market. What is essential is the ability to adapt and be flexible in one's approach and attitude towards employment and its changing style.'
'Check before you start that your qualification is relevant to the career of your choice or for future education, e.g. post-

graduate courses. Check the age limits. You may be too old by the time you have qualified.'

'I would advise all mature students to attend a study skills course before embarking on their course. I didn't and found it took a long time to re-acquire skills I had had at school.'

'Choice of course is important. With the current job situation, those with a science/maths/computer content are almost certainly more useful. Choice of course depends on motive, self fulfilment and career development. If you are already in a secure job that has prospects of promotion I would advise a prospective student to consider carefully before giving up that job. I am earning less than I would have been without a degree in my old job. Despite this I thoroughly enjoyed my time at university and feel it was time well spent. I am now looking for another job with more professional content, fewer daily "chores" and more money.'

So, you have to decide what to do. A degree may lead to a more interesting, better-paid job with prospects of promotion, but there is no guarantee that it will, and a number of students said they had to start with a lower salary than they had hoped. You have to ask yourself why you want to take a degree. If you can provide yourself with satisfactory answers, then go ahead. All we can suggest, once again, is that you try to find out what the snags are likely to be before you commit yourself to taking a course. Giving up your job is risky, but if you know fully what all the implications are, then you at least make an informed decision to take the course, rather than a snap decision that you might regret later.

Many have gone before you and the thousands of people who have succeeded in gaining London external and Open University degrees provide powerful evidence of the fact that age has little to do with ability to study. Give yourself the best chance of success. Prepare thoroughly, consider all options, try to be realistic in your applications and then . . . enjoy your course.

101

PART TWO

Access to higher education:
A survey of admission regulations
and procedures, special schemes
and special provision for
mature students

The information in this Part was obtained from the institutions themselves in response to a survey carried out in 1985. Each institution was circulated with a questionnaire and was asked to provide information on the following points.

1. *Percentage of mature students.* What percentage of students were aged 21 and over on starting undergraduate courses in 1984.
2. *Establishment policy.* Whether there was any establishment policy relating to the admission of mature students, including the age at which students were designated mature and any special schemes relating to the admission of 'unqualified' mature students.
3. *Introductory/study skills courses.* Whether such courses were provided, together with brief details of any such provision.
4. *Special literature.* Information about any literature, other than the prospectus, produced specifically for mature applicants or students.
5. *Upper age limits.* Information about the operation of upper age limits in the institution as a whole, and in individual departments, when considering applicants for undergraduate courses.
6. *Additional provision.* The existence of crèche facilities, mature students' unions and societies and any special provision in the way of advisers and contact people for mature students was sought.
7. *Part-time degrees.* Institutions were asked to list any part-time first degrees provided and to comment on any future plans.

Each institution returned a completed questionnaire and there are two points which should be borne in mind when examining responses. The first relates to the *percentage of mature students.* In order to provide a degree of comparability, mature students were defined in the survey as being 21 and over on their initial enrolment on courses leading to a first degree, and institutions were asked to give the percentage of students aged 21 and over on starting undergraduate courses. However, the age designated as mature does vary considerably, ranging from 19 to 26, and it was not always possible for institutions to provide 21 + statistics. Where age variations occur, they are noted in the individual entries.

Percentages quoted include students over 21 with conventional entry qualifications in addition to those with non-standard entry qualifications and accepted under special entry procedures. The actual number of students in the latter category and accepted under special schemes is still very small.

The second point relates to the fact that, in order to avoid a large amount of negative information, categories to which an institution's response was an unqualified 'no' have been left out.

Universities

All forty-nine universities and the constituent colleges of the University of Wales responded to the questionnaire and their individual responses are included in this Part, on pp. 109–50.

Polytechnics

All thirty polytechnics responded to the request for information and their responses are given on pp. 151–72. Many polytechnics referred to the policy as laid down by their validating body, the Council for National Academic Awards (CNAA), and two relevant documents relating to this policy are:

1. *Extension of Access to Higher Education* (22 September 1980). The purpose of this publication was to make institutions more aware of the flexibility inherent in the Council's Principles and Regulations 1979 and to encourage institutions to take greater advantage of the regulations to extend access to higher education to a wider range of students.

2. *Opportunities in Higher Education for Mature Students.* A booklet for distribution to students outlining CNAA policy, defining entry qualifications and selection procedures and giving advice on course choice, the demands of study, transfer arrangements, how to apply and where to go for a grant. Information on how to obtain this pamphlet is given in the Bibliography.

Colleges and Institutes of Higher Education (including the Scottish Central Institutions)

Seventy-nine responses were received and the individual responses are included in this Part, on pp. 173–213.

Universities

Aberdeen University

Percentage of Mature Students. Between 7 and 10 per cent of undergraduates admitted to the University are aged 23 or over at the time of admission.

Establishment Policy. The University welcomes applications from mature students, defined by the Scottish Universities Council on Entrance as those aged 23 or over on the date of proposed entry. Each application is considered on its merits but candidates are normally required to show evidence of recent academic study relevant to the course which they wish to study. Mature candidates are more likely to be interviewed than other candidates.

It is possible for mature students to enrol on a part-time basis for the University's existing day time courses leading to the degrees of MA (Ordinary), MA (Ordinary) Social Science, BSc (Pure Science) and BTh (Bachelor of Theology). For some of these courses, no formal entry qualifications are required. A student who has doubt about his or her ability to take a degree course, or who is simply not interested in taking a full degree, can either:

1. Enrol for a single subject course as a non-graduating student or,
2. Take an 'access' course specially designed to introduce students to study at university level.

Part-time students apply direct to the University and can obtain further information from the Continuing Education Adviser. Full-time students must apply through UCCA.

Special Literature. A leaflet on part-time facilities is available, as is the normal prospectus. The University is always pleased to answer individual queries and to comment on an appropriate course of study particularly if candidates are embarking on a programme of study with the aim of entering University.

Mature Students' Union/Society. Mature students are able to use all student facilities; there is no separate Mature Student Society. We feel that it is important that mature students view themselves as part of an integrated student community.

Special Provision for Mature Students. We do not wish to isolate mature students but it is recognised that they may experience difficulties which are not so likely to affect school leavers. Advisors of Study, Regents, the Careers Service and Chaplaincy provide support for all students but are aware of the special needs of mature students.

The University of Aston in Birmingham

Percentage of Mature Students. 11 per cent of undergraduates; 46 per cent of all postgraduates are over 30.

Establishment Policy. The University is happy to consider applications for undergraduate courses from students who will be 23 years of age or above on entry and who have pursued study to a suitable level, even though they may not meet the formal entry requirements. 'Unqualified' mature applicants are considered on an individual basis.

Introductory/Study Skills Courses. These are not normally provided for all mature students but two four-week English and Study Skills courses are run each summer, aimed mainly at overseas students whose English is not up to the required standard.

Special Literature. None, but undergraduate prospectus or Postgraduate Studies Guide available.

Crèche Facilities. A nursery run by professional nurses is provided for under school age children of students and staff. Situated in a purpose-built unit on the campus, the nursery offers expert care from 08.45–17.00 hrs for up to forty children, for forty-two weeks per year.

Mature Students' Union/Society. No society as such. However, there is a Postgraduate Society open to all students engaged in postgraduate study, and any undergraduate over 21 may join as an associate member.

Part-time Degrees. For all faculties, at postgraduate level only – course or research, as detailed in the Postgraduate Studies Guide.

108

Future Plans. New courses are being introduced which it is hoped will prove equally attractive to mature students but age is not generally used as a major criterion in planning proposals. TVI (Tutored Video Instruction) is increasingly being used to provide tailor-made short courses and post-experience courses which are of particular value to mature students.

University of Bath

Percentage of Mature Students. 7 per cent.

Establishment Policy. Mature students above school leaving age are considered for admission to courses in the social sciences provided evidence of academic suitability for the course is submitted. Twenty-three students in this category were admitted in 1984. All other applicants have to satisfy the normal entrance requirements as defined by the University regulations.

Introductory/Study Skills Courses. Yes. Tuition provided in School of Humanities and Social Sciences.

Special Literature. No. Prospectus available on request.

Crèche Facilities. Yes.

Part-time Degrees. The full time courses offered in the School of Humanities and Social Sciences may be taken on a part-time basis.

Queens University of Belfast

Percentage of Mature Students. 7 per cent.

Establishment Policy. Mature age: over 23 on 1 June of year of entry. While some concessions are granted, and each case is considered individually on its merits, evidence of recent academic study at a suitably high standard would normally be required. In practice the majority of our mature candidates enter the faculties of Arts, Law and Economics and Social Sciences many with two 'A' levels or Open University credits.

Special Literature. Yes. A guidance leaflet *A Guide for Mature Students*. Prospectuses also available.

Upper Age Limits in Individual Departments. Yes, the Faculty of Medicine is reluctant to admit students over 30 years of age because of the length of the academic and professional training.

Crèche Facilities. Yes.

Part-time Degrees. BA in General Studies with maximum three years part time for the foundation programme and not more than five further years part time for the main programme. Also part-time study for the Degree of Bachelor of Divinity (BD) available.

University of Birmingham

Percentage of Mature Students. All entrants for the B Phil Ed degree are over 21. For other first degree courses mature students number about 7 per cent.

Establishment Policy. The University welcomes applications from mature students. As a member of the Joint Matriculation Board, it offers the Mature Entry Scheme for applicants where existing qualifications do not meet the General Entrance Requirement.

Introductory/Study Skills Courses. The University does not provide introductory courses linked to its own degree programmes. The Extramural Department offers courses for adults, which may directly or indirectly be helpful to applicants for degree courses. Many colleges in the West Midlands provide preparatory and study skills courses.

Special Literature. Yes. In addition to the prospectus there are leaflets, including the University's own notes of guidance for mature entrants to the University and to the affiliated Colleges (Westhill and Newman) and the JMB leaflet *21+ – Returning to Learning.*

Upper Age Limits in Individual Departments. Yes. In the Faculty of Medicine and Dentistry it is most unusual for a place to be offered on the MBChB course to anyone over the age of 30.

Crèche Facilities. Yes.

Mature Students' Union/Society. Yes.

Special Provision for Mature Students. There is a Tutor to Mature Students who provides a general counselling service, and other welfare services take account of the special needs of mature students.

Part-time Degrees. There are no part-time degree courses but there is provision for mature students to take part-time courses of study over two years, which are equivalent to the first year requirements for certain degree courses. These include the BA in English, the BA in Theology and the BSocSc in Economic History, Political Science, Public Policy Making, Social Administration or Sociology.

Future Plans. Possible extension of part-time first year study to other subjects.

University of Bradford

Percentage of Mature Students. 13 per cent (approximately) over 21; 8 per cent (approximately) over 23.

Establishment Policy. The University of Bradford Senate, on the recommendation of the appropriate Board of Studies, may accept that applicants over 23 who submit satisfactory evidence of appropriate study and of the capacity and attainments required to enable them to pursue the course for which they are applying, have satisfied the general entrance requirements. Special consideration is also given to holders of diplomas awarded by recognised adult education institutions.

Special Literature. Not at this time. Prospectus available on request; contains advice to mature students.

Crèche Facilities. Yes.

Mature Students' Union/Society. Yes.

Special Provision for Mature Students. None.

Part-time Degrees. BA Social Studies: five years part time. Holders of certain higher qualifications may be given entry to year 3.

University of Bristol

Percentage of Mature Students. 5 per cent over 21; 4 per cent over 23.

Establishment Policy. The University is willing to consider applications from older candidates, i.e. over the age of 23 years. When qualifications do not satisfy normal entry requirements the submission of sufficient evidence of previous education and attainments is required.

Special Literature. None. Prospectus available on request.

Crèche Facilities. Yes.

Part-time Degrees. Part-time degrees are not offered to undergraduates.

Brunel University

Percentage of Mature Students. 8.3 per cent.

Establishment Policy. Brunel University welcomes applications, in certain areas, from candidates without formal entrance requirements, but who are qualified by their maturity and are 25 or more on entry. The areas concerned are mostly those that do not

111

build on assumed knowledge or qualifications, e.g. psychology, systems and information management, or sociology.

Special Literature. None. Prospectus available on request.

Crèche Facilities. Yes.

The University of Buckingham

Percentage of Mature Students. 31 per cent aged 25 and over. The percentage is calculated on the basis of our latest figures, i.e. our total student population in January 1985 (Buckingham operates a January–December academic year).

Establishment Policy. Mature students are normally defined as those over the age of 25, although they may be considered mature at an earlier age, should they have acquired appropriate work experience. The University is anxious to provide opportunities for mature students and particularly for those who have gone into industry and commerce without any previous university experience. They can be considered both for the full degree course and also for shorter courses and, for these purposes, formal academic qualifications may be waived if the applicant has sufficient relevant practical experience. Mature candidates may be required to sit an entrance examination.

Introductory/Study Skills Courses. Pre-sessional courses in study skills are held prior to the commencement of a full degree course. They last ten weeks. Students work at developing their abilities in essay-writing, note-making from books and lectures, and reading and reference techniques. Materials are in subject units which provide background knowledge and vocabulary extension. One unit, for example, is about the EEC. The courses are designed particularly for mature students to re-introduce them to academic study and both British and overseas students attend.

Special Literature. None. Prospectus available.

Special Provision for Mature Students. All efforts are made to ensure that mature students are allocated older members of staff as their personal advisers.

Part-time Degrees. None.

University of Cambridge

Establishment Policy. The Cambridge Colleges accept applications from candidates of 25 or over who either have not previously attended a University, or who have begun, but not completed, a first degree course, and they may apply for

112

admission as mature students. Mature students may be given exemption from the University's matriculation requirements. Candidates write to the admission tutor or admissions secretary of one college and provide the following: (a) curriculum vitae; (b) the course they wish to follow at Cambridge and a statement of how it ties in with their other plans for the future; (c) their intended method of financing themselves at the University; and (d) the names of two referees who are willing to write about their academic potential.

Girton, Newnham, Clare and Churchill Colleges will normally require candidates to take papers from the Cambridge Colleges Examination and application to these Colleges must be made a year before the intended start of the course, and in general early applications will increase a candidate's chance of a place.

Special Literature. No special literature is produced by the University for mature students because anyone interested in applying to Cambridge is encouraged to write to a college, and individual colleges deal with enquiries from mature students after looking at their individual circumstances.

College Addresses
Enquiries should be sent to the Admissions Tutor of the relevant College. Please write, where possible, rather than telephone. Telephone numbers are given in brackets; the STD code for Cambridge is 0223.

Christ's College, CB2 3BU (67641)
Churchill College, CB3 0DS (61200)
Clare College, CB2 1TL (358681)
Corpus Christi College, CB2 1RH (59418)
Downing College, CB2 1DQ (59491)
Emmanuel College, CB2 3AP (65411)
Fitzwilliam College, CB3 0DG (358657)
Girton College, CB3 0JG (276219)
Gonville and Caius College, CB2 1TA (312211)
Homerton College, CB2 2PH (245931)
Hughes Hall, CB1 2EW (352866)
Jesus College, CB5 8BL (68611)
King's College, CB2 1ST (350411)
*Lucy Cavendish College, CB3 0BU (63409)

Magdalene College, CB3 0AG (61543)
New Hall, CB3 0DF (51721)
Newnham College, CB3 9DF (62273)
Pembroke College, CB2 1RF (352241)
Peterhouse, CB2 1RD (350256)
Queen's College, CB3 9ET (65511)
Robinson College, CB3 9AN (311431)
St. Catharine's College, CB2 1RL (59445)
St. Edmund's House, CB3 0BN (350398)
St. John's College, CB2 1TP (61621)
Selwyn College, CB3 9DQ (62381)
Sidney Sussex College, CB2 3HU (61501)
Trinity College, CB2 1TQ (358201)
Trinity Hall, CB2 1TJ (51401)
Wolfson College, CB3 9BB (64811)

*Cambridge College of particular interest to mature women.

113

Lucy Cavendish College. Lucy Cavendish College is one of the youngest Cambridge Colleges: the University recognized it as an Approved Society in 1965. It specializes in providing at Cambridge facilities for women whose University education has been postponed or interrupted.

The College admits up to a total of fifty undergraduates reading for their first degrees. They are either mature (over 25 years of age) or affiliated students (graduates of other universities). In addition, it admits postgraduate students. Candidates are accepted to read for all subjects covered by the Cambridge Tripos examinations. Directors of Studies, tutorial services and supervisors are provided by the College.

The College is a community particularly suited to able women who have decided to develop further their intellectual potential, after a break from the routine of school, or academic study.

The City University

Percentage of Mature Students. 11 per cent over the age of 23, the age at which a student is designated as mature.

Establishment Policy. Although there are mature students on all courses run by the University, they are to be found mainly in three areas: engineering, ophthalmic optics and social sciences. In engineering and ophthalmic optics, although they may be admitted with slightly lower grades than students coming direct from school, mature students will need some form of qualification, either 'A' levels, ONC, OND, BTEC, etc. Most come with industrial experience. In social sciences, students may be accepted with qualifications of a less formal nature but they must show evidence of recent academic study. In these cases students are often set special tests and essays before being admitted.

There is no set standard for mature students as each application is judged on its merit.

Special Literature. None. Prospectus available on request.

Mature Students' Union/Society. No.

Cranfield Institute of Technology

Percentage of Mature Students. 95 per cent over 21.

Establishment Policy. Cranfield Institute of Technology is a predominantly postgraduate institution which provides a wide range of full-time courses leading to higher degrees. Thus the students are mainly over 21 and graduates in possession of a first degree. Entrance requirements are laid down in the Guide to Courses and no alternative routes are provided.

Special Literature. None. Prospectus available on request.

University of Dundee

Percentage of Mature Students. 15 per cent.

Establishment Policy. Students aged 23 and over are classified as 'mature'. Depending on the nature of the subject of study 'normal' entry requirements may be modified for mature students.

Introductory/Study Skills Courses. Yes. The University's centre for continuing education offers a 'New Opportunities – Return to Study' course which can act as a preparation for unqualified entrants seeking entry to the Faculty of Arts and Social Sciences and the Faculty of Law.

Special Literature. None. Prospectus available which includes a section on mature student admission.

Mature Students' Union/Society. Yes.

Special Provision for Mature Students. Normal access to student counselling and other student welfare agencies.

Part-time Degrees. Some degree courses in the Faculties of Arts and Social Sciences, Engineering and Applied Science and Science can be attended by part-time students. Details are available on request from the Admissions Officer.

University of Durham

Percentage of Mature Students. 4 per cent.

Establishment Policy. No special policy relating to mature students in the University as a whole, due to two contributory factors in the registrar's opinion, namely that almost all courses are heavily over-subscribed with highly qualified applicants of normal age and the University is largely residential and collegiate and is located at some distance from any large centre of population.

Special Literature. None. Prospectus available on request.

Crèche Facilities. Yes. Run by Students' Union for staff and students.

Mature Students' Union/Society. Yes.

Special Provision for Mature Students. No, but union executive member is responsible for mature students.

Part-time Degrees. A two-year part-time Certificate in Social Studies is available and the award of the Certificate allows the student to transfer directly to the second year of the full-time honours degree in a social science subject.

University of East Anglia

Percentage of Mature Students. 15 per cent.

Establishment Policy. The University of East Anglia welcomes applications from candidates who are not coming straight from school and recognises that in some cases their experience and maturity will more than compensate for the lack of formal academic qualifications. Mature students are defined as over 23 and may be considered if they have a full practising professional qualification or other acceptable equivalent or by submitting satisfactory evidence of the capacity and attainments requisite to enable them to pursue the course proposed. The University looks for evidence of the basic intellectual capacity for degree level study, the ability to apply that capacity to disciplined and sustained work and the commitment necessary to face the demands of a three-year degree course. In order to check on the candidate's ability to apply intellectual capacity to disciplined and sustained work the sort of evidence looked for may be GCE 'A' level passes obtained part time or written work presented for assessment by the University, e.g. two 3,000-word essays or some equivalent project on a topic approved by the School of Studies concerned.

Special Literature. Prospectus available on request. Revised version of mature students leaflet in preparation. See also section on part-time degrees below.

Crèche Facilities. Yes. For children from six weeks to school age.

Mature Students' Union/Society. All registered students are admitted to ordinary membership of the UEA students' union which welcomes students of all ages.

Part-time Degrees. Part-time BA degree courses are available in American Studies, History, Art History, Philosophy and Sociology for mature local residents, and it is also possible to study for the University's higher degrees on a part-time basis. The School of Education runs an in-service BEd degree and part-time masters degree for practising teachers. A booklet on Part-time Study at the University of East Anglia, Norwich is available free on request.

University of Edinburgh

Percentage of Mature Students. 7.27 per cent.

Establishment Policy. The University is very willing to consider applications from mature students (i.e. those who are 23 years of age or over by the 1 October of the year in which they begin their degree courses) and the General Entrance Requirement may be modified in such cases. Such applicants are advised that the normal minimum level of attainment expected will be recent passes on the Higher grade in three subjects (or at 'A'-level in two subjects) including either mathematics or an approved science, or an approved language other than English. Alternatively, two full credits in Open University foundation level courses may be accepted.

Exceptional Admissions Procedure is available for selected mature applicants seeking admission at undergraduate level, to the Faculties of Arts, Divinity, Law, Music and Social Sciences. This procedure will be used only in a small number of cases for which it may appear that the normal modified entrance requirement for mature entrants may be inappropriate. Details may be obtained from the appropriate Faculty. The closing date for the receipt of completed application forms is 15 January, but enquiry should be made well in advance.

All mature students intending to apply are recommended to write as early as possible to the appropriate Faculty for guidance, giving full details of their educational background and their experience in employment.

The Faculty of Law does consider applications from mature students although such is the pressure on available places in the Faculty that mature students are invariably expected to possess qualifications which are higher than the minimum stated.

Special Literature.   Yes. A leaflet, *Mature Students at Edinburgh – a brief guide to University entrance*, is available, as is the prospectus, which contains information relevant to mature students.

Crèche Facilities.   Yes.

Part-time Degrees.   These are not widely offered at undergraduate level, though some developments are currently under consideration. For example, the Faculty of Divinity hopes to offer part-time degrees starting in October 1985. Candidates for admission should enquire with the Faculty of Divinity Office about entry requirements.

University of Essex

Percentage of Mature Students.   13.1 per cent over 23.

Establishment Policy.   The University welcomes applications from mature students (N.B. 23 or over on entry). The procedures for selection vary, but, where the candidate does not offer 'A' levels or equivalent, usually consist for arts, law and social science courses of an entrance test or examination, together with an interview. Selectors will normally wish to see some evidence of recent study. Various qualifications are acceptable as alternatives to 'A' level. A credit transfer agreement exists with the Open University and each year a number of candidates with one or more OU credits are admitted.

For sciences, where 'A'-level knowledge of a subject or subjects is a prerequisite for entry, mature candidates must recently have followed a course covering the content of the appropriate 'A'-level syllabus.

Introductory/Study Skills Courses. For candidates under 23 who have had a significant break since their schooling and are educationally disadvantaged the City and East London College (CELC) runs a one-year preparation course, devised jointly by CELC and the University. Successful completion of the course leads to admission to an undergraduate degree course in arts or social sciences at Essex.

A study skills course for any student, runs throughout the year – perhaps one day a week – as needed. This course covers study skills, examination techniques and essay writing and is mainly used by mature students.

An advisory evening is held annually in November for potential mature students. Attendance in 1984 was the highest ever with some 150 people from the area attending.

Special Literature. There is a leaflet containing information for mature applicants to the Schools of Comparative Studies, Social Studies and Law. Further, a special letter accompanies the prospectus if the enquirer is known to be mature, and the University is always pleased to answer individual queries and to comment on an appropriate course of study particularly if candidates are embarking on a programme with the aim of entering university.

Upper Age Limits in Individual Departments. No, but in engineering and science particular current academic skills are deemed essential (usually in terms of 'A' level, and BTEC/HNC/HND qualifications). Persons currently in employment may not have these qualifications and could therefore stand less chance of admission.

Crèche Facilities. Yes. For staff and students.

Mature Students' Union/Society. All students have an adviser. In addition there is an assistant dean of students for mature students. Special services include a half-term baby sitting service, hardship fund, etc . . .

University of Exeter

Percentage of Mature Students. 6.5 per cent.

Establishment Policy. The University welcomes applications from mature candidates who for a variety of reasons may not have had the opportunity of embarking upon a University education when they left school. Mature students are seen as a valuable addition to the undergraduate body and all applications are fully considered on their individual merits. Candidates who are aged over 23 by the time the course for which they are applying is due to commence and who cannot satisfy the normal entry requirements will be considered under the mature matriculation clause. The University looks for evidence of some recently undertaken systematic course of study during the three years prior to entry and also for evidence of literacy and numeracy. Mature students considered under the special clause in whom the University are interested are interviewed.

Introductory/Study Skills Courses. None, but if a mature student were to experience difficulties, the Teaching Services Centre would provide help.

Special Literature. None. Prospectus available on request.

Crèche Facilities. Yes.

Mature Students' Union/Society. Yes.

University of Glasgow

Percentage of Mature Students. 12.5 per cent over 21.

Establishment Policy. Mature students (over 23) will be considered for entry and the faculties have differing requirements as outlined below.

The Faculties of Arts, Divinity and Social Science will look favourably on mature applicants with three recent H passes or two recent Adv passes (or equivalent qualifications). Arts strongly prefers mature applicants to have an H or Adv pass in a foreign language or in Mathematics. Divinity strongly prefers H. or Adv. passes to include English. Additional Ordinary passes are not required in any of these Faculties. The Faculty of Law and Financial Studies (Law School) requires H or Adv passes to include English, and the number of H or Adv passes expected depends on whether your preliminary study is full or part-time.

A good performance in the *Introduction to University Study* course (see below) confers eligibility for admission to the Faculties of Arts, Social Sciences, Divinity and, occasionally, Law.

In Engineering, Medicine, Science and Veterinary Medicine, the

119

Admissions Officers are likely to insist on the possession of the full recent SCE or equivalent qualifications. This is because of the prior knowledge necessary to study these subjects successfully at the university.

Introductory/Study Skills Courses. Yes. The Department of Adult and Continuing Education offers courses in eight subjects, two of which are expected to be chosen; study time then comprises two evenings a week and additional tutorials. This programme, *An Introduction to University Study*, gives students the opportunity to gain an idea of the suitability of University work for them. It involves assessment by means of essays and a final short examination. Good performance is recognised by Glasgow University (see above), Strathclyde University and the Open University as a recommendation for degree work.

Heriot-Watt University

Percentage of Mature Students. 16 per cent over 23.

Establishment Policy. The general entrance requirements may be relaxed in the case of mature applicants, i.e. those who are 23 years of age or over by 1 October of the year of entry to the course. Such candidates must be able to satisfy the department concerned as to their ability and capacity to pursue successfully the course of study for which they have applied.

Special Literature. No. Prospectus available.

Part-time Degrees. In October 1984 twelve mature students were admitted to the part-time degree of BA in Business Studies. The period of study for this degree can extend to ten years. Also a general BSc studied over a minimum period of four years part time (maximum period of eight years) is available.

University of Hull

Percentage of Mature Students. 6 per cent.

Establishment Policy. The University of Hull welcomes mature students and has a long-standing commitment to the education of adults shown by its part-time degree schemes, its wide range of courses for adults provided by its Department of Adult Education over a wide geographical area and its encouragement of mature students to apply for full-time degree courses.

The University regulations say that students over 21, who submit to Senate such evidence, as it may deem sufficient, of previous serious study and who have the capacity and attainments required to enable them to pursue the course proposed can be declared eligible for matriculation, although Senate may require them to take an entrance examination conducted by the University. The Matriculation Committee is flexible and all applications are given careful and sympathetic consideration.

Introductory/Study Skills Courses. Some departments offer an introduction with emphasis on study skills.

Special Literature. The Prospectus provides a helpful and encouraging section on Mature Students and Adult Education.

Crèche Facilities. Yes.

Mature Students' Society. Yes.

University of Keele

Percentage of Mature Students. 10 per cent over 21.

Establishment Policy. The University of Keele is pleased to consider applications from mature students. Candidates who do not fulfil the general entrance requirements will be considered as 'mature' students if they are over 19, have been employed for three years and have attended systematic courses of study (e.g. adult education classes, FE courses).

Mature students applying for three-year courses have to fulfil any specific course requirements as detailed in the prospectus, but for four-year undergraduate courses there are no course requirements. All applications are treated on their merits and most mature applicants will be interviewed unless there is enough information on the UCCA form for a definite decision. Applicants may be required to sit a written examination or asked to submit essays or other written work and selectors look for a persevering interest in academic work and proof that applicants have tried to continue and extend their education, although examination passes are not necessarily required.

Introductory/Study Skills Courses. Yes. Study skills courses are available but not specifically for mature students.

Special Literature. The University supplies a leaflet, *Information for Mature Students,* which includes the above information, grants advice, alternative courses available and who to write to at Keele for advice on courses and admission. Prospectus and departmental leaflets also available on request.

Crèche Facilities. Yes. Student parents given preference.

Mature Students' Society. Yes.

Special Provision for Mature Students. University has an appointment and counselling service for all students. Student Union

121

has a loans fund and will answer enquiries from any prospective student.

University of Kent at Canterbury

Percentage of Mature Students. 16 per cent of total first-year intake in Oct 1984 (over 23).

Establishment Policy. It has been the policy of this University to welcome applications from older or mature students who have for some reason missed out on Higher Education or who simply want to return to academic life either by developing their previous careers or by making a fresh start. It is a policy that has worked well, and over the years we have found that the presence and participation of a significant body of mature students in the University has made a distinct and valuable contribution to our academic life.

In each Faculty applications from mature students receive careful and sympathetic attention, especially as in many cases applicants will not have the usual formal entrance qualifications. In such cases, it will be an advantage if candidates can provide evidence of some recent academic study. Whenever possible, applicants are interviewed, partly to test academic suitability, but also to ensure that personal circumstances affecting the choice of a university career can be fully discussed. It is not the practice of the University to treat mature students as a separate group requiring special arrangements for teaching – nor is it the desire of the large majority of mature students themselves. At the same time, the University is very conscious of the fact that the process for getting to University, of often having to combine academic work with continuing responsibilities outside the University, or of having to adjust to the pace and demands of academic life, does create special problems. The University therefore endeavours to provide mature students, once they are here, with the support and advice they may need. There is, in fact, a large variety of people to whom mature students can turn for help, including a very lively and supportive Mature Students' Society.

Introductory/Study Skills Courses. Not provided by the institution itself but a detailed booklet, 'Study Hints for Students', is available with much helpful information on study skills. Also see above.

Special Literature. Prospectus available and also the Faculty of Humanities publishes a special leaflet on the admission of mature students, copies of which can be obtained from the Senior Assistant Registrar for Admissions.

Crèche Facilities. Yes, but space limited.

Mature Students' Union/Society. Yes.

Special Provision for Mature Students. Yes.

Part-time Degrees. Kent has been active in the introduction of part-time degrees and diplomas and of courses preparing for degree level study. Also 'New Opportunities for Women' and 'Gateway' courses are run in Canterbury, Tonbridge and other centres in Kent on a regular basis. A number of students have moved from these courses on to part- or full-time courses, despite in most cases the lack of formal entry qualifications. Part-time degrees and diplomas are offered in a wide range of subjects (for example, English, Social Sciences and Ecology) and are available in the evenings at the main campus at Canterbury and in the School of Continuing Education's centre at Tonbridge.

The following part-time degree courses are offered through the School of Continuing Education:

BA in Modern European Languages (5 years).
BA in English/History (5 years).
BA in Social Sciences (4 years).
BA in a Social Sciences subject (4 years).
Diplomas in English, Philosophy, Local History, Ecology, Women's Studies, Adult and Further Education, Law and Society.

University of Lancaster

Percentage of Mature Students 11 per cent over 23.

Establishment Policy Lancaster is keen to welcome mature student applicants to its degree schemes and does not necessarily expect them to have achieved 'A'-level passes if they have other relevant qualifications/experience. It is flexible in its approach, accepting and encouraging students to apply with Open College preparatory courses, Open University foundation courses and a wide variety of other qualifications are documented in its leaflet *Admission of Mature Students*. The Lancaster degree can be studied full time or, in a number of subject areas, part time. In all subjects Part I may be studied on a part-time basis and the final two years of the course completed on a full-time basis. Unqualified mature students can also be considered where they can provide evidence that they are sufficiently able, motivated and prepared for a degree course and this normally means that the candidate has recently successfully undertaken a course of formal study of a level significantly higher than 'O' level and requiring directed reading, essay writing and preferably examination.

Candidates applying on the basis of their reading but no systematic study or writing cannot be accepted, but are advised to undertake more formal studies and re-apply later. Over 10 per cent of the undergraduate entry comes from mature candidates, but departments generally over-subscribed include psychology, social administration, sociology and English. Academic and counselling advice are available to all mature students or prospective mature students.

Introductory/Study Skills Courses.   Yes. Two-day courses immediately before the start of first term.

Special Literature.   Leaflets:
(1)   *Part-time Degree Study for Mature Students.*
(2)   *Open College – a new approach to part-time learning for adult students in the North West.*
(3)   *Admission of Mature Students.*
(4)   *Admission of Open University Students.*
Also prospectus and video available on request.

Crèche Facilities.   Yes.

Mature Students' Union/Society.   Yes, mainly social but some representational action.

Special Provision for Mature Students.   College admissions office, departments and counselling service will advise prospective mature students and try to welcome them. Students' Union will also handle enquiries as they arise.

Part-time Degrees.   BA Honours in Independent Studies is offered with mostly ad hoc arrangements (and no evening teaching at present). Other subjects may be available. Anyone interested is welcome to enquire about possibilities.

University of Leeds

Percentage of Mature Students.   8 per cent (approximately) aged 21 and over (undergraduate degrees, home and overseas).

Establishment Policy.   As a member of the Joint Matriculation Board the University welcomes mature students (over 21) who are admitted on the basis of their qualifications and suitability for the course chosen. Individual departments within the University are responsible for admissions and each applicant is treated individually on his/her merits. The JMB mature entry scheme operates with details as given in the relevant publications.

Special Literature.   No special literature produced for mature students by Leeds itself but the JMB booklet *21+ – Returning to*

Learning is used and distributed. University prospectus available on request.

Crèche Facilities. Yes. Students' Union run a crèche.

Mature Students' Union/Society. Mainly social activities.

Special Provision for Mature Students. Students' Union run an annual 'Returning to Learning' forum and a play scheme for school holidays. Informal advice to enquirers and responsive welfare section for students.

Part-time Degrees. The following postgraduate degrees are available:
MMus, MPH – taught courses only.
MA, MEd, MSc, MEng, MMed, Sc, MDSc, – taught courses (only certain schemes are part time) or research.
MPhil, PhD – research only
The University is currently considering the introduction of part-time first degrees for mature students.

University of Leicester

Establishment Policy. Applications from those who would be over 23 years of age on entry to the University can be considered on their merits if conventional qualifications are not possessed. Evidence of previous serious study is required and a credit obtained on an Open University foundation course is usually acceptable for the purposes of meeting the general entrance requirements. There may be additional course entrance requirements. The University does warn intending mature students of the need to ensure that they can obtain a local authority grant or finance.

Introductory/Study Skills Courses. Introductory courses are provided in many departments and a booklet is given to all new students.

Special Literature. None. Prospectus available on request.

Crèche Facilities. Yes.

Special Provision for Mature Students. No.

Part-time Degrees. A variety of part-time degrees is offered including BA with Honours in Combined Arts, Economic and Social History, Economics, Economics and Economic History, Geography, Politics, Politics with Economic History, Sociology and Applied Sociology. Part-time study requires four to eight years. Also a BSc with Honours in Combined Science,

Economics, Sociology and Applied Sociology can be studied over four to eight years part time.

University of Liverpool

Percentage of Mature Students. 9.9 per cent (over 21).

Established Policy. The University of Liverpool welcomes applications from mature candidates, and the Mature Matriculation Officer will be pleased to advise people who do not have standard entry qualifications. The University belongs to the JMB mature matriculation scheme, details of which are given in the booklet *21 + – Returning to Learning,* available from the University or the JMB.

Admission tutors will give advice and academic guidance to those considering applying for mature matriculation.

Moral support for all mature students is now available in the form of 'MATSOC', the Mature Students' Society.

Introductory/Study Skills Courses. Yes. 'British Society: An Introduction to the Social Sciences'. The course is designed to help those without formal educational qualifications to acquire basic study skills. It is aimed particularly, but not exclusively, at aspiring social scientists. This is run at present in Liverpool and Chester.

Special Literature. Yes, leaflet on introductory course, *An Introduction to the Social Sciences* + JMB leaflet *21 + – Returning to Learning.* Prospectus sent on request.

Crèche Facilities. Yes, a playgroup for 2 to 5-year olds is in operation.

Mature Students' Union/Society. Yes.

Special Provision for Mature Students. No, but the personal tutors, student counsellor, and the Mature Matriculation Officer are all available and willing to advise on any problems encountered.

University of London

Percentage of Mature Students. Not known.

Establishment Policy. Colleges of the University are willing to consider applications from mature students (not less than 23 years of age) who neither satisfy the normal admission requirements nor possess an alternative acceptable qualification. Candidates must first satisfy the college authorities to which they intend to apply that they are capable of following their proposed course. They will almost certainly be interviewed at length and may be required to take an ad hoc test to demonstrate their academic fitness. If the College wishes to offer a place it submits an application on the candidate's behalf to the University's Special Entrance Board which considers the case on its individual merits.

While an increasing number of mature students who do not satisfy normal entrance requirements are being admitted to degree courses, special consideration is not given on the basis of maturity and professional experience alone. Candidates must be able to provide acceptable evidence of relevant mature-age study such as success in an approved 'A'-level, extra-mural courses, 'Fresh Start' or 'Fresh Horizons' courses, Open University courses or the publication of written work.

Special mention should be made of *Birkbeck College*, a School of the University which specialises in providing degree-level teaching and research facilities for mature students, and in particular for those earning a livelihood during the day. It admits students by direct entry and not through UCCA and all essential formal teaching takes place between 6.00 p.m. and 9.00 p.m. Monday to Friday in term time. (See Chapter 5 for further information.)

Special Literature. No separate literature is provided by the University of London as a whole for mature students, but detailed information is contained in the University Entrance Regulations obtainable from the Secretary for Entrance Requirements, University of London, Senate House, Malet Street, London, WC1E 7HU and in the prospectuses produced by, and obtainable direct from, the Schools and Institutes and Birkbeck College.

A pamphlet of General Information for Internal Studies may be obtained from the Academic Registrar, Senate House, Malet Street, London, WC1E 7HU. The pamphlet gives the addresses of Schools and Institutes of the University and Institutions having Recognised Teachers, a synopsis of the courses, fees, and general facilities.

Upper Age Limits in Individual Departments. Yes, especially in some medical schools. If in doubt contact departments individually.

Crèche Facilities. Yes. Used by staff and students.

Mature Students' Union/Society. Yes. These unions operate at college level.

Special Provision for Mature Students. Yes. Special provision is available at college level.

127

Part-time Degrees. Goldsmiths College offers a BSc with Honours in Psychology or Anthropology and Psychology and BA with Honours in Sociology. Also a BEd in Education for serving teachers. Birkbeck College offers a very wide range of degrees studied part time and some degrees which incorporate part-time and full-time study. BA degrees are available with honours in Languages, Geography, History, History of Art, Philosophy, and Classics with a variety of combined honours degrees also available. BSc with honours is available in Biological Sciences, Chemistry, Geography, Geology, Mathematics, Physics, Psychology and other subjects and a wide range of combined honours degrees is also available.

Loughborough University of Technology

Percentage of Mature Students. 2 per cent.

Establishment Policy. Mature students' applications are welcomed by Loughborough and in general they are treated as all other students by the University. Loughborough is anxious to offer all possible help in the process of deciding to read for a degree. Students who do not satisfy the general entrance requirements but who will be over 21 years may be offered places provided they satisfy the appropriate Board of Studies of their fitness to undertake a degree course and to sustain it successfully.

Introductory/Study Skills Courses. None. Each case is treated on its merits and appropriate advice is given.

Special Literature. No special literature is produced, but a comprehensive section in the prospectus relates to mature students.

Upper Age Limits in the Institution. None. One recent PhD was 63.

Crèche Facilities. Yes, by arrangement with the Students' Union, subject to space.

Special Provision. None as such, but in certain cases special arrangements can and have been made.

Part-time Degrees. BLS (Honours) in Library Studies offered in two parts, both studied part time and BA honours in English can also be studied part time over five to seven years.

University of Manchester

Percentage of Mature Students. 9 per cent (approximately) over 21.

Establishment Policy. The University of Manchester is a member of the Joint Matriculation Board and so the JMB mature entry scheme operates. Applications from mature students, i.e. aged over 21 by 1 May in the year of proposed entry, are welcomed and where students have insufficient formal entry qualifications they are interviewed by the department and by the JMB representative and a special examination may be set.

Introductory/Study Skills Courses. Yes. Pre-entry courses for both full-time and part-time students are run specifically by the Extra-Mural Department of the University. Other courses in the Extra-Mural Department are also used by prospective students.

Special Literature. The university distributes the JMB pamphlet *21+ – Returning to Learning.* Prospectus available on request.

Upper Age Limits in Individual Departments. Yes. If in doubt contact individual departments.

Crèche Facilities. Yes.

Mature Students' Union/Society. Yes.

Special Provision for Mature Students. Mature Matriculation and Advisory Service specifically and also normal access to other student services.

Part-time Degrees. The University is developing a programme of part-time undergraduate degrees and the first students were admitted in October 1985. Degrees have modular structure (ten modules for unclassified, thirteen for Honours). Evening and/or day time attendance. Duration of degrees varies, dependent on student-determined rate of study. Initially BA/BA Honours in Adult and Community Education, American Studies, Economic and Social Studies, Education, History, History of Art, Language Teaching, Literary Studies, Nursing Education and Theology will be offered. The part-time programme will be expanded over the next few years especially into the sciences.

University of Manchester Institute of Science and Technology

Percentage of Mature Students. 1984: 12 per cent over 21.

Establishment Policy. The Institute welcomes enquiries from mature students over 21 who would be treated as any applicant and required to meet JMB and departmental requirements. The Institute has no formal policy towards mature students in particular and in September 1982 a total of 146 mature students were admitted to undergraduate courses; of these, two students entered the Institute under the JMB Mature Matriculation Scheme, although they would be happy to admit more.

Special Literature. None, but mature applicants are sent on request a copy of *A University Degree; A second chance at 21+* and *21+ – Returning to Learning*, both JMB publications. Normal prospectus available on request.

Crèche Facilities. Yes.

Special Provision for Mature Students. No, though admissions tutors will see mature enquirers and students' union welfare and advisory services are available for all students.

University of Newcastle upon Tyne

Establishment Policy. The University of Newcastle upon Tyne classifies mature students as being 25 years of over and each application is considered on its individual merits with particular reference to the applicant's opportunities for study since leaving school and the advantage taken of these, together with any alternative qualification or work experience relevant to the proposed course of study.

The mature student should be able to benefit from the course and particular attention will be given to the course selector's recommendation, especially if this be made in the light of an interview.

Introductory/Study Skills Courses. The adult education department runs a number of courses designed to 'bridge the gap' between school and university: they include New Opportunities and Study Link.

Special Literature. Yes. Guide for mature students available. Prospectus also available on request.

Upper Age Limits in the Institution. None.

Upper Age Limits in Individual Departments. None.

Part-time Degrees. A BA Honours in Philosophy is offered which can be studied full time or over five to seven years part time.

Nottingham University

Percentage of Mature Students. 6 per cent (approximately).

Establishment Policy. The University welcomes applications from mature candidates and is prepared to accept a variety of qualifications in lieu of the traditional 'O' and 'A' levels. There are

ACCESS TO HIGHER EDUCATION: UNIVERSITIES

no fixed quotas for any category of student and applications are considered on individual merit. Candidates over 23 who cannot matriculate in the normal way may be given permission, following an interview with the Head of Department, to take the Special Entrance Examination which is held in June each year. This consists of a three-hour paper in the Use of English and at least one but not more than three papers in relevant subjects. In practice students entering by this method are virtually all arts-based.

Special Literature. None. Prospectus available.

Upper Age Limits in Individual Departments. Because of the length of the training involved, it would be unusual for the medical school to offer a place to a candidate much over the age of 30.

Crèche Facilities. Playgroup operates.

Mature Students' Union/Society. Yes.

Special Provision for Mature Students. The welfare services are available to all students.

Part-time Degrees. Part-time degrees studied over five to seven years and leading to the qualification BA Honours in Archaeology, Philosophy, Politics, Social Administration, Sociology and Theology. A leaflet entitled 'Part-time First Degrees' is available.

The Open University

Percentage of Mature Students. 100 per cent (approximately) over 21. Regulations changed in 1985 to reduce age on entry from 21 to 18.

Establishment Policy. The Open University will normally accept any residents of the United Kingdom as students, provided they are over 18. No educational qualifications are required, since all applications are decided on a first-come, first-accepted basis, until the quotas on each course offered for study in each region are full. Students of the Open University study part time in their own homes and courses are based on a set of correspondence texts, supplemented where appropriate by face-to-face tutorials, television and radio broadcasts, slide and/or tape presentations, experimental kits and residential summer schools in conventional University environments. The Open University is based at Milton Keynes, but has thirteen regional centres throughout the British Isles, and maintains a network of study centres to meet the needs of its students. All undergraduate students with the Open University study for a BA or BA (Hons) degree by obtaining six or eight credits respectively and by studying, at their own pace, over an unrestricted period of time. Students can study any combination of courses chosen from those presented by the six faculties of Arts, Social Science, Mathematics, Science, Technology and Educational Studies but they commence their undergraduate study by choosing a foundation course in Arts, Social Sciences, Mathematics, Science or Technology.

Students with previous educational qualifications above 'A' level may be eligible for advanced standing and so may be able to obtain their degrees by studying less than the six or eight credits normally studied.

Introductory/Study Skills Courses. The Open University provides introductory, faculty-specific courses for registered OU students and each foundation course contains an introductory element, sent to students in the autumn before commencement of study. Students are advised about how to prepare for undergraduate study by means of University publications and by regional OU staff.

Special Literature. The University provides a *Guide for Applicants* which is updated each year, and a great deal of high quality publicity material is produced and available from the Open University headquarters at Milton Keynes, or from any of the thirteen regional offices.

Mature Students' Union/Society. All Open University students are members of the Open University Students' Association (OUSA) who organise social and educational activities at national, regional and local level.

Special Provision for Mature Students. All students are allocated to a tutor-counsellor in their local area who is the first contact for help with educational or other problems affecting study. Full-time staff in the regional offices work with tutors and counsellors in solving persistent, complicated or administrative problems on behalf of students.

Financial assistance for students of the University who are unemployed or on low incomes is available through the financial assistance fund.

Regional enquiry services deal with a large variety of enquiries from people seeking information on study with the Open University on its undergraduate, associate and community education programmes and they will be happy to advise on courses of study.

University of Oxford

Percentage of Mature Students – not known.

Establishment Policy. There are no special regulations for mature students (over the age of 25), but colleges are willing to consider applications for the very small number of places likely to be available. Mature students may be required to take the written entrance examination, or to submit specimens of their work or to take test papers, and in both cases attend for interview. A confidential report is required from a referee.

Candidates should apply through UCCA and through the Oxford Colleges Admissions Office, University Offices, Wellington Square, Oxford, OXL 2JD. Colleges may apply for dispensation from the University matriculation requirements on behalf of those candidates whom they have agreed to accept.

Special Literature. None, but contact individual colleges and halls for details.

A. Colleges (telephone numbers are given in brackets; the Oxford STD code is 0865)
(i) For men and women undergraduates.
Balliol, OX1 3BJ (249601)
Brasenose, OX1 4AJ (248641)
Christ Church, OX1 1DP (242201)
Corpus Christi, OX1 4JF (249431)
Exeter, OX1 3DP (244681)
Hertford, OX1 3BW (241434)
Jesus, OX1 3DW (249511)
Keble, OX1 3PG (59201)
Lady Margaret Hall, OX2 6QA (54353)
Lincoln, OX1 3DR (722741)
Magdalen, OX1 4AU (241781)
Merton, OX1 4JD (249651)
New College, OX1 3BN (248451)
Oriel, OX1 4EW (241651)
Pembroke, OX1 1DW (242271)
The Queen's, OX1 4AW (248411)
St Anne's, OX2 6HS (57417)
St Catherine's, OX1 3UJ (249541)
St Edmund Hall, OX1 4AR (245511)
St John's, OX1 3JP (247671)
St Peter's, OX1 2DL (248436)
Trinity, OX1 3BH (241801)
University, OX1 4BH (241661)
Wadham, OX1 3PN (242564)
Worcester, OX1 2HB (247251)

133

(ii) For women undergraduates.
St Hilda's, OX4 1DY (241821)
St Hugh's, OX2 6LE (57341)
Somerville, OX2 6HD (57595)

B. Permanent private halls.
(i) For men and women undergraduates
Mansfield, OX1 3TF (249175)
Regent's Park, OX1 2LB (59887)

(ii) Primarily for members of religious orders.
Campion Hall, OX1 1QS (240861–2) (primarily for members of the Society of Jesus).
Greyfriars, OX4 1SB (243694) (priority to members of the Franciscan Order).
St Benet's Hall, OX1 3LN (55006) (priority to members of the Benedictine community).

Crèche Facilities. A check with individual colleges is advised. Balliol, St Anne's and Somerville have regular play group facilities.

Part-time Degrees. None.

University of Reading

Percentage of Mature Students. 9 per cent (approximately).

Establishment Policy. Mature students (i.e. those aged over 21 or over 23 depending on the Faculty they wish to enter) who are able to satisfy the University's general entrance requirement are considered in the usual way and judged on the same criteria as the school leaver, although a good performance at interview may allow us to relax slightly the advanced level grades asked for, especially where applicants are studying part time. The University is also willing to consider mature applicants who do not satisfy the normal general entrance requirement; this exemption may not extend to course requirements, and, particularly in science-based subjects, we will need to be sure that the applicant has reached the appropriate 'jumping off point' for the particular course. Applicants for science courses will therefore normally need to have followed appropriate preparatory courses, either for GCE Advanced Level or some other form of preparation. A few selected applicants for entry to the arts or social sciences may be invited to take part in a special entrance test.

Under the special entrance test arrangements candidates are required to submit written work related in a general way to the course for which each candidate has applied, and this is followed by an interview. It should be emphasised that preference will be

134

given to applicants who can offer evidence of academic achievement at Advanced Level or at a comparable standard, and/or recent academic study.

Special Literature. None. Prospectus available on request.

Part-time Degrees. Not provided at undergraduate level.

Royal College of Art

Percentage of Mature Students. Postgraduate institution, so all students over 21.

Establishment Policy. The RCA is a postgraduate University institution empowered to award the degrees, Master of Arts (RCA), Master of Design (RCA), PhD (RCA), and Dr of Arts (RCA). The majority of students follow a two- or three-year course leading to the Master's Degree. Candidates should normally be over 21 and under 40 years old and hold a first degree, a diploma in art and design or have completed three years of approved study after the age of eighteen. UK students must also have the equivalent of five 'O' level GCE passes. Entry is by competitive examination for the 250 or so places available and candidates are required to send portfolios of work to the College. Selected candidates are then invited to the College for interview and practical tests may be set. One-year mid-career courses for artists, designers or teachers with at least five years professional experience are also available.

Special Literature. Prospectus available on request.

Upper Age Limits in Individual Departments. Yes, normally 40 years of age.

Mature Students' Union/Society. Yes.

Special Provision for Mature Students. Help is provided for all students by Professors and their schools.

University of St Andrews

Percentage of Mature Students. 6.9 per cent over 21.

Establishment Policy. For persons who are 23 years of age or over (called 'mature students'), the General Entrance Requirement may be relaxed.

Students are admitted by Faculty, but all admissions officers generally treat applications from mature students on their merits in open competition against other applicants; however, there are variations, as follows.

1. *Arts.* Evidence of academic success within the five years preceding application to university is sought and potential 'mature' students are usually interviewed.

135

2. *Science*. The foreign language element of the General Entrance Requirement is not normally required and Science may be prepared to accept two 'A' levels rather than the customary three.
3. *Medical Science*. In selecting from a very well-qualified group would probably be unwilling to relax main-line academic qualifications as sought. The language requirement might possibly be waived in some cases.
4. *Divinity*. Attracts a fair proportion of 'mature' applicants for vocational training in religion. Entry qualifications are relaxed when necessary, though competition amongst all applicants is the aim. Formal academic qualifications, previous training, professional experience, interview, etc. all have a part to play in the admissions process.

Introductory/Study Skills Courses. No course offered specifically for mature students but a study skills course is offered and available to all interested first students.

Special Literature. No. Prospectus available.

Upper Age Limits in Individual Departments. Candidates over 21 years of age are not normally considered for the Medical Science Course. Otherwise there are no age restrictions in the University.

Crèche Facilities. Yes, run by the Students' Union.

Special Provision for Mature Students. Mature students are integrated totally into the student body; it is policy to regard them as 'normal' members of the student population and, as such, they enjoy the same organisational benefits as all other students.

University of Salford

Percentage of Mature Students. 18 per cent over 21; 9.4 per cent over 23.

Establishment Policy. Mature candidates (23 years of age and over on date of admission who are unable to matriculate in the normal way) are required to satisfy the academic department concerned as to their ability and capacity to pursue successfully the programme of study for which they have applied. They may then, on the recommendation of the department and the resolution of the appropriate Board of Faculty, be declared to have qualified for matriculation.

Special Literature. None. Prospectus available on request, and booklet published by UCCA distributed.

Crèche Facilities. Yes. Arrangements often with local nursery schools, and facilities available at Manchester University used, although no crèche available on campus.

Mature Students' Union/Society. Yes.

Special Provision for Mature Students. Yes. Applicants are encouraged to contact the Admissions Tutor before a formal application is submitted through UCCA.

Part-time Degrees. BA in Politics and Contemporary History (Evenings), BSc in Sociology and BSc in Applied Physics with Electronics (day time) available.

University of Sheffield

Percentage of Mature Students. 1984: 9 per cent (approximately) over 21; 2 per cent (approximately) admitted via JMB mature entry scheme.

Establishment Policy. Sheffield welcomes applications from mature candidates. Those who are unable to satisfy the general entrance requirement of the University may apply through the Joint Matriculation Board's Mature Entry Scheme. Most applications through this scheme will result in an interview, after which there may be a special examination or some set essays before acceptance. There is no formal quota set aside for mature students.

Introductory/Study Skills Courses. Yes. The University's Division of Continuing Education runs a preparatory course for individuals considering higher education. This is not part of the formal entry procedure. Further details from the Division of Continuing Education.

Special Literature. Yes. A mature entry pack, including the JMB *21+* booklet, a mature entry application form, an UCCA handbook and an UCCA application form is available from the JMB Representative. Prospectuses are also available on request.

Upper Age Limits in Individual Departments. Yes. Faculties of Medicine and Dentistry.

Crèche Facilities. Yes.

Mature Students' Union/Society. Yes.

Part-time Degrees. None.

University of Southampton

Percentage of Mature Students. 15 per cent.

Establishment Policy. The University of Southampton welcomes applications from candidates who have had significant working experience since leaving school. There are no special entry regulations for such students, but each case is considered on its individual merits, particular attention being given to the referee's report on the UCCA form. Those over 21 at the start of the course and who do not have the normal entry qualifications may be exempted from the general entrance requirement. They are usually required to show evidence of recent serious study and of their capacity to pursue the course, e.g. one or two 'A'-level passes or successful completion of a foundation course at the Open University or of certain courses offered by a University Department of Adult Education could be appropriate.

Introductory/Study Skills Courses. Return to study courses are available in the University itself, currently in English, Spanish and General Subjects.

Special Literature. None. Prospectus available on request.

Upper Age Limits in Individual Departments. Yes. Medicine normally operates an upper age limit of 30 years while many departments will not normally admit 55+ and operate quotas for 40+

Crèche Facilities. Yes.

Mature Students' Union/Society. Yes.

Part-time Degrees. Yes. BSc Honours degrees are available in Biology, Botany, Chemistry, Environmental Sciences, Geography, Geology, Geophysical Sciences, Physics, Physiology and Biochemistry, Psychology and Zoology. These degrees are studied over four to eight years. Part-time degrees are also available in Mathematical Studies and Social Sciences.

Other. There are some specialist areas in postgraduate work open to candidates with relevant experience but without a first degree, e.g. social work.

University of Stirling

Percentage of Mature Students. 9 per cent (mature on entry).

Establishment Policy. Policy is to admit as many mature students who wish to come and who are suitably qualified. The University, in common with the other Scottish Universities, has adopted age 23 in relation to its definition of mature status. Each application is taken on its merits and the University is prepared to waive its general entrance requirement where there is evidence of ability to undertake degree work. The University normally interviews mature age candidates if they are not offering evidence of recent study.

Special Literature. No. Prospectus available.

Crèche Facilities. Yes.

Part-time Degrees. These are available for students living in the area only who are able to select units from the full-time degree course timetables and so spread their degree course over a longer period.

University of Strathclyde

Percentage of Mature Students. 21 years and over 21.8 per cent, 23 years and over 12.8 per cent.

Establishment Policy. Mature candidates aged 23 and over may be given separate consideration (Regulation 2.1.5, page 138), but the normal method of selection is on the basis of passes in recognised public examination and successful mature applicants normally have a group of SCE Higher grade or GCE Advanced level passes supported by Ordinary grade passes covering a range of approved subjects, with at least two of the Higher or Advanced level passes at good standards; a pass in English on at least the Ordinary grade or level is normally required. Consideration is given to the number and dates of sittings of examinations and whether the study has been full time or part time.

Special consideration may be given to mature candidates who, although lacking conventional entrance qualifications, have over the years shown an interest in their educational advancement and an aptitude for academic study. Such candidates, as well as those with old and unusual qualifications, **may be** considered for selection by means of a special Mature Entry Test held in the spring preceding the proposed date of entry. The test is used in connection only with proposed students in Arts and Social Studies and Strathclyde Business School and not Science and Engineering.

There is no special application procedure for mature candidates, who should apply in the usual way through UCCA. On the basis of this application, a candidate may be invited to sit the Test, which consists of a series of aptitude tests, an essay chosen from a varied list of topics and an interview. Extra references are also sought.

Introductory/Study Skills Courses. There are introductory study skills lectures for all undergraduates grouped by subject of study.

Special Literature. None. Prospectus available on request.

Crèche Facilities. Yes, crèche facilities provided by the students' association.

Mature Students' Union/Society. Yes.

Special Provision for Mature Students. Each student has his/her own academic counsellor and there is a Student Advisory Service of the University. There is a study centre to advise students on study skills at all times during their course and, there is an Advisor on Educational Methods available for consultation by appointment at any time and one half-day a week without appointment.

University of Surrey

Percentage of Mature Students. 8.9 per cent (66 students) of new entrants to undergraduate courses in October 1984.

Establishment Policy. The University of Surrey welcomes applications from mature students and applicants who are 23 years of age or over and who do not otherwise satisfy the general entrance requirement may be eligible for admission if they are able to submit satisfactory evidence of the requisite capacity and attainments to enable them to pursue successfully the course for which they are applying. The students' applications are then considered by the academic department in consultation with the Registry, and most of the annual intake designated 'mature' do possess 'A' level or equivalent qualifications. A very few students without formal qualifications are admitted to courses usually in the Faculty of Human Studies.

Introductory/Study Skills Courses. No formal study skills but the University's Institute of Educational Development is available to assist any students with learning difficulties and such help would be available to mature students on returning to study.

Special Literature. None. Prospectus available on request.

Upper Age Limits in the Institution. None.

University of Sussex

Percentage of Mature Students. 30 per cent admitted to arts and social studies courses. 20 per cent admitted to science courses. Total 26 per cent.

Establishment Policy. The University welcomes applications from mature students because of their greater experience and motivation and the proportion of mature students at Sussex is significantly above the national average. In general there are special entry schemes for mature and/or unqualified candidates who need to be over 19, resident in the UK and have ceased formal full-time education at least three years prior to intended date of entry. After applying to UCCA, candidates that we are interested in complete a supplementary application form provided by the University.

Candidates will be required to write an essay of not more than 2,000 words based on a book nominated by the University and related to their proposed course of study, although in some cases alternative work will be accepted. Selected candidates are then interviewed and unqualified candidates will be required to sit the University's entrance examination. The special entry schemes are not available in the science area except for students applying for Biology, Experimental Psychology and Human Sciences; 'A'-level or equivalent knowledge in certain subjects is a prerequisite for the other science subjects.

Special Literature. Yes. The University provides a leaflet called *Special Entry Scheme for Mature and/or Unqualified Candidates* which describes the special procedures. There is also a comprehensive section in the Prospectus on unqualified students and mature students. Prospectus available on request.

Crèche Facilities. Yes.

Mature Students' Union/Society. Yes.

Part-time Degrees. BEd in-service studied over two years part time.

The University of Ulster

Percentage of Mature Students. Full time, 16.4 per cent; part time, 97.5 per cent.

Establishment Policy. With effect from 1985/86 applicants for admission to first degree courses who will be 21 years of age or more at the date of entry, who do not satisfy the general entrance requirements, but who have useful experience to bring to university studies and to a future career, may be considered for admission.

Introductory/Study Skills Courses. 1. Certificates in Foundation Studies for mature students, aimed particularly at those who left school early and who wish to return to some form of academic

discipline. Successful completion is regarded as satisfying the University entrance requirements for undergraduate courses.
2. Students Counselling Service offers to *all* students workshops on learning and communication skills.

Special Literature. See Undergraduate Prospectus, Postgraduate Prospectus and also literature published by the Department of Adult and Continuing Education.

Crèche Facilities. Yes.

Special Provision for Mature Students. None, but all students have advisers and the counselling service is available to *all* students.

Part-time Degrees. A number of part-time higher degrees are offered – see prospectus. Also part-time undergraduate degrees in Business Studies, Public Sector Administration, Catering Administration, Hotel and Tourism Management, Education, Humanities Combined, Biological Sciences, Nursing Studies, Psychology, Sociology, Engineering.

The University of Wales

The University of Wales has long made provision for the admission of mature students over 23 years of age who have been recommended by the Constituent Institutions of the University as having reached a satisfactory standard of general education. In recent years the University has consciously attempted to increase provision in this area and recent innovations include external schemes for the degrees of BA/BSc/LLB/BD and for the Diploma in Theology. It is also possible for certain mature students whose relative lack of formal qualifications is compensated for by age and relevant experience to carry out study/research for master's degrees.

University College of Wales – Aberystwyh

Percentage of Mature Students. 12 per cent.

Establishment Policy. The University College of Wales welcomes applications from mature students (over 23) and is anxious to offer all possible help in the process of deciding to read for a degree. Mature students can matriculate under modified regulations which is, simply, on the recommendation of a constituent college of the University. Applicants over 23 are given sympathetic consideration by the College and normal entry requirements can be waived or modified providing course selectors are satisfied that the applicant has a reasonable chance of completing the course successfully. Where a particular degree course assumes a prior knowledge of the subject up to GCE 'A' level, then that level is essential. Candidates lacking formal academic qualifications, but who are well motivated, are invited to attend for interview and take an essay-type test based on a wide range of topics (current affairs, literature, etc.). The prospectus entry is helpful and encouraging and the CVCP/TUC booklet 'Mature Students – A Brief guide to University entrance' is circulated to prospective applicants.

Special Literature. CVCP/TUC booklet. Prospectus available on request.

Crèche Facilities. Yes.

Mature Students' Union/Society. Yes.

Special Provision for Mature Students. Yes, all students are assigned to a personal tutor.

Part-time Degrees. BA (External Degree) available only through the medium of Welsh.

University College of North Wales

Percentage of Mature Students. 7 per cent over 23 (1984); 12 per cent over 21 (1984).

Establishment Policy. The University College of North Wales, Bangor welcomes applications from candidates over the age of 23 who do not possess the normal entry requirements, and such applications are considered on their merits in competition with all other applications. Mature aged applicants are required to attend for an interview to discuss the demands and suitability of courses. The final decision with regard to acceptance rests with a Sub-Committee of the Senate. Mature-aged candidates who are admitted are recommended for matriculation to the University of Wales as having reached a satisfactory standard of general education, but in some cases such applicants may be advised or required to follow courses prior to entry, e.g. 'A' level or Open University or Extra Mural courses.

Special Literature. None. Prospectus available on request.

Crèche Facilities. Yes. Facility available in the Students' Union on weekdays.

Mature Students' Union/Society. Mature students are free to participate in all college societies.

143

Special Provision for Mature Students. Mature students have a personal tutor as do all undergraduate students. They may also if the need arises take advantage of the counselling service.

Part-time Degrees. None.

University College, Cardiff

Percentage of Mature Students. 17.7 per cent over 21 on first degree courses, excluding a special BEd course for overseas students.

Establishment Policy. University College, Cardiff usually interviews mature age students (i.e. those over 23 years and who are unable to satisfy the normal requirements of matriculation in the University of Wales) and attempts to assess the candidates' suitability for entry to a degree course.

A special Mature Age Matriculation examination has been replaced by the special interview and a consideration of examination results which can often be of lower standard than those requested from a normal applicant. The College admits some seventy candidates every year under the Mature Age Regulations, representing 50 per cent of the total number of mature entrants.

Introductory/Study Skills Courses. Short evening course for mature age entrants who live locally held during September preceding enrolment.

Upper Age Limits. None.

Special Literature. Yes. The college produces an information sheet entitled *Notes for Prospective Mature Students* based on that produced by the Association of Graduate Careers Advisory Services Working Party on the Training and Employment of the Older Graduate. It also distributes the CVCP/TUC document *Mature Students – A brief guide to University entrance.* Prospectus also available on request.

Mature Students' Union/Society. Yes.

Crèche Facilities. Yes.

University of Wales Institute of Science and Technology

Percentage of Mature Students. 16 per cent.

Establishment Policy. Applications for admission by mature students are dealt with individually on their merits by the course selectors. Applicants must apply on the UCCA form but they may contact UWIST direct for advice before making formal application. Candidates for Science and Engineering courses will be required to show that their academic background and/or experience will allow them to pursue a degree course.

Introductory/Study Skills Courses. A mathematics refresher course, not designed specifically for mature students, is available access to higher education; to first-year students.

Special Literature. None. Prospectus available on request.

Crèche Facilities. Yes.

University College of Swansea

Establishment Policy. This is set out on page 40 of the current edition of our prospectus. The College welcomes application from mature-age students and they are given careful, individual attention. The College looks for genuine commitment demonstrated, for example, by the pursuit of Open University qualifications, Advanced-level passes or Extra-Mural work. The view is taken that mature-age candidates must be adequately prepared before they can embark upon an advanced scheme of study. Experience shows that in the majority of cases candidates without such preparation admitted in the past came to grief since they could not cope with the level and volume of work.

Introductory/Study Skills Courses. The College's Department of Adult and Continuing Education offers one-year preparatory courses in English, Philosophy, Politics and Sociology specially created for mature-age students. These courses have been in operation for two/three years and seem to be working successfully. There are plans to broaden the range of subjects on offer in the next few years subject, of course, to the availability of financial and other resources. Day-long induction courses are mounted at the beginning of each session for all new students. Special note is taken of the individual needs of mature students.

Special Literature. A brochure, *So you want to get a degree? A second chance at 23+*, is available (in English and Welsh) on request.

Upper Age Limits in the Institution. There are no upper age limits but, in practice, Admissions Tutors are rather reluctant to admit those over the age of, say, 60 who wish to read for a degree merely for personal satisfaction. This is because the competition for places from well-qualified school-leavers is so intense at the moment and it is felt that the latter must be given priority.

Crèche Facilities. The Students' Union operates a crèche during term time.

Special Provision for Mature Students. The College has, for many years, recognised the special needs of mature-age students and all applications in this category are considered by the Mature-Age Matriculation Committee. The Committee receives recommendations from individual departments and has authority from the Senate to take executive action. It seeks to ensure that the College operates a consistent and fair policy for all candidates of mature-age. Every year, it receives a report on the progress of the students admitted in this category in order to ensure that its procedures are working satisfactorily.

The Student Union also has a Mature-Students' Society. Its aim is to bring together all those over the age of twenty-three, to represent their interests in the College and to provide a forum for discussion of matters of common interest.

St David's University College

Percentage of Mature Students. 10.75 per cent.

Establishment Policy. See also the general entry under 'University of Wales'. Applications from mature students are welcomed. Each is given full consideration on its merits. Those without formal entry qualifications are normally interviewed so that their abilities and capacity to work successfully for a degree may be assessed. At this point evidence such as recent essay work helps to prove motivation, preparatory study etc.

The University of Wales Diploma in General Studies offered at Coleg Harlech is an acceptable entry qualification and suggested to those who are at present inadequately prepared for degree work. (See Chapter 8 for further information about Coleg Harlech.)

Introductory/Study Skills Courses. Yes. Open Seminars for mature students are held to discuss difficulties and to share experiences.

Special Literature. None. Prospectus available on request.

Crèche Facilities. Yes. Run by Students' Union.

Mature Students' Union/Society. Yes.

Special Provision for Mature Students. Individual tutors and a careers and a counselling service.

146

Part-time Degrees. See entry for 'University of Wales'.

University of Warwick

Percentage of Mature Students. 12 per cent (approximately).

Establishment Policy. The University is keen to encourage applications from mature students – that is, students aged over 21 at their proposed date of entry who have been unable for one reason or another to complete a normal secondary education. Each application is considered on individual merit. Special provision can be made to waive the General Entrance Requirement for suitable candidates who can show evidence of previous study and of the capacity necessary to pursue the proposed degree course. Certain course entry requirements, however, particularly in the Faculty of Science, cannot normally be waived.

There is no special University entrance examination for mature students. Some Departments may be able to accept candidates with very few formal educational qualifications and set their own written work in the form of essays. However, as fierce competition for places inevitably results in a restriction of the flexibility exercised by selectors when considering mature applicants, it is increasingly the case that they may be expected to obtain some qualifications before applying for admission. Potential applicants are therefore encouraged to contact the University well in advance for advice.

Special Literature. None, but information on part-time degrees in arts and prospectus available on request.

Crèche Facilities. Yes.

Mature Students' Union/Society. Yes.

Part-time Degrees. Four- and five-year part-time (daytime only) degree courses are offered in the following arts subjects: Classical Civilisation, English and American Literature, English and European Literature, European Studies, French Studies, French and European Literature, History. Leaflet and application forms are available from the Academic Registrar.

It is hoped to extend the range of part-time degree courses in the future.

University of York

Percentage of Mature Students. 9.5 per cent (over 21).

Establishment Policy. The University welcomes applications from 'mature candidates' (that is, those aged 21 or over at the time of application), and a number of such students are admitted each year. Prospective applicants are advised to write in the first instance (stating their qualifications, if any) to the Undergraduate Admissions Officer at the University. Each application by a mature candidate is considered on its merits. Some of those admitted have had qualifications such as the diplomas issued by the universities concerned to students at Ruskin and Plater Colleges, Oxford; Coleg Harlech, Wales; and Newbattle Abbey, Scotland; also qualifications in banking, accountancy, journalism and nursing. The University has also entered into a transfer agreement with the Open University, whereby Open University students with appropriate and sufficient credits may be considered eligible for entry into undergraduate courses at York.

Special Literature.   Yes, leaflet *Mature Students at the University of York* and prospectus available on request.

Crèche Facilities.   No, but there is a private nursery adjacent to the University site.

Mature Students' Union/Society.   Yes.

Special Provision for Mature Students.   Care is taken to ensure that as far as possible mature students are assigned to supervisors whose own experience of life has given them an awareness of the sort of problems, both academic and personal, that mature students are likely to face.

Polytechnics

City of Birmingham Polytechnic

Establishment Policy. It is the policy of the Polytechnic to encourage applications from mature students without the normal entry qualifications. Applications are welcomed from students who have successfully taken access courses, Open University foundation courses, or units from the Polytechnic's Visiting and Listening Students' Scheme. Course Boards of Study, with whom the final decision rests, are also authorised to admit students over 21 without normal entry requirements.

Boards of Study may also admit students to second or later years of a course on the basis of studies completed at other institutions.

Introductory/Study Skills Courses. A variety of courses is available locally run by Colleges of Further Education and these include,

Access	One year, eighteen hours per week. Prepares students for subjects in the Polytechnic's Faculty of Social Sciences and Arts.
Mature Students Alternative Admissions Scheme	One-year part-time course can give entry to BEd Course in Polytechnic's Faculty of Education and Teacher Training.
New way	Two-year part-time course designed with Afro-Caribbean and Asian students in mind. Can give entry to a number of courses at the

New Way	Polytechnic, particularly those concerned with training for Teaching and Social Work.
Return to learn	Three stage progression from basic, through second-chance, gateway. Can give entry to a variety of courses at the Polytechnic.

Full details from Adult Learner's Enquiry Centre, Central Library, Paradise Circus, Birmingham B3.

The Polytechnic also offers a Visiting and Listening Students programme. This programme enables mature students to study one or more units drawn from courses in most areas of the Polytechnic. *Visiting Students* are qualified to take units and may be eligible for transcripts of success in assessment; Listening Students may not be so qualified but 'sit in' on lectures and may be eligible for transcripts of satisfactory attendance. Students can thus gain experience of Higher Education before deciding to enter it more fully.

Special Literature. There are special leaflets on all of the above mentioned courses. Reference to mature students is made in the Polytechnic prospectus and in individual course literature.

Upper Age Limits in Individual Departments. Upper age limits for teacher training.

Crèche Facilities. Under discussion, but there is some cover during school half-terms. Students may bring in school-age children.

Special Provision for Mature Students. Yes.

Part-time Degrees. Business Studies, Law, English, Economics, Government, Mechanical Engineering and Electrical Engineering are offered. Plans for 1986 and beyond include the development of part-time degree courses in Estate Management, Quantity Surveying and Building Surveying. The polytechnic is switching to unit-based, multimode courses where possible. Students will be able to change from part time to full time and vice versa to suit their own needs.

Brighton Polytechnic

Percentage of Mature Students. 20 per cent (approximately).

Establishment Policy. A mature candidate (aged 21 and over by 31 December in the year of entry) may be admitted to the beginning of a course without the formal entry requirements if the Polytechnic is satisfied that the student has had relevant experience and is likely to follow the course successfully and beneficially, having the necessary motivation, potential and knowledge to do so.

Special Literature. None. Prospectus available.

Crèche Facilities. Yes. Used by 50 per cent staff and 50 per cent students.

Special Provision for Mature Students. Yes.

Part-time Degrees. BA (Hons) Business Studies, BA (Hons) Combined Studies (Humanities), BEd (Hons) for serving teachers, BSc (Hons)/BSc Applied Chemistry, BSc Nursing.

Bristol Polytechnic

Percentage of Mature Students. 23 per cent.

Establishment Policy. Applicants over 21 may be admitted without meeting normal minimum academic entry requirements. All mature students who do not meet entry requirements may be interviewed. The interview takes the form of (a) selection interview and (b) counselling session. The Polytechnic is currently reviewing policy and has set up a working party to consider open access to polytechnic courses with particular reference to mature students. Applicants with Open University background are welcomed.

Special Literature. None. Prospectus available.

Upper Age Limits in Individual Departments. Yes; if in doubt consult the departments of interest individually.

Crèche Facilities. Yes (on two sites).

Special Provision for Mature Students. Careers adviser available.

Mature Students' Society. Yes.

Part-time Degrees. BA and BA (Hons) Business Studies, BSc Applied Physics, BEd (Hons), BEd (Hons) Special Education, BA and BA (Hons) Law, B.Eng Electrical Engineering and BSc Mechanical Engineering. Bachelor Town Planning, BSc (Hons) Applied Biological Sciences. Also wide variety of courses from HNC to research degree level and many professional qualifications.

City of London Polytechnic

Percentage of Mature Students. 27 per cent.

Establishment Policy. The Polytechnic strongly favours the admission of students over the age of 21 years.

Introductory/Study Skills Courses. Study Skills courses are provided though not specifically for mature students.

Special Literature. No. Guide for Applicants available.

Crèche Facilities. Yes.

Special Provision for Mature Students. No, but the Student Advice Centre is available for help and advice.

Part-time Degrees. Large selection of part-time degrees including BA and BA (Hons) in Business Studies with Business Finance, Manpower Studies and Marketing, BSc and BSc (Hons) in Metallurgy and Materials Engineering, BA and BSc with Honours in Accountancy, Biology, Chemistry, Economics, Geography, Law, Mathematics, Metallurgy and Materials Engineering, Physics, Politics, Psychology, Sociology, Statistics.

Coventry (Lanchester) Polytechnic

Percentage of Mature Students. 12 per cent.

Establishment Policy. The Polytechnic welcomes applications from mature students with standard or limited entry qualifications, and many such students have successfully completed courses. Applicants contact the course tutor for advice and information and where departmental admissions tutors are satisfied and wish to admit mature students without conventional qualifications, they request the academic registrar to approve a 'special case' admission.

Special Literature. None. Prospectus available.

Crèche Facilities. Yes. Organised by the Students' Union.

Special Provision for Mature Students. Yes, Students' Union financial aid fund set up as an independent charity. Welfare Students' Officer deals with most queries and offers advice.

Part-time Degrees. BSc in Engineering, BSc in Mathematics, BA and BA (Hons) in Modern Studies, BA and BA (Hons) in Applied Economics.

The Hatfield Polytechnic

Percentage of Mature Students. 39 per cent (first-year, first-degree students aged 21 and over).

Establishment Policy. A policy adopted in May 1979 stipulates that, where appropriate, programmes be designated to amalgamate full-time and part-time participants. The Polytechnic maintains close contact with the community and can respond in a flexible way to meet the community needs. Thus the needs of the mature student are well catered for with preparatory courses to assist them in returning to study, short courses, part-time degree courses and a variety of services described in the literature.

Students are assessed by interview and essay and other tests of ability.

Introductory/Study Skills Courses. An opportunity for a return to study is given by Polyprep – two linked short courses leading to a Polytechnic first certificate of preparatory studies.

Special Literature. Yes. *The Adult Way to Continue Your Education,* a polytechnic-wide leaflet, and leaflets outlining the opportunities for mature students in various study areas produced by the five schools of study describe the variety of opportunities available at Hatfield Polytechnic.

Crèche Facilities. Yes.

Special Provision for Mature Students. A centre offering free educational guidance for mature students – The E.G.A. Centre, P.O. Box 109, College Lane, Hatfield, Herts.

Part-time Degrees. BA degrees in Social Science, Contemporary Studies or English with Historical Studies. BSc degrees in Computer Science, Mathematics, Applied Biology or Applied Chemistry and a BEd degree by part-time study.

Huddersfield Polytechnic

Percentage of Mature Students. 25 per cent (approximately).

Establishment Policy. There are opportunities on some courses for older applicants who lack the formal entry requirements. Such people, i.e. those who will be 21 or over, should indicate on their application forms that they wish to be considered for 'mature student' entry. Candidates who appear to show potential are always interviewed. Applicants who have been out of full-time education for some time, or who can offer little tangible evidence of their academic capacity, may be advised to follow a preparatory 'A' level, OU Foundation or Access course, to bridge the formal educational gap and to provide some measure of their ability. Courses which are especially appropriate for 'mature-student' entry are degrees in Humanities, Behavioural Sciences and possibly Human Ecology. Mature candidates for Engineering or Chemistry degrees should be aware that they must be able to offer the 'A'-level subjects or National Diploma required, otherwise they are unlikely to be sufficiently well equipped to cope with degree level studies in their chosen disciplines.

Students from the Middle and Far East and Africa would not necessarily be treated as 'mature' at 21, as in most cases their education has started about two years later than their English contemporaries.

Special Literature. No. Prospectus available.

Crèche Facilities. Not yet, but being negotiated.

Mature Students' Union/Society. Yes.

Special Provision for Mature Students. Yes.

Part-time Degrees. BA (Hons) Social Welfare Administration, BEd (for teachers and lecturers in FE and related fields), BEd with Honours (in-service), BA (Hons), BA Humanities, BA (Hons) Business Studies, BSc (Hons) Textile Technology.

Kingston Polytechnic

Percentage of Mature Students. 16 per cent (1st year intake), which includes BTEC Higher Diplomas and CNAA undergraduate courses. If first-year, part-time degree and part-time HNC students are included the figure is 18.5 per cent.

Establishment Policy. The institution welcomes mature students designated as over 21. There are no formal schemes relating to the admission of unqualified mature students. Admissions tutors consider past experience, performance at interview and references when considering people with non-standard entry qualifications.

Introductory/Study Skills Courses. In most courses there is an emphasis upon the acquisition of adequate study skills, and assistance is given to students through the Learning Resources Department: sometimes these schemes are formal and in other cases by individual arrangement.

Special Provision for Mature Students. Yes.

Special Literature. There is literature for mature students which is administered by the Learning Resources Department in conjunction with study skills schemes operated within courses.

Part-time Degrees. BA and BA (Hons) in Modern Arts, Economics, Applied Social Science and Geography. BEng and BEng (Hons) in Civil, Aeronautical, Mechanical and Production Engineering. BSc and BSc (Hons) in Geography. BEd (Hons) in Education.

Lancashire Polytechnic
(formerly Preston Polytechnic)

Percentage of Mature Students. 45 per cent.

Establishment Policy. Mature students are positively encouraged to apply for Lancashire Polytechnic's regular full- and part-time courses. For many courses it is possible for mature students (over 21) to be admitted without the normally required formal qualifications under the 'exceptional entry' rules. This takes into account factors like maturity and experience, continued study and evidence of development, the motivation and commitment of the student. Each mature student application is treated on its merits and course tutors have to be satisfied that applicants can cope with and benefit from a particular course. The main problems are in the linear subjects – in Science, Technology, Maths and Languages where 'A'-level standards of knowledge are necessary to cope with the course.

Introductory/Study Skills Courses. There are a number of courses – mainly part time which serve as an introduction to part-time or full-time degree programmes at the Polytechnic. These give adults in particular the opportunity to sample life at the Polytechnic, to acquire study skills and to become familiar with the basic elements of advanced study – notably practical work, lectures, seminars, reading, essay writing and independent study. As well as preparing mature students for a return to study such courses will assist in familiarising students with the nature and demands of the chosen subject area. In some instances a foundation course is essential to bring the student up to the academic standard required for entry to particular courses. (See prospectuses for details.) We offer such courses in:

Accountancy	various times and levels
Some Management areas	typically one day per week or afternoon and evening – one year
Physics (Polyphysics)	one or two evenings per week – one year
Mathematics (Certificate courses)	similar if available
French	intensive extra courses on BA Humanities degree
Pre-degree course	one evening per week – two terms

The pre-degree course concentrates on return-to-study aspects offering an introduction to Higher Education with tasting of various subject areas, essay writing, etc. There is no formal examination at the end of the course but it provides a diagnostic base for students and admissions tutors.

Associate Student Scheme. Most courses are divided into smaller units which can be taken individually, and in some cases aggregated for an award. This provides a useful taster.

Open College. The North West Open College offers an alternative to 'A'-level courses for entry into higher education.

These are validated by Lancashire Polytechnic and Lancaster University. The polytechnic takes twenty to thirty local mature students each year from this route.

Special Literature. Yes. Booklet *Opportunities for Adults in Education and Training at Lancashire Polytechnic* is available together with the prospectus.

Upper Age Limits in the Institution. No.

Upper Age Limits in Individual Departments. There is no formal policy to preclude any age but individual departments may have restrictions placed upon them by professional bodies as far as certification is concerned.

Crèche Facilities. Yes.

Special Provision for Mature Students. A co-ordinator for Continuing Education is available to offer advice and information: Tony Goddard, Preston (0772) 22141. Student Services also assist mature students as regards personal career needs bearing in mind the majority of students at Preston are mature.

Part-time Degrees. These include a BA (Hons) Business Studies, BA (Hons) Law, BSc Physics, and a Combined Studies Programme leading to BSc Hons, BSc, BA (Hons), BA. Full details of all part-time courses are available in the part-time prospectus.

Some first year subjects in the Combined Studies Degree can now be studied in local Colleges of Further Education thus making them accessible to local mature students in particular.

Leeds Polytechnic

Establishment Policy. General policy is to admit mature students in small numbers to all courses. They are individually considered by the respective teaching schools and may be admitted without the usual entrance qualifications, if they can be integrated into courses. Where there are specific course requirements these must be met or an appropriate academic standard reached by the mature applicant. Particular information is available on the regulations relating to the entrance of mature students to a BA (Hons) Social Policy and Administration course. Candidates for mature entry should normally be 21. Applicants are interviewed and a written examination may be necessary.

Special Literature. A leaflet, *BA (Hons) Social policy and Administration, Regulations relating to the Entrance of Mature Students,* is available together with the prospectus.

Upper Age Limits in Individual Departments. Yes where students are embarking on BEd and PGCE courses.

Crèche Facilities. No, but nursery facilities are available.

Part-time Degrees. BSc and BSc (Hons) Electrical Engineering, BEd and BEd (Hons), BSc Nursing Studies, BA and BA (Hons), also Dip HE Management and Administration, BA and BA (Hons) Combined Studies, BA and BA (Hons) Law. BSc Production Engineering, BA Librarianship.

Leicester Polytechnic

Percentage of Mature Students. Approximately 5 per cent embarking on first qualification, i.e. first degree and HD/HND.

Establishment Policy. Leicester Polytechnic welcomes applications from mature students (21 years and over). The procedures for selection vary, where prospective entrants do not hold GCE 'A'-level subjects or equivalent qualifications. Candidates are interviewed in depth and for arts and related disciplines some form of written test is required – often taken before or at the time of the interview. For science and other related disciplines candidates are encouraged to register on 'Open College' courses available at Further Education Colleges and other centres, to first obtain certificates in those schemes which the polytechnic has agreed are an acceptable basis to meet minimum entrance qualifications for mature students.

Part-time Degrees. BA and BA (Hons) in Social Science, Business Studies, Law. BSc and BSc (Hons) in Applied Physics, Architecture and Surveying.

Liverpool Polytechnic

Percentage of Mature Students. Approximately 48 per cent of intake on all undergraduate courses (full time, sandwich and part time) fall into this category.

Establishment Policy. The Polytechnic as a general policy adopts a flexible attitude towards mature applicants, accepting where appropriate alternative qualifications to the more usual 'O' and 'A' levels and implementing as widely as possible, on degree courses, the CNAA policy of admitting mature applicants without formal qualifications who nevertheless indicate that they have the necessary motivation, potential and knowledge to follow the course successfully. Applicants aged 21 years or over are regarded as mature students.

Introductory/Study Skills Courses. Many departments provide study skills schemes, personal counselling support, and it is hoped within the very near future to make this a feature of all departments.

Special Literature. No, but details of mature student entry are available through the main prospectus, although it is expected, within the near future, to produce material with special reference to mature students.

Upper Age Limits. Not generally, although exceptions may apply where restrictions are imposed by professional bodies, as on certain other courses. Students are advised to consult individual departments concerning age limits.

Crèche Facilities. Yes.

Special Provision for Mature Students. Yes.

Part-time Degrees. Biology, Chemistry, Business Studies, Electrical and Electronic Engineering, Law, Mechanical Engineering, Surveying, Social Studies, Psychology and Literature, Life and Thought, together with future developments in Fine Art and Sports Science. The polytechnic expects to be able to offer, by 1986–87, a wide range of part-time courses at degree level, but also a large number of other part-time courses at other levels.

Manchester Polytechnic

Percentage of Mature Students. 20 per cent (approximately). Includes students on sandwich, full-time and part-time undergraduate courses.

Establishment Policy. The first Manchester Polytechnic *Policy for Development Statement* actively welcomed mature students to the institution and this policy has been subsequently confirmed in course development and faculty activities. Polytechnic staff are involved in the Manchester Eductional Advice for Adults Network and counselling facilities are always available. The Council for National Academic Awards attitude has always been most encouraging and their access policy for exceptional admission can be a positive incentive to adult returners. Ultimately, discretion on admission rests with each course committee.

Introductory/Study Skills Courses. Yes, there is a study skills unit in the Department of General Studies and this serves the Polytechnic as a whole. Individual and group sessions are arranged by appointment. Students may approach the study skills unit direct or through that department.

Special Literature. Yes. The Careers Advisory Officer, Mr Colin Sills, provides special literature to departments and on application. The Polytechnic Community Liaison Officer, Mrs Clare Debenham, is producing the second edition of the 'Mature Students Handbook'. As well as giving particulars of grants, child care arrangements, etc, it also features the experience of mature students from all faculties. Other leaflets, e.g. *CNAA Mature Admissions,* are available through the Manchester Educational Advice for Adults Network.

Mature Students Union/Society. Yes.

Special Provision for Mature Students. Manchester Educational Advice for Adults Network. Dip HE student counsellors. Certain degrees make special tutors accessible.

Part-time Degrees. Wide variety of part-time degrees available including BA (Hons) – Psychology, Public Administration, BA and BA (Hons) – Humanities/Social Studies, Law, Librarianship, BA (Hons) BSc (Hons) – Business Studies, BSc and BSc (Hons) – Biological Sciences, Engineering, Polymer Science and Technology, Applied Chemistry, Applied Computing, Combined Studies, Physics, Mathematics; BSc – Nursing Studies, Environmental Health, Electronic Engineering Studies, Production Engineering, Manufacturing Metallurgy.

Middlesex Polytechnic

Percentage of Mature Students. 40 per cent (approximately).

Establishment Policy. Mature students are in general actively recruited and most courses are designed accordingly, including flexibility (within the CNAA framework) towards people without formal qualifications but presenting evidence of suitable potential.

Introductory/Study Skills Courses. Yes, various courses are available including (a) self-contained short courses, (b) preparatory return to study pre-degree course, (c) Diploma of Higher Education, a leading example of continuing education that is part of the Polytechnic's modular scheme in which students are recruited part and full time to specific programmes across an extensive subject range but can defer their choice of award until the pattern of studies becomes clear, the programmes extending to degrees in Humanities and Combined Studies.

Special Literature. Yes. Separate leaflets are available in some fields and reference to mature students is found in general course literature and in prospectus.

Upper Age Limits in Individual Departments. No, but certain courses are suited to 'A'-level school leavers.

Crèche Facilities. Limited nursery and playgroup provision.

Part-time Degrees. Yes, and full details are given in the current prospectus, and see also entry under Introductory/Study Skills Courses.

Newcastle upon Tyne Polytechnic

Percentage of Mature Students. 57 per cent of all students on advanced level courses in 1983–84 were 21 or over.

Establishment Policy. The Polytechnic encourages enquiries from mature students, and is always prepared to consider applications from those without the normal entry requirements. Admission is permissible under these circumstances when the Polytechnic is satisfied that such students are likely to benefit from, and successfully complete, the courses of study proposed. The Polytechnic and local colleges provide the Higher Education Foundation Course as a means of preparing mature students for degree-level studies, and the Polytechnic will also consider applicants who have completed other such preparatory or introductory courses. Mature students are defined as those aged 21 years or over.

Introductory/Study Skills Courses. The Higher Education Foundation Course, run in collaboration with local FE Colleges, provides courses in ten subject areas, successful completion in three of which can provide entry to appropriate degree, diploma and certificate courses at the Polytechnic. The Associate Student Scheme allows mature students to enrol for part(s) of existing courses for the purposes of retraining, updating, personal interest or to 'taste' a particular course.

Special Literature. Leaflet for Higher Education Foundation Course and leaflet for Associate Student Scheme available, together with prospectus.

Upper Age Limits in Individual Departments. BEd normally has upper age limit of 35 years.

Crèche Facilities. Yes. Students' Union crèche.

Special Provision for Mature Students. Yes. Continuing Education Service.

Part-time Degrees. Yes. An extensive range of part-time degrees is available and full details are included in the prospectus.
Current plans include exploring the assessment of prior learning (i.e. taking into account the full range of experience of mature students when considering applications), and extension of

the Associate Student Scheme. Future plans include further moves towards part-time versions of full-time courses.

North East London Polytechnic

Percentage of Mature Students. Over 50 per cent.

Establishment Policy. North East London Polytechnic (NELP) is concerned to give the opportunity for higher education not only to sixth-formers and college students but also to those whose background, experience and attainment have not made their entry to higher education seem an obvious or straightforward step. In particular applications are encouraged from older people with or without the normal entry requirements for a course of higher education. The Polytechnic accepts applications under CNAA regulations on mature entry, or from students who have done Open University preparatory courses. Some courses are specifically designed to meet the needs of mature students.

Introductory/Study Skills Courses. Yes. An induction course is held at the beginning of the first term. As part of the induction procedure the student will be acquainted with the content and structure of the course, the nature of assessment and learning methods. Study skills programmes are provided according to need, as far as resources permit.

Special Literature. No special literature but there are sections relating to mature student entry in both the part-time and full-time prospectus.

Crèche Facilities. Yes. At Barking Precinct, nursery facilities for 2½ to 5-years olds are available daily.

Special Provision for Mature Students. A personal tutor is assigned to all students and is responsible for dealing with course related and personal problems.

Part-time Degrees. Yes. A wide range available but some have specific entry requirements. Degrees available in Architecture, Education, Business Studies, Law, Mathematics, Civil Engineering, Applied Biology, Health Studies, Life Sciences, Archaeological Science, Psychology. Dip HE and BA/BSc by Independent Study, and a modular (multi-subject) Dip HE which offers opportunity for progression to degree courses also available. The Polytechnic expects a continuation of its present policy of encouraging applications from and seeking to meet the needs of mature entrants.

North Staffordshire Polytechnic

Percentage of Mature Students. 14 per cent.

Establishment Policy. North Staffordshire Polytechnic encourages applications from mature students in all subject disciplines, making extensive use of the flexibility within CNNA regulations to admit mature students to undergraduate courses. Mature students are defined as persons aged 21 years or over on 31 December in the academic year in which they enrol. In addition North Staffordshire Polytechnic offers a comprehensive range of courses under the auspices of its Continuing Education Programme, which include Associate Student Scheme, Study Experience Course, Open College Course, Sampler Short Course Programme and Specialist Short Courses.

Introductory/Study Skills Courses. Yes. The Economics Study Experience Course is a one-year part-time course designed to give students an opportunity to acquire and improve their study skills. There are no entry requirements for mature students wishing to join this course and successful students may use this qualification to gain entry to a degree course. This course is based at Stoke.

The Open College Course is a two-year part-time course run at Stafford in conjunction with the Stafford College of Further Education. Again, considerable emphasis is given to the acquisition of study skills in addition to the study of several subject options.

Special Literature. Advice for mature students is included within general literature for all potential students seeking admission to the Polytechnic, i.e. in the prospectus.

Crèche Facilities. Yes.

Mature Students' Union. Yes.

Special Provision for Mature Students. North Staffordshire Polytechnic makes special provision for mature students in that all students entering under the Associate Student Scheme are counselled by 'contact staff' prior to admission. A comprehensive student services/counselling provision is available to mature students within the polytechnic; the Students' Union is affiliated to the national Mature Students' Union, and supports an active Mature Students' Society.

Part-time Degrees. Business Studies, Law, International Studies, Economics and Sociology available.

162

Oxford Polytechnic

Percentage of Mature Students. Full-time and Sandwich, over 15 per cent, part-time, over 90 per cent.

Establishment Policy. Applications from mature students are encouraged by all courses. Students aged 21 and over are classified as mature, and special arrangements for admission may be made for those who do not possess the normal minimum entry requirements. On the modular course, 'unqualified' mature students can attend part time on a trial basis, and if progress is satisfactory, then move on to a full-time course. The Polytechnic cooperates with a local community college which provides an access course for mature students.

Study Skills Courses. There are study skills courses offered to all students, and individual study counselling, run by Student Services. Such courses have on occasion been offered specifically to mature students.

Special Literature. Prospectus available.

Crèche Facilities. Facilities are available for eighteen children (age range two to five years).

Special Provision for Mature Students. No one is allocated by the Students' Union, but there are mature students as Union officials.

Part-time Degrees. Oxford Polytechnic offers a wide range of part-time degrees – BA, BSc, BEd, and DipHE modular courses. Masters degrees in Urban Planning and Urban Design, Research degree (MPhil and PhD) supervision in various disciplines.

Plymouth Polytechnic

Percentage of Mature Students. 20 per cent.

Establishment Policy. Whilst there are no specific procedures for mature students, the Polytechnic welcomes and encourages applications, even from those without the minimum formal entry requirements. A place will be offered if it is felt that the student will benefit from and complete satisfactorily the particular course.

Introductory/Study Skills Courses. Mature students may take advantage of the counselling service available and may attend the study skills courses provided for all students.

Special Literature. None. Prospectus available.

Part-time Degrees. BSc and Dip HE Combined Studies in Science and Social Science. BSc in Mathematics.

The Polytechnic of Central London

Percentage of Mature Students. 37 per cent on full-time and sandwich undergraduate courses.

Establishment Policy. Candidates who do not hold the conventional entry qualifications are considered on merit, provided that their admission is possible under the regulations of the validating body. Every encouragement is given to older students who can demonstrate an aptitude for study and who are likely to benefit from the course. PCL operates a very flexible policy (within the rules of validating bodies) on entry requirements to its course. In addition to the many full-time and sandwich undergraduate courses, a number run in part-time (evening) modes (usually over five years). There are also a large number of diploma, postgraduate and other part-time evening courses, at various levels, which are suitable for the mature student who is busy during the day with a job or family responsibilities. Some courses in Management Studies also operate special modes designed for 'women returners' – e.g. mornings only.

Introductory/Study Skills Courses. Various levels of provision; varies from faculty to faculty. In many cases intending students are counselled to take such courses outside the polytechnic prior to entry.

Special Literature. None. Prospectus available.

Crèche Facilities. Yes.

Special Provision for Mature Students. Yes.

Part-time Degrees. BSc in Computing, BSc for the Remedial Professions, BA in Social Science.

Polytechnic of the South Bank

Percentage of Mature Students. 67 per cent (for undergraduate courses in 1984).

Establishment Policy. The Polytechnic is keen to admit mature students and sympathetic consideration is being given to applicants over 21 who lack all or some of the normal entry requirements. In considering applicants the prime concern is to assess, in the light of the applicant's particular background and experience, whether he/she would be likely to benefit from and complete the course.

Course directors are happy to speak to and advise potential applicants.

Introductory/Study Skills Courses. Access courses are run in conjunction with local colleges to prepare mature students without formal qualifications for entry into various Polytechnic courses, e.g. Town Planning, Building Administration, Civil Engineering, BEd Degree Course, BA Hons Law, BSc Hons Social Sciences, Mathematics and Computing, BA Hons Business Studies, Electrical Engineering, Modern Languages.

Special Literature. Prospectus and special leaflets on access courses available from the Central Registry.

Crèche Facilities. Yes.

Special Provision for Mature Students. Yes. The appointment of a counsellor within the Student Services Department with special responsibility for mature part-time and continuing students.

Part-time Degrees. The Polytechnic offers part-time degree courses in the following subjects: Building, Business Studies, Chemical Engineering, Civil Engineering, Electrical and Electronic Engineering, Environmental Engineering, Mechanical Engineering, Physics, Social Sciences, Surveying, Teaching Studies, Town Planning.

The Polytechnic of Wales

Percentage of Mature Students. 30 per cent (approximately).

Establishment Policy. The Polytechnic follows the CNAA's policy on the admission of mature students, which is that applicants over 21 years of age without the normal entry requirements can be admitted if they can provide evidence that they are likely to benefit from study on a degree course. The Polytechnic encourages mature students to apply and has had considerable experience in teaching mature students.

Introductory/Study Skills Courses. A study skills course is provided which is open to all students.

Special Literature. None. Prospectus available.

Part-time Degrees. Part-time degrees in Public Administration, Humanities (English, History and Philosophy), Law, Civil Engineering, Police Studies.

The Polytechnic Wolverhampton

Percentage of Mature Students. 24 per cent (approximately).

Establishment Policy. It is an agreed policy of the Polytechnic, approved by Academic Board, to encourage the admission of mature students and this is prosecuted through course advertising and course literature. The mechanisms for entry and for demonstrating candidates' suitability are left to schools.

Introductory/Study Skills Course. Wolverhampton Polytechnic validates 'access' courses offered by Bilston College of Further Education and Dudley College of Technology.

Special Literature. None. Prospectus available.

Upper Age Limits in the Institution. None.

Upper Age Limits in Individual Department. None.

Mature Students' Union/Society. Yes.

Special Provision for Mature Students. Although no special facilities exist for mature students *per se*, the Student Services section of the Polytechnic is sympathetic to the needs of mature students and is able to give counselling in this area.

Part-time Degrees. Variety of part-time degrees and courses for professional examinations, BTEC courses, Dip HE, and other certificates and diplomas. BA and BA (Hons) in Humanities. Inter-disciplinary Studies, Business Studies, Economics, Law, Social Science. BSc and BSc (Hons) in Applied Sciences, Applied Chemistry, Biological Sciences, Computer Science, Metals Technology. BEd and BEd (Hons) for serving teachers. MEd and MA in West Midland Historical Studies. Postgraduate degrees in Education Management and Management Studies and MSc in Instrumental Chemical Analysis or the Applications of Psychology.

Future plans include the development of BEng and BEng (Hons) in Industrial Engineering and Building Services Engineering.

Portsmouth Polytechnic

Percentage of Mature Students. 11 per cent (approximately).

Establishment Policy. Applications from candidates who do not hold the minimum CNAA qualifications are welcome. Applicants are advised to seek advice from the appropriate Head of Department before submitting an application.

Introductory/Study Skills Courses. Not generally provided but individual departments may encourage applicants to undertake reading, etc., before admission.

Special Literature. None. Information in prospectus relates to mature students.

Crèche Facilities. Yes. Facilities for 2½- to 5-year-olds available.

Special Provision for Mature Students. Yes, careers counsellors and advisers are provided.

Sheffield City Polytechnic

Percentage of Mature Students. 16.1 per cent.

Establishment Policy. The admission of mature students (over 21) is encouraged by Academic Board policy on the admission of students. CNAA Policy is used as a guideline but departments and tutors exercise their discretion on each application.

Introductory/Study Skills Courses. Yes, a variety of introductory and study skills courses are provided and associated centres also run preparatory courses for higher education. Examples include pre-study courses such as pre-Polymaths, New Opportunities for Women, Wider Opportunities for Women, pre-Diploma in Applied Statistics. Study Skills courses are run by the Education Department in the first term of each academic year.

Special Literature. *Careers Advice* leaflet is provided as well as the prospectus.

Crèche Facilities. Yes, a crèche is provided on one site. The Department of Applied Social Studies has a timetable adjusted to suit mature students with school-age children and has a school holiday child-minding scheme run voluntarily by staff/students.

Mature Students' Union/Society. No. Research has shown this is not desired by the mature students.

Part-time Degrees. BSc in Engineering, BSc (Hons) in Applied Chemistry, BSc and BSc (Hons) in Computer Studies, Metallurgy and Microstructural Engineering. BA and BA (Hons) in Fine Art, Social Studies, Business Studies, English Studies. BA (Hons) in Humanities and Social Dimensions of Health. BEd.

Sunderland Polytechnic

Percentage of Mature Students. 6 per cent.

Establishment Policy. Although there are minor differences in attitudes which occur in the separate departments and faculties, the advice of the CNAA is adhered to. Admissions tutors will normally satisfy themselves as to the motivation, potential and knowledge of candidates by interview.

Introductory/Study Skills Course. Continuing Education Certificate Course (Humanities Bridging Course) linked to the BA Combined Arts degree part time and full time.

Special Literature. Yes. Prospectus available.

Special Provision for Mature Students. Continuing Education programme provides an information, advice and counselling service. The Polytechnic policy is to encourage adults to participate and see Continuing Education as an important provision. We offer (1) an Open Lecture programme – Lectures selected from the Polytechnic programme; (2) facilities for adults to associate with regular students on the BA Combined Arts degree, BSc Science Subjects degree and Engineering for Women course; (3) Polyarts programme of Dance, Music and Film events including workshops available to the wider community.

Part-time Degrees. Range of part-time degrees available with details in the Part-time Prospectus available on request.

It is hoped that an 'Access Centre' will be established in the Polytechnic by the beginning of the 1985–86 session.

Teeside Polytechnic

Percentage of Mature Students. 25.7 per cent, 21–24 years, 33.5 per cent, 25 and over.

Establishment Policy. Mature students welcome in all departments. Admissions individually assessed by departmental tutors.

Introductory/Study Skills Courses. Administrative and Social Studies and Humanities department operate a study skills introductory course.

Special Literature. Reference made in departmental literature and prospectus, to mature students.

Crèche Facilities. Day nursery.

Part-time Degrees. BSc and BSc (Hons) in Metallurgy, Chemistry, Mathematics, Chemical Engineering. LLB (Bachelor of Law). BA (Hons) in Humanities.

Thames Polytechnic
(see also Avery Hill College)

Percentage of Mature Students. 26 per cent of undergraduates starting full-time and sandwich courses. NB: Most of the undergraduate courses are also offered in a part-time mode.

Establishment Policy. Mature students not less than 21 years of age who, although they lack the usual entry qualifications, have shown exceptional ability in appropriate fields, or who are able to show by appropriate means that they have achieved competence in their chosen field of study, may be admitted as concessional entrants.

Introductory/Study Skills Courses. Yes. The Continuing Education Unit initiated Poly study courses in October 1982 and these will give direct access to Polytechnic degrees in Humanities and Sociology. The Poly study course consists of a variety of course units.

Special Literature. Yes. Leaflets are available. Information for mature students is contained in full-time and part-time prospectus.

Special Provision for Mature Students. Yes. Assistant Registrar (Admissions) and/or Head of Continuing Education Unit act as advisers/contact people.

Part-time Degrees. BA and BA (Hons) in Architecture, English or Business Studies, BSc and BSc (Hons) in Computing Science, Civil Engineering, Electrical and Electronic Engineering, or Mechanical Engineering. BSc in Quantity Surveying.

Trent Polytechnic

Percentage of Mature Students. 10.75 per cent of undergraduates (over the entire student body 19.5 per cent of students are in the mature category).

Establishment Policy. There is no special policy covering the admission of mature students. Like any other applicant, they are assessed on their qualifications and their ability to profit from the course they have applied for. In the absence of the former the latter obviously plays a major part. Most of our degree schemes allow the admissions tutor discretion regarding applicants who do not possess the minimum entry qualifications and the clause regarding ability to benefit from a course is not infrequently applied.

Introductory/Study Skills Courses. Study courses are organised early each academic year by the student counselling service for all students and specifically for mature students.

Special Literature. No, but sections relevant to mature students are included in most literature produced. Prospectus available.

Upper Age Limits in the Individual Departments. None, but departments may take the clause regarding ability to profit from the course into account.

Crèche Facilities. Yes.

Special Provision for Mature Students. No, but sections relevant to mature students are included in most literature produced. Prospectus available.

Part-time Degrees. MA Fine Art, BSc Computer Studies, MSc Computer Aided Engineering, BEng, BSc Quantity Surveying, BSc Urban Estate Surveying, MA Economics, MA Politics and Public Administration, BA (Hons) Humanities, BA (Hons) Modern European Studies, BSc (Hons) Biological Studies, BSc (Hons) Applied Chemistry, MA Accounting and Finance, BA Business, BA (Hons) Law, MEd Primary Education, BEd (Hons) In-service and many part-time BTEC and professional qualification courses.

Trent Polytechnic keeps its provision for mature students under constant review and this area of work seems likely to continue to develop, particularly in the part-time mode. The Polytechnic is also keen to encourage mature students and others to study part time for research qualifications, e.g. PhD, MSc, MA, MPhil, etc.

Colleges and Institutes of Higher Education

Colleges of Education

Colleges of Technology

Scottish Central Institutions

Aberdeen College of Education

Percentage of Mature Students. 12 per cent of students who started on undergraduate courses in October 1984 were over 23.

Establishment Policy. Student 23 years of age and over would normally be designated mature. For entry to college courses no special concession would be given. All applicants are judged on merit – not age.

Special Literature. None. Prospectus available.

Upper Age Limits in the Institution. None.

Upper Age Limits in Individual Departments. None.

Avery Hill College, London (see also Thames Polytechnic)

Percentage of Mature Students. A significant number on both BEd (Hons) degree and existing DipHE courses, and BA (Hons) Theological Studies.

Establishment Policy. This College is interested in mature applicants and it provides two preparatory courses at present. One, an 'access' course in conjunction with a number of FE Colleges, is designed to bring students, particularly from ethnic minority groups, to the standard required for teacher education courses and the other is a 'second chance' course to bring mature students, over 21, to a higher education level. The 'access' course to the BEd (Hons) include specific routes, particularly in the fields of craft design and technology, youth and community studies, maths and primary education. In addition the College operates a common exceptional entry procedure, namely an initial screening interview followed by college tests. Exceptional entry for mature students aged 21 and over who show evidence of potential and successful recent study can be obtained on BEd (Hons) degree courses. Exceptional entry for students over 21 to other degree level courses can be available where students have appropriate experience but insufficient entry qualifications. The College degrees are validated by CNAA so it operates remission within current CNAA regulations for candidates transferring to and from other institutions. A recent Academic Board statement underlines the fact that 'Primarily College admissions policy seeks to offer a variety of entry points and a variety of routes into FHE rather than open access *per se . . .*'.

Introductory/Study Skills Courses. Yes. Second chance course. 'Positive action courses for Women' are currently being developed and the college is negotiating with other FE institutions to provide special Joint Access Courses.

Special Literature. Leaflet on *Second Chance*. Prospectus and individual courses leaflets have all the information required by potential mature entrants and a personal advisory interview system operates. Other literature is being developed.

Upper Age Limits in the Institution. For BEd (Hons) age limit of about 40 years is accepted but this is not totally rigid and it depends on individual circumstances, the subject to be studied and possible future career openings in teaching.

Special Provision for Mature Students. Advisory interviews arranged – contact Gavin Farmer at Eltham Campus, Bob Wilmot at Mile End Campus.

From September 1985 Avery Hill College has been amalgamated with Thames Polytechnic to form a new faculty of the Polytechnic at Avery Hill.

Bath College of Higher Education (incorporating Bath Academy of Art)

Percentage of Mature Students. 8.5 per cent.

Establishment Policy. CNAA validated courses – mature students are those aged 21 or over. Bath University validated course – mature students are those aged 26 or over. There are no special schemes relating to the admission of 'unqualified' mature students. All such applications are considered on an individual basis.

Special Literature. None. Prospectus available.

Upper Age Limits in the Institution. The College would be unlikely to accept a candidate over 50 for training on a BEd degree course as their years of professional service would be so short.

Part-time Degrees. None at present but the possibility of part-time degree courses is being discussed at Academic Board level.

Bedford College of Higher Education

Percentage of Mature Students. 9 per cent.

Establishment Policy. 25 is designated as mature. 'Unqualified' mature candidates are considered on their particular merits, bearing in mind academic background and experience for a particular course. For the BEd degree *all* candidates must have 'O' level English Language and Mathematics.

Introductory/Study Skills Courses. These are provided for all students.

Special Literature. None. Prospectus available.

Upper Age Limits in Individual Departments. For BEd courses 45 is generally regarded as upper age limit.

Part-time Degrees. BA Combined Studies and in-service BEd degrees are available by part-time study. A proposed distance learning in-service BEd degree in Human Movement is under discussion but has yet to be validated.

Bishop Grosseteste College (Lincoln)

Percentage of Mature Students. 3 per cent.

Establishment Policy. Mature students are welcomed by this College, particularly those in the local area, as there is little other higher education in the area. Advisory interviews are offered and as favourable a view as possible of all factors likely to raise difficulties for mature students is taken. The College produces no special literature for mature students, but feels that access and preliminary visit with interviews is more satisfactory than special literature.

Upper Age Limits in the Institution. As this College simply trains for the primary classroom, it rarely accepts mature students who will be in their late 30s at the end of the degree programme.

Part-time Degrees. BEd degree (part-time in-service for qualified teachers only).

Bolton Institute of Higher Education

Percentage of Mature Students. 62 per cent of first degree students (includes BSc (Hons) Psychology and BA (Hons) Humanities which are part time and all students must be 21 and excludes BEd (Hons) degree course for serving teachers).

Establishment Policy. First degrees offered at the Institute are validated by CNAA and the University of Manchester. Mature candidates (aged 21 years or over) may be accepted on CNAA degree courses in accordance with CNAA regulations, i.e. a mature student may be admitted to the beginning of a course without normal course entry qualifications or their equivalents, provided that he/she shows the necessary potential, motivation and knowledge to follow the course successfully. Departments offer advisory interviews. The BEd (Hons) degree course for serving teachers is validated by the University of Manchester and has specific regulations for entry obtainable from the Institute.

Special Literature. None. Prospectus available.

Special Provision for Mature Students. All students are assigned course tutors to whom they can take any academic and personal problems. The Students Services Unit has a number of specialist staff who, as well as providing a counselling service, can offer advice and factual information on problems and issues associated with student life.

Part-time Degrees. CNAA validated BSc in Mathematics (Stage 1), BSc and BSc (Hons) in Civil Engineering, BA (Hons) in Humanities. University of Manchester validated BEd (Hons). BA Business Studies (Foundation Stage) subject to CNAA approval.

Bradford and Ilkley Community College

Percentage of Mature Students. 60 per cent.

Establishment Policy. Within Bradford and Ilkley Community College there is a major commitment to 'access for mature students'. The college has, for the last five years, run a mature students' certificate course which provides access to its DipHE/BEd/BA programme for successful students. It also has contractual arrangements with a number of other Colleges in the district who also offer preparatory courses for mature students. Students who successfully complete the Mature Students' Certificate course, or courses in other colleges with whom it has an arrangement, are able to gain entry to its degree programme. Possession of an OU Foundation credit is recognised as an entry qualification, and students possessing appropriate post foundation credits may be considered for exemption from part of the DipHE programme. It has established an 'Access' Unit which offers not only advice but a process whereby students receive information and are counselled into programmes.

Introductory/Study Skills Courses. Study skills programmes are available for mature students during the early part of their courses. These address particularly the development of the skills of reading and analysing texts, organising and structuring material in essay form and other basic study skills related to the above. In addition, all first-year students in the DipHE undertake diagnostic tests in Mathematics and on the basis of their preference are referred to support programmes where necessary. A part-time 'return to study' course is offered on the Ilkley Campus.

Special Literature. Literature concerning the nature of the Mature Students' Certificate and progression from this to the Dip HE and degree programme is produced.

Crèche Facilities. Yes.

Special Provision for Mature Students. Yes and an advisory service covering counselling and careers for all students operates.

Bretton Hall College of Higher Education (Wakefield)

Percentage of Mature Students. 19 per cent of undergraduate students in 1984.

Establishment Policy. The degrees in Bretton Hall College are awarded by the University of Leeds, a member of the JMB. Mature students (over 21) are welcomed and encouraged to enter either by standard 'O/A' level route or by JMB Mature Matriculation examination. A BA ordinary degree in Combined Studies operates a modified time-table to facilitate the attendance of mothers with school-age children.

Departments offer advisory interviews. The BEd (Hons) degree course for serving teachers is also validated by the University of Leeds and operates in both a one-year full-time and two-year part-time version.

Introductory/Study Skills Courses. 50 per cent of the autumn term Access courses provide study skills tuition and some study skills are also included in the spring term courses and summer term introductory study week-ends.

Special Literature. A Distance Learning Pack is available incorporating study skills advice and some lead into OU Foundation courses and Mature Matriculation exam content.

Upper Age Limits in the Institution. With students over 50 or so the College may look at career opportunities to follow and the chances of moving into employment.

Special Provision for Mature Students. All students are assigned course tutors to whom they can take any academic and personal problems. The Students Services Unit has a number of specialist staff who, as well as providing a counselling service, can offer advice and factual information on problems and issues associated with student life. The District Adult Educational Counsellor and the College Internal Counsellor are those known to have particular interest in mature students.

Part-time Degrees. None, other than In-service BEd degrees. Future plans include a speedy admission of mature students and possibly increase in the number of handicapped students and members of ethnic groups.

Buckinghamshire College of Higher Education (High Wycombe)

Percentage of Mature Students. 28 per cent.

Establishment Policy. There is no overall establishment policy relating to the admission of mature students at this college. Each degree course has its own general policy and reserves the right to consider each individual case on its own merit.

Introductory/Study Skills Courses. Yes. Open University Preparatory Course (twelve weeks, two hours per week). Literature and Thought (one year, three and a half hours per week).

Special Literature. None. Prospectus available.

Bulmershe College of Higher Education (Reading)

Percentage of Mature Students. 35 per cent on BEd and BA degree programmes.

Establishment Policy. The College has a well established tradition of admitting mature students to teacher training courses and more recently to BA degree programmes, social work courses and the Community and Youth Certificate course. CNAA regulations allow discretion to vary the normal admission requirements where a candidate is able to demonstrate his or her

176

ability to follow the course by virtue of non-standard qualifications and/or experience. Mature students are usually interviewed by the Academic Registrar before their applications are processed, and are advised on the College and courses available; any pre-entry study required and domestic problems which might arise are discussed. The above procedure had been accepted by the Academic Board.

Introductory/Study Skills Courses. No courses as such but the student counsellor offers study skills sessions to mature students.

Special Literature. None. Prospectus available.

Upper Age Limits in the Institution. In general, no. Students aged 60+ have been admitted to the BA programme, but due to poor job opportunities candidates over 45 are not encouraged on the BEd programme.

Crèche Facilities. Yes, but very limited.

Special Provision for Mature Students. The student counsellor, careers co-ordinator and the Academic Registrar all have a particular interest in mature students. As Bulmershe is a small institution, mature students have ready access to the above individuals and they keep in close touch with the special needs of mature students.

Part-time Degrees. A variety of BA and BA (Hons) degrees are offered at Bulmershe majoring in English Literature, History, Geography and Development Studies, with a wide choice of minor subjects. BEd and BEd (Hons) for serving teachers.

Camborne School of Mines

Percentage of Mature Students. 5 per cent.

Establishment Policy. Mature students are classified as those of age 23 or over when they apply. Mature students who have not obtained normal entry qualifications may sit entrance tests which cover relevant subjects and skills.

Upper Age Limits in the Institution. Upper age limits are considered in the institution and in its departments and would be discussed on an individual basis.

Cambridgeshire College of Arts and Technology (Cambridge)

Percentage of Mature Students. 19 per cent.

Establishment Policy. Mature applicants are welcomed and considered individually on their merits. They are usually advised to take a course of academic study if they have no 'A' levels and/or have not studied recently. For some degrees specific 'A'-level subjects will be required, e.g. English for English Literature, and French if French is being taken in the Modern Languages Degree.

Introductory/Study Skills Courses. Return to Study Course – a short course for people with no qualifications or qualifications that have become rusty includes study skills and also information and advice on future courses.

Special Literature. Yes. A leaflet called *Opportunities for Mature Students at CCAT.* Information and advice for mature students is included in the College's *Degree and Advanced Courses Prospectus.*

Special Provision for Mature Students. All students enrolled on full-time courses are assigned to a tutor who is available for consultation on any personal or academic problems. The welfare service includes a counselling service which offers help on practical and personal problems.

Part-time Degrees. BA/BSc (Hons) Geography and BA (Hons) Humanities/Social Studies – two from English, Economics, European Thought, Literature, Geography, History, Sociology, Study of Art, Spanish, (French, subject to CNAA validation). Future plans include a wish to offer a DipHE in Languages with Business Studies (subject to CNAA validation) which could be taken via a part-time route.

The College holds an Open Evening annually for mature students who live locally where advice is available on full- and part-time vocational and academic courses.

Canterbury College of Art

Percentage of Mature Students. 32.8 per cent of students 21 and over were admitted to the first year of advanced courses in 1984–85.

Establishment Policy. All applications for course entry are assessed on merit and should be supported by a portfolio of the applicant's recent creative work in the visual arts. The College takes a sympathetic view of applications from mature persons over 25 who for acceptable reasons have not gained the minimum educational qualifications normally required for entry, and has always been prepared to consider offering places to underquali-fied mature applicants on the strength of their abilities and ex-perience.

Introductory/Study Skills Courses. The College offers a one-year pre-degree Foundation Course to which prospective mature students may apply, but it is quite usual for the mature applicant to be offered a place on a degree course in Art/Design on the strength of his/her talent and previous experience, omitting the Foundation Course element which is a normal requirement for entry to degree courses in Art/Design.

Special Literature. No. General prospectus available.

Canterbury Christ Church College

Percentage of Mature Students. 25 per cent.

Establishment Policy. This College welcomes applications from mature students: where such students lack formal entry qualifications, they are considered under the mature entry procedure. Mature entrants are considered individually on their merits: they are invited for advisory interviews and one relevant GCE 'A'-level pass is nearly always required before beginning a degree course. All candidates must have 'O' level English Language and BEd candidates must also have 'O' level mathematics or the equivalent. BEd, BA and BSc degrees are awarded by the University of Kent at Canterbury.

Special Literature. None. Prospectus available with section relevant to mature students.

Upper Age Limits in Individual Departments. BEd degree courses are unlikely to consider applications from candidates over 40. No age limit for BA and BSc degree course.

Crèche Facilities. Yes.

Charlotte Mason College of Education (Ambleside)

Percentage of Mature Students. 8 per cent.

Establishment Policy. This College is much in favour of 'mature' students defined as those over 25, and will be as helpful as possible over entry. They are bound by the University of Lancaster requirements as their degrees are validated by the University, and in practice the mature students need at least one 'A' level or equivalent. The College welcomes mature students on their courses and finds that in general they do well.

Special Literature. None. Prospectus available.

Upper Age Limits in Individual Departments. For teacher training, in view of reasonable job prospects for successful students, the College does not normally encourage anyone over 50, although they have no absolute law.

Chelmer Institute of Higher Education (Chelmsford)

Percentage of Mature Students. 41 per cent (part-time and full-time degree courses).

Establishment Policy. Mature students are welcome at the Chelmer Institute. From September 1983 all degree courses have been validated by the CNAA whose regulations allow the Institute to take a percentage of mature candidates not necessarily possessing the normal entry requirements (with the exception of the BEd degree where students must still have 'O' level Mathematics and English Language). For the last three years, the Institute has obtained a grant from the EEC to run Foundation Courses to retrain women in predominantly male-orientated areas.

Introductory/Study Skills Courses. Yes, where necessary and individual tutorials are also given if necessary.

Special Literature. No, but specific details relevant to mature students are contained in the prospectus, under 'Entry Requirements', for each course.

Upper Age Limits in Individual Departments. Each case is normally decided on merit and circumstances.

Crèche Facilities. Half-term crèche facilities only at present.

Special Provision for Mature Students. A counselling service is offered to all students to cope with problems of all types. A careers advisory service is also offered to help people nearing the end of their course.

Chester College of Higher Education

Percentage of Mature Students. 14 per cent.

Establishment Policy. Applications from mature students (i.e. 21+) are welcomed and we operate an advisory interview service for such candidates. Entry for 'unqualified' mature students is available under the JMB's mature entry scheme outlined in the leaflet *21+ – Returning to Learning.*

Special Literature. Information sheet *Entry to a degree course as a mature applicant with insufficient qualification for entry in the normal way.* Prospectus and *21+ – Returning to Learning* also available.

Upper Age Limits in Individual Departments. Because of poor job opportunities candidates over 40 are only considered for teacher training in exceptional circumstances.

Special Provision for Mature Students. All students are assigned to a personal tutor.

Part-time Degrees. The BA in Combined Studies and Health and Community Studies are available over five years (six years for Honours) with reduced day-time attendance for at least three days per week.

College of Ripon and York St John (York)

Percentage of Mature Students. 28 per cent of full-time students are aged 21+.

Establishment Policy. This college has its degrees validated by the University of Leeds, a member of the JMB. Students can be accepted with suitable 'O' and 'A'-level qualifications or under the mature matriculation scheme.

The College offers programmes leading to the award of the BA or BSc Collegiate degrees of the University of Leeds by full-time study (three years for the Ordinary degree and four years for the Honours degree) and half-time study (six years to the Ordinary degree). The half-time degree scheme has been validated with a view to admitting mature students who are able to give a two day per week commitment to study.

Introductory/Study Skills Courses. Yes, mature students entering upon the half-time degree scheme are encouraged to take an induction course during the few months prior to entry.

Special Literature. Yes, leaflet *Study for a Degree Part-time* is available in addition to the Prospectus.

Part-time Degrees. Yes (see section on establishment policy). Subjects studied include American Studies, Art, Chemistry, Drama, Film and Television, Design and Technology, Educational and Community Studies, English, Geography, History, Human Movement, Dance and Recreation Studies, Language Studies, Mathematics, Music, Rural Science, Theology and Religious Studies.

The College of St Mark and St John Foundation (Plymouth)

Percentage of Mature Students. 45 per cent (approximately) on full-time courses.

Establishment Policy. All applications from mature students are considered on an individual basis. Special admission procedures through CNAA and the University of Exeter; normally one 'A'-level pass is required, in addition to 'O' levels, as well as some evidence of recent study. Agreements between CNAA and OU observed. Age of mature students: University of Exeter courses – 23, CNAA courses – 21.

Special Literature. No special literature. Prospectus available.

Upper Age Limits in the Institution. Although there is no written rule, it is normally expected that candidates for teacher training course are under 50 years of age. No limit for other courses.

Crèche Facilities. Yes. Run by the Students' Union at school half-term only.

Special Provision for Mature Students. Students' Union services available to all students.

College of St Paul and St Mary (Cheltenham)

Percentage of Mature Students. 13 per cent.

Establishment Policy. BA (Combined Studies), BSc and BEd Honours Degrees are validated by the CNAA. Mature candidates (over 21) who lack the normal entry qualifications are offered an advisory interview, followed by a formal interview with appropriate staff, if it seems likely that a recommendation for 'special entry' could be made. The College is always glad to consider mature candidates as staff experience of them has been a happy one.

Introductory/Study Skills Courses. Yes, a pre-BA Honours course (eleven weeks from January onwards) which is also appropriate for those wishing to enter other degree courses. Preliminary reading can also be arranged for candidates in some subject areas (e.g. Religious Studies) and written work submitted on the basis of this reading.

Special Literature. None. Prospectus and course leaflets available.

Upper Age Limits. None except for BEd courses where anyone between 40 and 49 is asked with the aid of an interview to think seriously about embarking on the BEd and anyone over 50 is asked to think about a different course. The College has no absolute limits.

Crèche Facilities. Yes.

Mature Students' Union/Society. No, but all students are full members of the Students' Union.

Special Provision for Mature Students. No, but every student has a personal tutor.

182

Part-time Degrees. BA Combined Studies in English and Geography, Geography and Religious Studies, English and History, English and Religious Studies, History and Religious Studies.

Craigie College of Education (Ayr)

Percentage of Mature Students. 25 per cent.

Establishment Policy. In line with the Scottish Education Department regulations, all mature students (over 23) entering teacher training must hold the same entry qualifications as school and university leavers.

Introductory/Study Skills Courses. Yes. A very brief two-day course is provided for all entrants to the college.

Special Literature. No. Prospectus available.

Upper Age Limits in the Institution. Yes. Except in special circumstances applicants for teacher training are not given consideration if they are likely to be over 45 years of age on completion of training (this policy is related to the award of students grants).

Special Provision for Mature Students. Yes, when required.

Crewe and Alsager College of Higher Education

Percentage of Mature Students. 45 per cent.

Establishment Policy. Mature applicants welcomed and in fact a significant proportion of college students do fall into the category of mature students. A flexible scheme operates, enabling a proportion of candidates (usually mature) who do not hold the normal entry requirements but who have relevant experience to be admitted. The acceptance of 'mature' entry students depends on whether the College considers that an individual student can follow the degree course successfully. The College also operates a system of mutual credit transfer with the Open University and other colleges and polytechnics offering a DipHE.

Introductory/Study Skills Courses. Yes.

Special Literature. None. Prospectus available.

Part-time Degrees. A part-time DipHE and a BA Hons (Combined Studies) by Independent Study are offered.

183

Colchester Institute

Percentage of Mature Students. 2.5 per cent.

Establishment Policy. The Institute observes CNAA policy in that mature students (less than 10 per cent of student population) may be admitted without the formal entrance requirement. All such students take an entrance examination, interview and audition as part of this selection process. This currently applies to the BA Music Course.

Introductory/Study Skills Courses. Open University preparatory course (evening). A number of Flexistudy courses of relevant content are also available.

Special Literature. None. Prospectus available.

De La Salle College of Higher Education (Manchester)

Percentage of Mature Students. 12 per cent (approximately).

Establishment Policy. The policy of De La Salle College of Higher Education is determined by the JMB's provisions for candidates of mature years. The College welcomes and wishes to encourage mature students.

Special Literature. No special literature but the JMB leaflet *21+ – Returning to Learning* is used.

Mature Students' Union/Society. Mature Students join the Students' Union.

Special Provision for Mature Students. It is not considered advisable to treat mature students as a separate category. They are expected to join in the normal life of the college and most do so and make a very valuable contribution.

Part-time Degrees. In-service degree of BEd with Honours in Education.

Derbyshire College of Higher Education (Derby and Matlock)

Establishment Policy. The College has recently expanded its provision for continuing education including direct access to advanced further education for mature students. In Education, Humanities and Social Sciences there is a strong tradition of recruiting a substantial minority of mature students and it is the intention of the College to expand this type of provision in other areas of its work. A mature student wishing to return to study would normally be offered an advisory interview.

Introductory/Study Skills Courses. Two courses are provided: a 'Gateway' course designed to prepare mature students for a return to study, and a 'Pathway' course which is a valuable programme in its own right but in appropriate cases does afford the possibility of entry into certain Honours degree courses.

Special Literature. Prospectus available. Further details of the course structure and range of subjects offered in 'Gateway' and 'Pathway' are available on request.

Dorset Institute of Higher Education (Poole)

Percentage of Mature Students. 43 per cent (Full time and part time).

Establishment Policy. The Institute, as part of its degree course programme, offers a four-year sandwich BA (Honours) degree in Business Studies and a BA (Honours) degree in Combined Studies. Both degrees have part-time routes specifically aimed at mature students.

On all courses in the Institute mature students without entry qualifications can apply for 'exceptional entry'. Applications are considered individually by a committee of the Academic Board. Work experience and, in some cases, performance in an entrance test may be taken into account.

Special Literature. No general literature for mature students is produced by the Institute, but course literature is available for both degrees explaining the full-time and part-time routes.

Special Provision for Mature Students. All students have a personal tutor.

Part-time Degrees. In addition to those mentioned under establishment policy, it is planned to offer a BEng in Computer Aided Engineering from September 1985, subject to validation and a part-time BSc Information Technology Degree will be offered from September 1986, subject to validation.

Duncan of Jordanstone College of Art, (Dundee)

Percentage of Mature Students. 7 per cent.

Establishment Policy. Age, in itself, is no bar to entry, excepting 17 minimum on commencing a course. For art and design courses entry can be on the merit of portfolio work alone to a limit of 7 per cent of the total intake (ninety-six in 1984). For all other courses the stated academic requirements cannot be waived.

Special Literature. None. Prospectus available.

Crèche Facilities. Yes.

Dundee College of Education

Percentage of Mature Students. Social Work 100 per cent, Community Education 60 per cent, Teacher Training 20 per cent.

Establishment Policy. Requirements vary from one department to another and are summarised below.

Social Work	For CQSW students, designated mature at 25 years and over. Normal entry requirements waived and candidates must be deemed capable of completing the academic work of the course. This is assessed via candidates' other qualifications, i.e. nursing, and by all candidates completing a written English test. For CSS, designated mature at 21 years. Normal entry requirements waived and procedure as above. For ICSC, no formal entry requirements.
Community Education	Students over 23 years are designated mature, and can be admitted to a two-year course of training (students under 23 years to follow a three-year course) for community education provided that the students possess relevant fieldwork experience. Students who have not the full academic qualifications needed (two Highers and four 'O' grade SCE passes) may be admitted if it is the view of the interviewing panel that they would be able to complete the academic work of the course satisfactorily.
Teacher training	Students over 23 years may be admitted with very slightly lower formal requirements than those set for students under 23 years, but the requirements of the Scottish Education Department must be met.

Introductory/Study Skills Courses. Not for Community Education and Teacher Training but for Social Work students a pre-course reading list is forwarded and pre-course exercises are set which are the subject of class discussion after commencement.

Special Literature. None. Prospectus available.

Upper Age Limits in Individual Departments. Whilst there are no upper age limits set, age is a factor considered during interviews – other things being equal, there is less chance of a candidate over the age of 55 being accepted for professional training in social work.

Dundee College of Technology

Percentage of Mature Students. 34 per cent.

Establishment Policy. The College welcomes enquiries from mature students but has no overall policy relating to their admission. Applications from mature students are considered on similar terms to all other applicants able to satisfy the normal admission requirements. Candidates not possessing the qualifications prescribed for entry to particular courses may be admitted subject to their qualifications being acceptable to the college and to the CNAA or other such awarding body. Applicants are normally required to attend for interview before an offer of admission is made.

Special Literature. No, but College prospectus available.

Part-time Degrees. BA (Hons) Commerce (two years' part time, entry with advanced standing), BSc Nursing (five years' part-time post registration). Postgraduate Diploma in Management Studies (two years part time). All are validated by CNAA.

Dunfermline College of Physical Education

Percentage of Mature Students. BEd (Physical Education) 2½ per cent; BA (Recreation) 27 per cent.

Establishment Policy. Mature students are expected to possess the same entry qualifications as other students but individual consideration is given to applicants with a considerable amount of post-school experience. Selection procedures include interviews (BA, BEd) and practical tests (BEd).

Special Literature. None. Prospectus available.

Upper Age Limits in Individual Departments. Mature candidates for BEd (Physical Education) are required to take the same performance tests as other applicants, and although no upper age limit is specified older candidates are likely to be disadvantaged.

Special Provision for Mature Students. Course Directors are available to help and advise mature students.

Part-time Degrees. BEd (Physical Education) for teachers of physical education holding a Diploma.

187

Ealing College of Higher Education

Percentage of Mature Students. 40 per cent (full time and undergraduate students).

Establishment Policy. Normal minimum requirements are five GCE passes, including two at 'A' level, or an equivalent such as ONC or BTEC certificate. Mature candidates without these minimum requirements are selected very carefully by seeking evidence of candidate's capacity to meet successfully the demands of the course for which they have applied. This selection is then approved by a Special Entry Committee.

Introductory/Study Skills Courses. Yes. Part-time day and evening one year 'Fresh Start' courses available.

Special Literature. None. Prospectus and handbook available.

Crèche Facilities. Yes, but half term playgroup only.

Special Provision for Mature Students. Yes, within individual departments.

Part-time Degrees. BA/BA (Hons) Humanities five to six years (six to eight hours per week); BA/BA (Hons) Law four to five years (two evenings per week); BA/BA (Hons) Business Studies four to five years (two evenings per week). Schemes for further part-time degree courses are under active discussion.

Edinburgh College of Art

Percentage of Mature Students. Architecture 7.6 per cent, Town and Country Planning 3.7 per cent, Art and Design 9.3 per cent.

Establishment Policy. The College has no special policy on the admission of mature students. Mature students are accepted into degree courses on the same basis as any other applicant. In Art and Design there is, however, provision for exceptional entry (up to 7 per cent of annual intake) for candidates who do not possess the required minimum entrance qualifications but who submit a portfolio of work of exceptional merit. While entry by this provision can apply to any applicant, it is more often invoked in the case of mature applicants.

Introductory/Study Skills Courses. Yes.

Special Literature. None. Prospectus available.

Part-time Degrees. By arrangement with Fine Art area Heads of Department/School 'Special' courses can be provided to suit the needs of the individual.

188

Edge Hill College of Higher Education

Percentage of Mature Students. 12 per cent.

Establishment Policy. College policy is to encourage the application of mature students, and since college degrees are validated by Lancaster University the flexible entrance qualifications as designated by that University apply. The normal academic requirement of two 'A' levels can be replaced by ONC, OND, HNC, HND or one Open University credit. Mature students can gain admission through 'Open College' schemes or the successful completion of a higher education Access Course and there is still the *ad hoc* consideration of any candidate by the University Exceptional Admissions committee for entry into degree courses. The most substantial piece of evidence to aid mature applicants in entering degree courses would be evidence of recent successful academic study at an appropriate level. For students who, through full-time employment or isolation, find themselves unable to follow a course in academic study, the College exceptionally can tutor them through a series of assignments, but this can only be done for a small number of students. Part-time degree courses with mature students in mind are now available.

Introductory/Study Skills Courses. Yes. A short 'Return to Study' course is held in the summer for appropriate mature students prior to starting degree courses in the following September.

Special Literature. There is a short section in prospectus and pamphlets for part-time courses.

Upper Age Limits in Individual Departments. Not normally, but in teacher training (BEd degrees) an upper age limit of about 40 years would apply.

Special Provision for Mature Students. Yes. Advisers are Mr D. Matthews, senior tutor in charge of admissions, and Mr G. W. Barrett, principal lecturer in charge of adult studies. Advisory interviews are arranged on request.

Part-time Degrees. BA, BSc and DipHE programmes can be studied on a part-time basis through day, day/evening and evening study. MA Crime Deviance and Social Policy is offered as a two-year part-time evening study course. Further plans include an extension of courses available on a part-time basis.

Essex Institute of Higher Education

Percentage of Mature Students. 40 per cent.

Establishment Policy. Mature students are very welcome and students may be admitted without the normal entry requirements.

Special EEC Courses are run for women wishing to retrain in predominantly male-orientated areas.

Introductory/Study Skills Courses. These are provided where necessary.

Special Literature. None. Prospectus available.

Special Provision for Mature Students. Normal counselling services are available to all students, including mature students.

Part-time Degrees. BSc Quantity Surveying, BSc Mathematics, BEd, MEd, LLB, are available by part-time study. A new option currently being developed is a DMS/MBA in Industrial and Educational Management.

Glasgow College of Technology

Percentage of Mature Students. 5 per cent (approximately).

Establishment Policy. The College welcomes applications from mature persons who have been away from full-time formal education for some time. In general such persons should meet the normal minimum entrance requirement for the course concerned. Exceptionally, a mature applicant may be admitted who does not meet that requirement but who presents evidence which, in the opinion of the Academic Board, indicates that he or she has the capacity and attainment to pursue and benefit from the proposed course.

Special Literature. None. Prospectus available on request.

Gloucestershire College of Arts and Technology (Gloucester)

Percentage of Mature Students. Approximately 10 per cent of the total student population are mature students on advanced courses.

Establishment Policy. Mature students are considered for entry to all courses offered in the College. Degree courses, validated by CNAA are available in Fashion, Fine Arts, Landscape Architecture, Computing and Mathematics. All applicants are given a personal interview to provide an opportunity for academic qualifications and individual experience and background to be considered in the context of the needs of the course.

Introductory/Study Skills Courses. The College runs an Open University preparatory course and study skills help is provided to all students either through short courses or individual attention.

Special Literature. No. A College prospectus is available and separate course leaflets providing further information.

Crèche Facilities. Not available at present but under consideration.

Special Provision for Mature Students. No special provision, but assistance for mature students is available through course tutors, the student services sections and other responsible college officers.

Part-time Degrees. Yes. Available in Mathematics and Computing.

Gwent College of Higher Education

Percentage of Mature Students. 40 per cent of undergraduate students are 23 or over; 35.5 per cent of undergraduates are 25 or over.

Establishment Policy. Mature students defined as 23 or over are welcomed on all courses and many courses have been explicitly mounted to cater for the needs of mature students. Some of the College degrees are validated by the University of Wales so the matriculation requirements are as detailed by that University, but they can be modified for suitable candidates over 23. Mature students are usually excused one 'A' level and may be accepted with only 'O' levels.

Introductory/Study Skills Courses. Yes, the Faculty of Education and Combined Studies provides an induction week in which study skills is one of the courses offered. In addition, the Faculty is running 'Gateway' courses which are an extension of 'New Opportunities for Women' courses. 'Gateway' courses are also offered to men.

Special Literature. No, but reference is made to supportive services of special interest to mature students in College literature; some of the literature assumes that a significant proportion of students will be mature.

Upper Age Limits in Individual Departments. Only people under the age of 50 are considered for teacher education courses, but students who are over 50 are welcomed on other courses such as BA Combined Studies.

Crèche Facilities. Yes, but half-term only on the Caerleon site.

Harrow College of Higher Education

Percentage of Mature Students. 14 per cent and all DipHE students.

Establishment Policy. (a) All students admitted to the part-time degree course referred to in this entry are over 21 years of age. Admission requirement is that applicants must have substantial proof of experience, i.e. over four to five years (it is a mid-career post

191

experience course). (b) No restriction is placed on entry to full-time course (BA (Hons), CNAA) in Applied Photo Film and TV.

Introductory/Study Skills Courses. A six-weeks Effective Study Skills Programme with appropriate tutorial follow-up is included in the part-time degree course. A 'Learn to Study' preparatory course for intending DipHE students runs from January to June.

Special Literature. A detailed booklet on the DipHE is available on request as well as the prospectus.

Crèche Facilities. Playgroup for 3- to 5-year olds.

Part-time Degrees. A Photographic Media Studies BA is available by part-time study and future plans include the expansion of the DipHE Scheme to provide a range of part-time degrees.

Hertfordshire College of Higher Education (Watford)

Percentage of Mature Students. BEd degree 30 per cent. BA degree 64 per cent.

Establishment Policy. The College has long experience of admitting mature entrants to the BEd degree. More recently a substantial proportion of those admitted to the BA Combined Studies programme have been over the age of 21 and are therefore classified as mature.

The experience of the College is that mature entrants invariably perform well and have much to contribute. The College operates a flexible admissions policy in the context of CNAA guidelines. Mature students without minimum entrance requirements are considered for admission on the basis of individual experience and background but recent experience of academic study at an appropriate level is highly desirable. The College is willing to arrange an advisory interview for prospective mature applicants.

Introductory/Study Skills Courses. Mature students are given any special help which may be necessary in the normal course of their first-year work.

Special Literature. None. Prospectus available.

Homerton College (Cambridge)

Percentage of Mature Students. No information.

Establishment Policy. Mature students are considered together with younger students. Study such as that with the Open

University is taken into account in assessing a student's academic competence. All teacher education students must have 'O' level English Language and Mathematics or an approved equivalent.

Special Literature. None. Prospectus available.

Upper Age Limits in Individual Departments. None, but on a vocational course it is not sensible to admit students whose contribution to teaching will be short – and who will probably not obtain a post in teaching.

Humberside College of Higher Education (Hull)

Percentage of Mature Students. 15 per cent.

Establishment Policy. It is difficult to state one policy for Humberside College of Higher Education in relation to mature students as policies differ within the various schools, but in most instances mature students are sympathetically treated, within the confines of the course entrance regulations. In the humanities/social sciences area it is felt academic qualifications are only equal in importance to understanding and ability and are not the primary consideration. In this area of studies some mature students are given a written assignment to help in their assessment in lieu of academic qualifications. The degree courses are validated by CNAA and so flexibility on mature entrants is possible within their guidelines.

Introductory/Study Skills Courses. Yes. All students have the opportunity of developing study skills and the college produces packages specifically designed to assist in this respect, together with tutorial help if required.

Special Literature. None, other than prospectus entries.

Part-time Degrees. BSc and BSc (Hons) in Combined Science or Applied Biology. BA and BA (Hons) Business Studies, Humanities, Secretarial Studies, Social Studies, Visual Studies, Combined Studies. BSc in Engineering. BEd and BEd (Hons) in-service.

Jordanhill College of Education (Glasgow)

Percentage of Mature Students. (1984) Bachelor of Education 5 per cent, BSc Speech Therapy 20 per cent, Youth and Community Work Course 55 per cent, Social Work Course 100 per cent, Technical Course 44 per cent.

Establishment Policy. The College welcomes applications from mature persons who have been away from full-time formal education for some time. A special career change course exists in the Social

Work Department limited to students aged 30–50. 'Mature' is defined in various regulations which lay down entrance requirements and may allow some concessions to applicants aged 23 and over in the case of Bachelor of Education, Bachelor of Science and Youth and Community courses and 25 or over in the case of the Social Work Regular course. All students are selected on the basis of qualifications, interview, etc. irrespective of whether they are 'mature' or not. For all courses they must meet the minimum entry requirements as laid down in the course regulations.

Introductory/Study Skills Courses. No. In view of the high level skills necessary in teacher training we do not provide any introductory skills course as we feel it is better to approach such courses either direct from school or university. Candidates at a mature age have usually attended other Further Education colleges prior to applying to this College.

Special Literature. Various course brochures, prospectuses.

Upper Age Limits in the Institution. The College policy is that a student cannot be considered if he or she would reach the age of 56 before the end of the course, except with the explicit approval of the Board of Governors.

Part-time Degrees. A number of courses are offered on an 'In-service' basis to teachers already employed on a full-time basis.

King Alfreds College (Winchester)

Percentage of Mature Students. 35.9 per cent.

Establishment Policy. The College treats each application individually, offers personal encouragement and gives advisory interviews when required. The Diploma of Higher Education and part-time BA/BA (Hons) course in History with associated English are recruited as second opportunity courses, and mature students without normal qualifications but with work experience are particularly welcome. Associate students are also admitted for elements of the part-time BA degree on a probationary basis if uncertain about their ability to persevere with full studentship. There is a DipHE outlet from this course.

Introductory/Study Skills Courses. Yes. A five-week introductory course for the part-time BA (Hons) degree in History with Associated English is available.

Special Literature. A general prospectus is available, and separate leaflets for each degree course.

Upper Age Limits in Individual Departments. No, but the college would be concerned in teacher training to ensure that a reasonable period of service was possible and probably would not accept students over 50.

Special Provision for Mature Students. All course directors are available to advise mature and non-mature students.

Part-time Degrees. BA and BA (Hons) History with English. BEd and BEd (Hons) in Education.

La Sainte Union College of Higher Education (Southampton)

Percentage of Mature Students. 13 per cent.

Establishment Policy. College degrees are validated by the University of Southampton which allows 'candidates over the age of 21 on their submitting to the faculty such evidence as it may deem sufficient of previous serious study and of the capacity and attainments requisite to enable them to pursue the course proposed', to be admitted as mature students. Interested mature candidates are interviewed and each applicant is judged sympathetically on his/her merits. More restrictions apply to intending teachers than to those wanting to take other degree courses. The College offers advisory interviews to prospective applicants.

Special Literature. None. Prospectus available.

Upper Age Limits in Individual Departments. Yes. For teacher training.

Special Provision for Mature Students. La Sainte Union is a small college and the normal pastoral procedures can be extended when required. Students and staff help in looking after school-age children in half-term holidays and baby-sitting is available through the Student Union Community Service. There is a house set aside for day students with simple cooking facilities as well as study rooms.

Part-time Degrees. BA/BA (Hons) and DipHE in Modern Languages and European Studies.

Liverpool Institute of Higher Education

Percentage of Mature Students. (a) In-service BEd seconded from LEAs 5 per cent; (b) Undergraduate courses generally 5 per cent.

Establishment Policy. Liverpool Institute of Higher Education has its degrees validated by the University of Liverpool, a member

195

of the JMB, so students can be accepted with suitable 'O' and 'A' levels or under the mature matriculation scheme. With JMB every support and encouragement is given to ensure students so motivated may follow an undergraduate course.

Special Literature. JMB document, *21+ – A Second Chance* is available together with prospectus.

Part-time Degrees. In-service BEd (Hons) degree and an in-service BEd specialising in the primary area.

Liverpool Polytechnic C.F. Mott Campus (formally City of Liverpool, College of Higher Education COLCHE)

Percentage of Mature Students. 1981, 12.7 per cent, 1982, 12.4 per cent.

Establishment Policy. This Campus gives special consideration to mature students and has had over 3,000 mature students qualifying in recent years. Applicants with formal qualifications are welcome and also exceptional entry is possible with Open University, HND, TEC/BEC, BTEC and other qualifications considered. The campus has a section on mature students in the Prospectus and produces a booklet, *Continuing Education*, for mature students, giving information and offering advice on entry, grants, applications and advisory interviews.

Introductory/Study Skills Courses. Study Skills help is offered to all students.

Crèche Facilities. Yes.

Special Provision for Mature Students. It has been found that mature students prefer not to be considered separately from the rest of the student body. Although no formal provision is made to provide special study advisers for mature students, we do try to ensure that mature students are advised by tutors who over the years have acquired experience of mature students' needs.

Luton College of Higher Education

Percentage of Mature Students. Roughly 75– 80 per cent of students are aged 18 or over, almost half of whom are aged 25+.

Establishment Policy. The College has a formal policy for continuing education. As part of this, the College is committed to removing as many barriers to access to higher education as possible, including provision for the admission of students with 'non-standard' qualifications.

Introductory/Study Skills Courses. Return-to-study programme available; also forms part of other courses, e.g. 'Preparation for retirement', 'New Horizons for Women'.

Special Literature. College Prospectus + additional course information available.

Crèche Facilites. Playgroup available for children 1½–5 years of age.

Moray House College of Education (Edinburgh)

Percentage of Mature Students. BEd 12 per cent, two-year Social Work 100 per cent, three-year Social Work 15 per cent, two-year Community Education 100 per cent, three-year Community Education 13 per cent, one-year Technical Education 0 per cent, two-year Technical Education 100 per cent, three-year Technical Education 100 per cent.

Establishment Policy. Mature students are considered for entry to all courses offered in the College. The lower entry requirements for mature students and the age at which students are designated mature are not the same for each course, so it is advisable to contact the college for detailed information.

Introductory/Study Skills Courses. Mature students frequently receive advice, before entry to the College, on relevant preliminary study/practical work. The College has an extensive collection of study skills materials and academic advisers are able to direct students to those materials best suited to individual needs.

Special Literature. No. Prospectus available.

Upper Age Limits in the Instituion. Although there is no statutory age limit the restriction on intake to teacher training courses makes it less likely that applicants of over 40 years of age will be selected.

Part-time Degrees. In-service BEd (Primary) Degree/Honours Degree, for experienced, finally registered teachers.

Napier College (Edinburgh)

Percentage of Mature Students. 5 per cent.

Establishment Policy. The College welcomes applications from mature persons (i.e. those over 23 years, usually with work experience) who have been away from full-time formal education for some time. In general such persons should meet the normal minimum entrance requirement for the course concerned.

Exceptionally, a mature applicant may be admitted who does not meet the minimum entrance requirements but who presents evidence which in the opinion of the Board of Studies indicates that he or she has the capacity to pursue and benefit from the proposed course.

Introductory/Study Skills Course. All students follow an induction programme during which study skills courses or supplementary study courses can be identified and made available, if necessary.

Special Literature. No, but full-time, part-time and postgraduate/professional prospectus available on request.

Upper Age Limits in the Institution. Many of the College courses include periods of industrial attachment and, occasionally, employers may be reluctant to take mature students. The College may therefore operate an unofficial upper age limit (approximately 30 years) if the applicant is unlikely to be offered industrial experience, thus jeopardising their prospects of qualifying. This is not seen as a hindrance to making an application.

Special Provision for Mature Students. Student adviser and the Student Services Unit will assist any mature student.

Part-time Degrees. BSc Quantity Surveying, BA Business Studies, BSc Life Sciences and various part-time postgraduate/professional courses.

Nene College (Northampton)

Percentage of Mature Students. 31.2 per cent.

Establishment Policy. Special consideration is given to mature students who apply for admission to advanced courses. The prospectus invites such applicants to make an appointment for an advisory interview preferably at least a year prior to entry to the course. The advisory interview deals, *inter alia*, with the applicants' possible programmes of studies, the entry requirements for the course, what further qualifications might be needed and whether some directed study is appropriate. The applicants normally also discuss the proposed course with two subject tutors and any directed study is then arranged with the tutors. Applicants who do not possess the normal entry requirements are also given an advisory interview and this is used to collect information for presentation to the Admissions Board of the University of Leicester. Directed study may be recommended where there has been some considerable interval since formal academic study was undertaken, in lieu of formal qualifications.

Introductory/Study Skills Courses. Each subject is obliged to include a study skills course for all students. Nothing specific for mature students.

Special Literature. None. Prospectus available.

Crèche Facilities. Yes. The mature students group under the aegis of the Student Union organises crèche facilities during school half-terms and other holidays.

Mature Students' Union/Society. Yes, there is a Mature Students' Group, for which an officer of the Student Union is responsible.

Part-time Degrees. BSc in Health Science Studies. In-service BEd and BEd (Hons) degrees.

New College Durham

New College Durham offers opportunities for further and higher education in pleasant surroundings, on the outskirts of an historic city, with residential accommodation and excellent sport, music, drama and other facilities.

Courses Offered. Degrees, Higher Diplomas and Higher Certificates, Certificates and Professional Qualifications for BEC/TEC/DATEC/PROFESSIONAL BODIES in Travel and Tourism, Accountancy and Finance, Computer Studies, Bi-lingual Secretaries, Personal Assistants, Housing, Business Studies, Chiropody, Hotel and Catering, Graphic Design, Technology, Electrical, Electronic, Mechanical, Production and Building.

Details of all full- and part-time day and evening courses available from: The Principal, New College Durham, Framwellgate Moor Centre, Durham, DH1 5ES. Telephone: Durham 62421.

Newman College (Birmingham)

Percentage of Mature Students. 13 per cent.

Establishment Policy. All degree courses are validated by the University of Birmingham, a member of the JMB. Students can be accepted either with normal matriculation requirements or by the mature matriculation route. Pre-entry courses are offered at two local further education colleges and these provide the techniques and background needed for academic work at university level.

199

Special Literature. *A University Degree for the Older Student* published by the University of Birmingham and *A University Degree – a second chance at 21+* produced by the JMB are available together with the prospectus.

Upper Age Limits in the Institution. Yes.

Upper Age Limits in Individual Departments. Yes.

Special Provision for Mature Students. No, but all students have personal tutors.

Nonington College (Dover)

Scheduled to close academic year 1985–86.

North Cheshire College (Warrington)

Percentage of Mature Students. 20–25 per cent.

Establishment Policy. Students are designated 'mature' when they have reached 21 years of age by 1 May in the year of entry. 'Unqualified' mature applicants may qualify for entry to undergraduate courses via the Joint Matriculation Board's 'Mature Entry' scheme. Degrees are validated by the University of Manchester.

Introductory/Study Skills Courses. Potential mature applicants for undergraduate courses and others who wish to enhance their education may take a three-term part-time 'Jigsaw' course, comprising one day's attendance per week, which is designed to introduce different approaches to study at undergraduate and other levels. The College also offers a wide range of full-time and part-time GCE courses at Ordinary and Advanced level.

Special Literature. Leaflet on 'Jigsaw' course and prospectuses are available.

Upper Age Limits in Individual Departments. Mature applicants for the BA ordinary course in sports studies are advised at interview of the possible physical demands of the course and are required along with other students to furnish before entry a medical certificate attesting to their physical fitness to pursue the course.

Crèche Facilities. Playgroup facilities are available on campus.

Special Provision for Mature Students. Before entry potential mature students may have access to the advice of the admissions tutor, to members of the 'Jigsaw' course team and to other members of the academic staff. The members of the academic staff have gained substantial experience in advising mature students.

The North East Wales Institute of Higher Education (Wrexham)

Percentage of Mature Students. 60 per cent.

Establishment Policy. For BEd (Hons) and BA (with Hons) in Combined Studies, students over the age of 23 with less than minimum entry qualifications will be considered. These degrees are validated by the University of Wales (see insert in University section). A BSc in Computer Studies validated by the University of Salford is also on offer.

Introductory/Study Skills Courses. The College has commenced a 'Gateway Course' for mature females to advise and inform on what is available to them by way of further study. This is a programme of meetings where potential students can learn about recent changes in education, modern study methods and new areas of study.

Special Literature. None. Prospectus available.

Special Provision for Mature Students. There is no special provision but all students have an academic adviser and personal tutor irrespective of age.

Part-time Degrees. In-service BEd degree.

North Riding College of Education (Scarborough)

Percentage of Mature Students. 7 per cent.

Establishment Policy. The education degrees offered by this College are subject to validation by the University of Leeds and so all unqualified mature entrants are subject to JMB regulations.

Special Literature. None. Prospectus available.

Upper Age Limits in the Institution. Entrants over 40 would be accepted only in very special circumstances.

Paisley College of Technology

Percentage of Mature Students. 10.5 per cent – overall College percentage. 18.9 per cent in the School of Social, Planning and Management Sciences.

Establishment Policy. Paisley College welcomes applications from mature candidates even if they do not necessarily meet the formal minimum entrance requirements. Special consideration may be given to mature candidates who, although lacking conventional entrance requirements, have over the years shown an interest in their educational advancement and an aptitude for study. Such candidates as well as those with old or unusual qualifications should not be deterred from applying by a lack of formal academic qualifications. Mature candidates who do not meet the formal minimum entrance requirements are invited to contact the appropriate academic department for further information.

Special Literature. Not produced by the College but the AGCAS *Notes for Mature Students* is issued by the Student Advisory Service. Prospectus available.

The Queen's College, Glasgow

Percentage of Mature Students. Overall 10 per cent. Home Economics 12½ per cent, Physiotherapy 8 per cent, Dietetics 10 per cent.

Establishment Policy. College degrees are validated by CNAA and the regulations allow flexibility within certain guidelines. College welcomes applications from older students on all its courses and increasingly encourages the younger students to defer entry for a year. A three-year Social Work Course is designated mainly for students over 30.

Introductory/Study Skills Courses. Not specifically for mature students but for all students.

Special Literature. Leaflet relating to three-year Social Work Course and prospectus available.

Special Provision for Mature Students. All candidates are interviewed and advisory interviews are offered to candidates without the normal entry requirements. Careers advice for mature students is important. The College offers a number of short post-qualifying courses for mature students seeking refreshment in professional and academic studies.

Robert Gordon's Institute of Technology (Aberdeen)

Percentage of Mature Students. In session 1984–85 10 per cent of the intake to undergraduate courses were aged 21 and over (this does not take into account postgraduate courses and post-experience courses). Two of the post-experience courses in particular attract mature students and these are Health Visiting and Social Work where all students are over 21.

Establishment Policy. RGIT has no firm policy on this matter. However, we regard students over 23 as mature students and normally we allow these students to enter our courses with less than the minimum entry requirements. We also give serious consideration to those students with relevant work experience provided they have some educational background on specified subjects needed for the course of their choice. To our professional course in Social Work students over 23 need not have any educational qualifications but must have proven ability in Social Work.

Special Provision for Mature Students. There is no special provision as such but our student services section would have responsibilities for assisting mature students and in general course tutors do take a special interest in assisting mature students with advice and information.

Roehampton Institute of Higher Education (London)

Percentage of Mature Students. 10 per cent.

Establishment Policy. The degree courses in this Institute are validated by the University of Surrey, so the policy as described in the Universities section is relevant. Roehampton Institute encourages mature students to apply within the limits of the University Special Entry scheme for applicants aged 23 and over. The Institute would welcome more mature applicants especially on BEd courses.

Special Literature. None. Prospectus available.

Part-time Degrees. BA Health Studies – four years part-time.

Rolle College (Exmouth)

Percentage of Mature Students. 20 per cent.

Establishment Policy. The College is happy to consider mature students for both BA degree and teacher training courses. For the purposes of regulations governing admission, the college is bound by Exeter University policy which sets the general entrance requirement (described in the section on Universities), but exceptional admission can be arranged for candidates over 23 who have a broad educational background who have undertaken some systematic course of study within the three years prior to admission.

Introductory/Study Skills Courses. A number of introductory courses are in planning and will probably start in 1985–86.

Special Literature. No special literature other than course leaflets produced for courses on which mature students only are accepted. Prospectus available.

Crèche Facilities. A half-term crèche is run by the Students' Union.

Special Provision for Mature Students. The College authorities and Students' Union co-operate in trying to achieve a good working situation for mature students, and there is a special section of the Students' Union which looks at the needs of mature students.

Royal Scottish Academy of Music and Drama (Glasgow)

Percentage of Mature Students. Drama 36 per cent, Music 6 per cent.

Establishment Policy. There is no individual establishment policy relating to the admission of mature students. Mature students are welcomed in both music and drama providing that our high standards of performance criteria are met. We do not differentiate between mature and other students.

Special Literature. None. Prospectus available.

St Andrews College of Education (Glasgow)

Percentage of Mature Students. 11.2 per cent.

Establishment Policy. There is no establishment policy for the admission of mature students, designated as 23 and over, although credit is given for prior experience deemed to be useful for the intending teacher. There is a slight modification to the entrance requirements in the case of mature students.

Special Literature. None. Prospectus available.

Upper Age Limits in the Institution. 45 years is the normal upper age limit but is not rigidly adhered to.

Part-time Degrees. In-service BEd for qualified primary teachers.

S. Martins College (Lancaster)

Percentage of Mature Students. 3 per cent.

Establishment Policy. Students are designated as 'mature' at 23 years of age. We offer advisory interviews to mature students. We consider it important that anyone aiming at doing 'A' levels,

Open College or Access Courses in order to prepare for a BEd course here should first be advised as to their *personal* (as opposed to academic) suitability for teacher training. We hope to avoid situations where candidates undertake protracted study only to be told they are not suitable for professional training. We also advise on appropriate academic courses for preparation for our BA and BEd courses, as we would normally require some evidence of recent academic study at an appropriate level. 'Unqualified' mature students whom we consider capable of embarking on a course without further preparation receive College support to the validating body for acceptance under exceptional admissions procedures.

Special Literature. None at present, but it is hoped to produce some for the next academic year. Prospectus available.

Upper Age Limits in Individual Departments. None, but BEd candidates who are over 40 are advised that they might experience more difficulty in securing employment than younger colleagues. We recommend that applicants should be under 50 on completion of the BEd course. No age limits apply for BA courses.

Crèche Facilities. The University of Lancaster close by the college has a crèche.

Special Provision for Mature Students. There are relatively large numbers of in-service students on site, who are mature. The College tutorial system offers personal and academic support to all students.

Part-time Degrees. MA in Religious Education (two years part-time).

This college welcomes enquiries from mature applicants and attempts to be sympathetic to their needs.

St Mary's College (Belfast)
[Incorporating St Joseph's College (Belfast) from September 1985]

Percentage of Mature Students. 4 per cent.

Establishment Policy. Each case is considered individually on its merits. Evidence of recent study at a suitably high standard is desirable.

Special Literature. None. Prospectus available.

St Mary College (Twickenham)

Percentage of Mature Students. 3–5 per cent.

Establishment Policy. Students are designated mature if they are at least 23 years old. All applicants are given individual consideration. Whilst alternative entry qualifications may be considered, mature students join the normal undergraduate courses. There are no courses specifically designed for mature students. All cases of mature students with alternative qualifications to the usual two 'A' and three 'O' levels or three 'A' and one 'O' level must also be approved by the University of Surrey.

Introductory/Study Skills Courses. Sessions on study skills are provided as part of the first-year induction programme. They are open to all first-year students but are not compulsory. There is no specific course for mature students.

Special Literature. None. Prospectus available.

Special Provision for Mature Students. All mature students are counselled pre-entry. The attitude of staff towards mature students is supportive, and since the number of mature students is very small individual consideration is given to the students' requirements. It is intended to continue the present policy of dealing with applicants on an individual basis.

Slough College of Higher Education (Slough)

Percentage of Mature Students. 60 per cent (approximately).

Establishment Policy. The College policy is to welcome applications from mature students (over 21). All such applications are considered on their merits along with those of other students. Exemption from part or all of the entry requirement may be possible on certain courses. The postgraduate courses offered are validated by the CNAA.

Introductory/Study Skills Courses. Mature students are given any special help which may be necessary, in the normal course of their first-year work. Particular attention is paid to literacy.

Special Literature. None. Prospectus available.

Mature Students' Union/Society. All students belong to the Students' Union.

Special Provision for Mature Students. Student Counsellor will advise if help is needed.

South Glamorgan Institute of Higher Education (Cardiff)

Percentage of Mature Students. 5 per cent (approximately).

Establishment Policy. Applications from mature students are welcomed and considered on their merits, but subject to the policy of the validating body, e.g. Art and Design (CNAA); other degree courses including BEd – University of Wales (over 23 designated as mature).

Special Literature. None. Prospectus available.

Part-time Degrees. MA in Ceramics, MEd in Art Education.

Southampton Institute of Higher Education

Establishment Policy. The College policy is to welcome applications from mature students. All such applications are considered on their merits. Exemption from part or all of the entry requirements may be possible for certain courses. The degrees are validated by the CNAA, or Southampton University.

Introductory/Study Skills Courses. Institute Certificate and Diploma Vocational Courses in Fine Art for Mature students. BTEC Certificate in Fashion for Mature Students. Polymaths refresher course in traditional and modern mathematics.

Special Literature. Entries in part-time prospectus.

Mature Students' Union/Society. Yes.

Stanmillis College (Belfast)

Percentage of Mature Students. 6 per cent.

Establishment Policy. Establishment policy is largely as described for Queen's University of Belfast, i.e. 'Mature age: over 23 on 1 June of year of entry. While some concessions are granted and each case is considered individually on its merits, evidence of recent academic study at a suitably high standard would be required.' Future plans may enable suitably qualified mature students to enter the second year of the Bachelor of Education Course in Craft, Design and Technology. Such students would follow an accelerated course in Education and Professional Studies. In placement for school experience, special consideration is given to mature students with family responsibilities.

Special Literature. None. Prospectus available.

Trinity and All Saints College (Leeds)

Percentage of Mature Students. 4 per cent.

Establishment Policy. The College is very pleased to consider applications from mature students who satisfy the general matriculation requirements of the Joint Matriculation Board and from students without 'A' levels who apply through the mature matriculation scheme of the JMB.

Special Literature. Prospectus available. The College also sends out the JMB leaflet on mature entry to appropriate students.

Future plans include the establishment of a crèche, given resources.

Trinity College (Carmarthen)

Percentage of Mature Students. 36 per cent.

Establishment Policy. The degree courses in this college are validated by the University of Wales and so the regulations relating to mature matriculation are as described under the University of Wales. Candidates over the age of 23 and possessing five 'O' level passes or other recognised qualification can be considered for entry to the BA and BEd courses. These candidates are asked to attend for an advisory interview.

Special Literature. None. General prospectus available on request.

Part-time Degrees. Part-time BEd (In-service).

West Glamorgan Institute of Higher Education (Swansea)

Percentage of Mature Students. 20 per cent (approximately).

Establishment Policy. The Institute admits students as mature if they are over the age of 23 for the University of Wales courses and they are subject to special admission procedures under the University of Wales standing orders. For those candidates wishing to do a BEd, they are expected to show evidence of recent academic study and are required to take tests in numeracy and literacy.

Introductory/Study Skills Courses. An induction programme for all new students including study skills lecture and handouts.

Special Literature. Yes. Handouts on coping strategies and time management are especially geared to the mature student. The prospectus is also available.

Mature Students' Union/Society. Yes.

Special Provision for Mature Students. No, because adequate provision is already available for all students.

Part-time Degrees. Yes. LLB (London) external and MPhil, PhD (CNAA). Future plans include the possibility of a BA in Humanities by part-time study.

Westhill College of Higher Education (Birmingham)

Percentage of Mature Students. 18 per cent.

Establishment Policy. Degree courses are validated by the University of Birmingham, a member of the JMB. Students can be accepted either with normal matriculation requirements or by the mature matriculation route, as described in the Universities section. There are pre-entry courses at two local further education colleges and these provide the techniques and background needed for academic work at University level, as well as enabling mature students to fulfil the general requirements for matriculation.

Special Literature. *A University Degree for the Older Student* published by the University of Birmingham and the JMB booklet *A University Degree – a second chance at 21+* are used to advise mature students on pre-entry courses and mature matriculation schemes respectively.

Crèche Facilities. Yes, mornings only.

Mature Students' Union/Society. Mature Students' Liaison Group is available.

Special Provision for Mature Students. A Students' Union Welfare committee deals with enquiries. The Students' Union gives informal advice to enquirers, etc. and has a hardship fund.

Part-time Degrees. BEd and BEd (Hons) in Teaching Studies, Art and Design or Religious and Theological Studies, for serving teachers.

West London Institute of Higher Education

Percentage of Mature Students. 7–10 per cent.

Establishment Policy. From 1983 CNAA regulations apply, i.e. for students 21 or over at the start of the course, CNAA Regulations 8.11–17, which stress necessary motivation, potential and knowledge.

Introductory/Study Skills Courses. Yes, 'Fresh Start' part-time preparatory course is offered two evening a week over a year.

Special Literature. Special literature for 'Fresh Start' course is available; other literature is in preparation.

Upper Age Limits in Individual Departments. Possibly BEd students in older age groups may have difficulty in obtaining places.

Crèche Facilities. Yes.

Special Provision for Mature Students. Yes.

Part-time Degrees. Adult Education BA Degree Courses with a DipHE awarded at the end of the third year for students unable to complete the degree course (five years part-time CNAA).

West Midlands College of Higher Education (Walsall)

Percentage of Mature Students. 30 per cent.

Establishment Policy. The policy of West Midlands College of Higher Education is to consider each application on its individual merit and the basic requirements on the student's part is to demonstrate the ability to study at degree level. Where a 'mature' candidate over 21 has inadequate formal qualifications, an internal examination may be set. This can be completed under exam conditions or as an assignment to be completed with access to libraries and other facilities. BA courses will not be provided from September 1984.

Introductory/Study Skills Courses. Access course for local candidates over 20 years wishing to enter the BEd course (one full time) run jointly with Warley College of Technology. Successful completion ensures entry to BEd.

Special Literature. None. Prospectus available.

Upper Age Limits. No age limits set but would seldom accept candidates over 45 years for entry to initial teacher training.

Crèche Facilities. Half-term crèche facilities.

Special Provision for Mature Students. No, but all mature students have a personal tutor as do all students in the College.

Westminster College (Oxford)

Percentage of Mature Students. 5 per cent.

Establishment Policy. The College welcomes applications from mature students over the age of 21 years. Advisory interviews are available for candidates without normal minimum entry requirements.

Mature students often join the DipHE course and then transfer into Part Two (years 3–4) of the BEd (Hons) course, if qualified in English and Mathematics.

Introductory/Study Skills Courses. Study skills are included in all the major degree and diploma courses. Staff responsible for counselling pay particular attention to the problems faced by mature students.

Special Literature. None. Prospectus available.

Upper Age Limits in Individual Departments. Candidates for teacher training courses are advised of the problem of employment, particularly if they are tied to the local area. It is unlikely that candidates over the age of 45–50 would be admitted.

West Sussex Institute of Higher Education (Chichester/Bognor Regis)

Percentage of Mature Students. 22 per cent.

Establishment Policy. We have a policy of particularly encouraging the admission of mature students. We find that they are a valuable group within the student community. All students over 21 are designated mature. We have a special scheme for the admission of unqualified mature students. The scheme is intended for those students who did not complete a conventional 'A'-level course but who have the academic and personal potential to complete a degree course. The mature entry scheme consists of a preliminary essay, an interview and an unseen examination.

Introductory/Study Skills Courses. There are no introductory skills courses for mature students. They are accepted as being on a parity with other students once they have completed the mature entry test procedure.

Special Literature. Yes.

Upper Age Limits in the Institution. The Institute does not have an upper age limit for BA courses, but generally regards candidates for initial teacher training as unlikely to receive posts over the age of 50. Therefore they would not normally recruit any candidate who would be 50 or over on completion of the course.

Special Provision for Mature Students. Special Adviser, the Dean of Students (Student Services), discusses possible courses with mature candidates.

Worcester College of Higher Education

Percentage of Mature Students. 15–20 per cent.

Establishment Policy. Mature students are welcomed at Worcester College of Higher Education. Each person is considered individually on his or her merits. The College prefers intending mature students to come for an explanatory/advisory interview before making a formal application. This has proved very helpful in saving time and putting applicants at ease, especially if a formal interview is part of the admission process.

Mature students are accepted with less than the minimum formal qualifications, other appropriate qualifications and/or experience being desirable but not essential. The College has an increasing number of links with institutions offering 'Access' or similar types of foundation, preparatory or bridging courses thus making admission to Worcester easier.

For BEd courses English 'O' level and Mathematics 'O' level are essential and some form of 'A'-level study or equivalent, is desirable. A DipHE normally requires no formal qualification but applicants must submit a test essay, attend for interview and where possible attend a weekend summer school. The Diploma is offered part time as well as full time. Successful diplomates can progress on to a BA/BSc course (validated by CNAA). The College now also offers the BA/BSc programme to suitable mature students (unqualified) rather than channelling them all via the DipHE route. The minimum age for consideration is 21 years.

Introductory/Study Skills Courses. A summer school (three days in August) has been held for DipHE students for some years. In 1984 it was opened to all mature students and was so successful that it is now standard College practice.

Throughout the rest of the year mature students are not deliberately separated from the rest of the student body. However, such students do have easy access to tutors who have considerable experience in dealing with the needs of mature students.

Special Literature. A booklet for mature students. Prospectus available.

Upper Age Limits in Individual Departments. No. However, the College would be concerned, in the case of applicants for courses of teacher training, to ensure that a reasonable period of service was possible.

Crèche Facilities. A crèche for children 3 months–5 years operates all year, Monday to Friday, with the exception of bank holidays. Play weeks for children 5–16+ organised in school half terms.

Mature Students' Committee. Yes.

Special Provision for Mature Students. Yes.

Part-time Degrees. The DipHE (three years part-time). Successful diplomates have automatic right of transfer to either BA (Hons) or BSc (Hons) in Combined Studies. The degree is currently full time only but future plans include the possibility of part-time degrees.

PART THREE

Bibliography of materials relating to mature students and higher education

Bibliography of materials relating to mature students and higher education

This bibliography has been classified in five sections, as follows:

Works of reference/information
Mature students
Grants and awards
Guidance and counselling
Study and examination skills

Many of the items included will be available from libraries or bookshops. In some cases (and particularly where pamphlets or booklets are provided free by an organisation) the name and address of the supplier is provided. Otherwise addresses are included in the Useful Addresses section.

As always in exercises of this kind, we had different views about what should go where. There is inevitably some overlap and some works could be classified equally well in two or more sections. In a few cases we have duplicated references, though we have tried to avoid duplication whenever possible.

In recent years there has been a publishing boom in works aimed at and intended for mature returners – particularly women. In this bibliography we are only able to include a selection and so we have chosen works which we think will be of interest to mature learners, to advisers and to teachers of adults and which we think are likely to be available in major libraries, from publishers or from bookshops.

Works of reference and information
Adult Education

Handbook of Adult Education in Scotland (annual). *Scottish Institute of Adult Education*
A useful directory, similar to the NIACE Yearbook but with detail of Scottish provision.

Never Too Late to Learn: the complete guide to adult education, Bell, J M and Roderick, G W (1982), *Longman*
Is, as its title suggests, a guide to adult education and therefore of particular value to mature students. It attempts to answer questions and offers advice and information.

Second Chances for Adults: the guide to adult education and training opportunities, Pates, A and Good, M. *Great Ouse Press*
Published annually as a guide to adult education and training opportunities.

Yearbook of Adult Continuing Education (annual). *National Institute of Adult Continuing Education (NIACE)*
A directory of organisations concerned with adult continuing education.

Agricultural Studies

Agriculture, Horticulture and Forestry Courses (annual). *National Consultative Committee for Agricultural Education*
Price 40p post free.

Architectural Studies

Schools of Architecture Recognised by the RIBA. *Royal Institute of British Architects (RIBA)*
Available from RIBA Publications Department, Finsbury Mansions, Moreland Street, London EC1V 8VB. Price £1.

Business Studies

Business Education Handbook. *Stonehart Publications*

Guide to Business Schools for Prospective Students and Employers, Coulson-Thomas, C (1981). *Business Graduate Association*

Dental Studies

Careers in Medicine, Dentistry and Mental Health, Humphries, J (1981). *Kogan Page*

The Dental Profession in Great Britain and Ireland: Educational Directory.
Obtainable from the British Dental Journal Professional and Scientific Publications BMA House, Tavistock Square, London WC1H 9JR. Price £1, post free.

Entry to Schools of Dentistry for Mature Students. *Sheffield Careers Service* (1981)

Design Studies

Design Courses in Britain. Design Council (1980)
Details of foundation, non-degree and post-graduate courses. The subject area covers all facets of industrial design, graphics and fashion textiles, three-dimensional design, design history and multi-disciplinary courses. Includes the courses available throughout the United Kingdom.

Further and Higher Education

Access to Higher Education: non-standard entry to CNAA first degree and DipHE courses, CNAA Development Services Publication 6 (1984). *Council for National Academic Awards (CNAA)*

Chapters on : (1) The enquiry: (2) Profile of non-standard entry; (3) Criteria and procedures for non-standard entry, etc. A policy statement and includes the relevant part of the CNAA's Principles and Regulations regarding admission of students who do not meet formal minimum entry requirements.

CH/1 Leaflet, *Central Register and Clearing House Ltd (CRCH),* 3 Crawford Place, London W1H 2BM.
Information leaflet giving details of all degree and other advanced courses within the Central Register and Clearing House. Sent to all candidates with their CRCH application forms.

Choice and Transition: Preparation for Entry to Higher Education: a manual for tutors and careers advisers, Ball, B & L (1984). *William's Press*

Commonwealth Universities Yearbook (annual), *Association of Commonwealth Universities* (4 volumes.)
As its title suggests the Yearbook covers the universities of the Commonwealth countries, includes approximately 600 pages on the universities of Britain. This includes a descriptive article, a section on each university, index of subjects and a brief survey of entrance requirements.

Compendium of University Entrance Requirements for First Degree Courses in the United Kingdom (annual). *Association of Commonwealth Universities*

Published by the Association of Commonwealth Universities for the Committee of Vice-Chancellors and Principals. An annual publication giving a detailed description of the minimum requirements in terms of GCE, for entry to first degree courses in United Kingdom universities and university colleges. This is designed primarily for school leavers but does contain some information in the appendix of relevance to mature students. Appendices include: (1) Non-GCE qualifications; (2) Alternative mathematical qualifications for course requirements; (3) Integrated sandwich courses; (4) Mature students; (5) Other printed sources of information on higher education. There are indexes to courses and subjects. Available from Lund Humphries, The County Press, Drummond Road, Bradford BD8 8DH.

Degree Course Guide, Careers Research and Advisory Centre (CRAC). *Hobsons Press*

These are available either in the form of individual booklets or a bound version.

Business and Social Studies, Science, Engineering and Technology, Arts and Humanities. Degree Course Index 1984. *Segal Information Services*

Degree Course Offers (annual). Heap B W, *Careers Consultants*

Annual publication giving information concerning selection procedures and listing the offers in 'A'-level grades for each subject at each university, polytechnic and college in the United Kingdom. Its aim is to provide the most up-to-date information on selection procedures to all degree courses. The information does however relate to the previous year and may not necessarily apply to the current year as selection procedures are based on a large number of variables. Main body of the work consists of an alphabetical subject listing giving the institutions and their offers as well as information on selection procedures, etc. Subject tables form the bulk of the publication. Each subject is divided down into average entry grades, annual intakes, applications, acceptability of general studies 'A' level, admissions tutors' advice, applicants' comments. Also contains advice on choosing a degree course, choosing a college, how to apply, interviews and clearing scheme.

Directory of First Degree and DipHE Courses (annual). *Council for National Academic Awards (CNAA)*
Lists all first degree courses and DipHE courses validated by CNAA. Published annually, as are most of the CNAA directories. Available free from CNAA, Publications Officer, 344/254 Gray's Inn Road, London WC1X 8BP

Directory of Further Education, (D. Curtis), Careers Research and Advisory Centre (CRAC). *Hobsons Press* (Updated regularly)
An annual publication which provides a comprehensive list of both degree and non-degree courses, which is arranged in subject order: Agriculture and horticulture; Arts, crafts and design; Arts and languages; Business, commerce and administration; Catering, hotel-keeping, food science, home crafts, hairdressing; Architecture, building and construction, surveying, planning; Science and applied science; Social sciences, health and welfare.

Directory of Postgraduate and Post-Experience courses (annual). *Council for National Academic Awards (CNAA)*
A preliminary guide to courses at postgraduate and post-experience level approved by CNAA.

Further Education in Scotland: Directory of day courses. Scottish Education Department. *HMSO* and available free from the SED

Getting Into Colleges and Institutes of Higher Education (1984). *Careers Consultants*
This 47-page booklet provides guidance on choice of college and course and how to apply. Lists all colleges and institutes.

Guide for Applicants (annual), *The Open University*
Obtainable free from the Open University, Walton Hall, Milton Keynes MK7 6AA

A Guide for Applicants to Universities, Polytechnics and Other Colleges Offering Degrees, ACE Advisory Booklet No. 5 (1982). *Advisory Centre for Education (ACE).*
A useful publication as an introduction, as it provides a step-by-step guide. It describes the different higher education establishments. Includes choosing a subject and course, entrance requirements, how to apply. Gives addresses. A starting point rather than a comprehensive guide.

Guide to Colleges and Institutes of Higher Education (annual). *Standing Conference of Principals and Directors of Colleges and Institutes of Higher Education*
A publication giving details of all courses offered by the colleges and institutions of higher education. Section of facilities and student activities. Useful, value for £1.

Guide to Further and Higher Education In Inner London. *ILEA,* County Hall, London SE1 7PS

Handbook of Degree and Advanced Courses in Institutes And Colleges of Higher Education, Colleges of Education, Polytechnics and University Departments of Education (annual). *NATFHE/Lund Humpries*
Published annually and describes a wide range of courses, including some specially designed for mature students. Includes BA, BCS, BSc, BTh degrees available in institutes and colleges of education, in addition to DipHE and BEd degrees. Particularly useful for courses leading to a teaching qualification. In addition to detailed information on subjects covered on each course, provides general background information relating to the institution.
Also covers colleges of music, drama and dance. Is the main source of information on initial teacher training.

Handbook for First Degree Classifications Transbinary Database, *Council for National Academic Awards (CNAA)* (1983)
For use by those in a higher education advisory capacity wishing to use the CNAA database.

Handbook of Scottish Central Institutions In Degree and Non- Degree Sections.
Provides information about courses and entry requirements. Available free from the Assistant Registrar, Paisley College of Technology, High Street, Paisley, Scotland.

Higher Education Annual Guide (B. Cossins and S. Downs), *National Association of Careers and Guidance Teachers (NACGT)* (1984)

The Higher Education Guide, Heap, B W (1983). *BBC*
A useful supplementary work, although most of the information can be found easily in the usual handbooks. In three main sections, *Preparing and choosing, Applying* and *Profiles.* Useful for linking 'A'-level results to relevant degree courses and careers entered by graduates in various disciplines. The profiles contain the usual factual data including

address, phone number, accommodation, sporting and cultural facilities, library, 'A'-level scores. A useful book list.

Higher Education: finding your way. A brief guide for schools and college students, Dixon, D (1981). *HMSO*
As its title suggests, a brief guide intended for school and college students about to apply for higher education. Includes sections on how to apply, taking a year off, grants and so on.

Higher Education in the United Kingdom – a handbook for students and their advisers, British Council and Association of Commonwealth Universities. *Longman*
A two-yearly publication although originally intended as a guide for overseas students, and as such containing information on the British way of life; it is also useful for home students. Provides an introduction to higher education, courses and qualifications.

How to apply for admission to a university. *Universities Central Council for Admissions (UCCA)*
An annual publication which is distributed through schools and other relevant educational establishments to applicants. For use in completing UCCA forms, includes a note for mature students. Includes England and Wales, listing all first degree courses. Available from: UCCA, PO Box 28, Cheltenham, Gloucestershire GL50 1HY

Mature Students: a brief guide to university entrance *Committee of Vice-Chancellors and Principals* and *TUC* (1979).
Leaflet giving advice to mature students considering undertaking a degree course. Available free from: Committee of Vice-Chancellors and Principals of the Universities of the UK, 29 Tavistock Square, London, WC1H 9EZ

National Conference on Degree Sandwich Courses, Universities Committee on Integrated Sandwich courses (1976) (E. F. G. Denbury). *Bath University Press*

Opportunities in Higher Education for Mature Students. *Council for National Academic Awards (CNAA)*
Leaflet, which outlines the wide range of opportunities available in polytechnics and colleges associated with CNAA, and the procedures for applying.

Part-time Degree Level Study in the United Kingdom, Tight, M (1982). *Advisory Council for Adult Continuing Education*
Outlines the provision of part-time advanced courses for adults.

The Polytechnics Central Admissions System (PCAS). Leaflet describing the PCAS system. Available from PCAS, PO Box 67, Cheltenham, Gloucestershire, GL50 3AP

Polytechnic Courses Handbook (annual), Committee of Directors of Polytechnics. *The Book Centre* A publication which lists all polytechnic courses. It gives details of the subjects studied for each course. The initial section lists polytechnics individually providing an introduction and description of each. Divided into four main sections which categorise courses by the qualifications to which they lead. Each section is subdivided initially into broad academic areas and then further subdivided into individual subjects. Each course entry lists the relevant polytechnics in alphabetical order giving the following information: (1) title of course and awarding body; (2) type and length of course; (3) subject content; (4) sandwich course arrangements (if appropriate).

The Polytechnics: full-time and sandwich courses (annual). *Committee of Directors of Polytechnics*

Professional and Vocational Degree Course Offers, 1984/5 Heap, B W (1984). *Careers Consultants* This is the second edition of this work. Deals with professional degree courses only and is therefore useful for mature students seeking information for vocational courses. It includes details on sandwich as well as full-time degree courses. The information includes details on the length and timing of placements on sandwich courses and details of professional examinations. The section on the exemptions is particularly useful.

Research Degrees (annual). *Council for National Academic Awards (CNAA)* Leaflet giving basic information about research degrees and how to register.

21 + – Returning to Learning. *Joint Matriculation Board* Leaflet which describes the JMB special scheme for mature students. Available free from the JMB, Manchester M15 6EU

Sandwich Courses (Eds M. Brewer and Wallace-Hadmill) (updated regularly), Careers Research and Advisory Centre (CRAC). *Hobsons Press*

Scottish Universities Entrance Guide (annual). Lists all subjects that can be studied at Scottish universities and gives details of entrance requirements. Available from:

Scottish Universities Council on Entrance, Kinnessburn, St Andrews, Fife KY1 9DR. Price £1. Supplements available from the same address also priced £1.

Selection for Admission to a University. *Assistant Masters Association (AMA), Gordon House, 29 Gordon St London WC1H OPT*

So You Want to Get a Degree? Bell, J M & Roderick, G W (1984). *Longman*
Useful for mature students for in addition to containing a chapter relating specifically to mature students includes chapters on applying for a place, finance, coping with life as a student, etc. Also contains lists of addresses plus a bibliography.

The Student Book: the applicants' guide to what and where to study (annual), Boehm, K & Wellings, N. *Macmillan Press*
Aims to be a 'dictionary' of advice on institutions, courses and problems relating to obtaining a place in higher education. The work is divided into three A – Z sections: (1) Getting your bearings; (2) United Kingdom colleges, polytechnics and universities; (3) Study areas. The first deals with 'A'-level grade requirements, interviews, grants, etc.; the second gives an outline description of the college, etc. together with personal accounts of student life, etc.; and the third with subjects available etc. Intended chiefly for school leavers, but also useful for mature applicants.

Student Eye: the CRAC guide to universities and polytechnics, as seen by students, Careers research and advisory centre (CRAC) (1983). *Hobsons Press*
Aims to give a student's view of life at individual universities and polytechnics. Divided into universities and polytechnics. Entry under each institution gives basic information on how to apply, UCCA code, degrees awarded and courses. Additionally includes special academic features, history and location, accommodation, government, academic life, library and resources, student life, sports, societies and clubs, health and welfare, careers, overseas students, mature students, disabled students, etc.

The Student's Guide to Graduate Studies in the UK, Careers Research and Advisory Centre (CRAC) (1985). *Hobsons Press*
Sub-divides into four sections: (1) Humanities and social sciences; (2) Biological, health and agricultural sciences; (3) Physical sciences; (4) Engineering and applied sciences.

Sub-divides further with an alphabetic arrangement for institutions. Contains a chapter on postgraduate awards and an index of subject headings together with an alphabetical list of institutions.

The Sunday Times good university guide, Wilby, P (1984). *Granada Publishing*
Although the title specifies university, it does include polytechnics, higher education colleges and other colleges. Aims to be a 'Good Food' type guide for universities, giving profiles of each institution, student numbers, largest departments, unusual courses, accommodation, library and recreational facilities. Includes both factual data and comments from students. Useful, though often relying on opinion, so use with care.

A Survey of 'Access' Courses in England, Lucas, S and Ward, P (1985). *School of Education, University of Lancaster*
A survey of courses which offer adults opportunities without 'A' levels to qualify for entry to higher education. This is a revised edition and reflects the increasing number of courses of this kind.
Includes detailed information on each scheme, its structure, content, etc, and is intended to be of use both to potential students and those assisting them.

Survey of Degree Course offers. *Kent Careers Service* (1985)
A survey containing information on offers made and results actually obtained by Kent students. Is useful however as it also contains sections on choosing a degree course, applications and interviews, sources of information, addresses, etc.

Survey of polytechnic courses in England, Wales and Northern Ireland, Whittington, E (1981). *Careers Consultants*
Intended for 'A'-level students considering vocational courses and gives comparisons between individual courses of the same topic, in differing situations.

Teaching information. *Scottish Education Department*
A series of leaflets giving information on registration and employment, teaching qualifications and obtaining a post. Available free from SED.

Your Choice of Degree and Diploma (2nd edn), Alan Jamieson (1985). *CRAC/Hobsons Press*
A useful guide for applicants to higher education. Explains the system, the courses and the terminology.

226

Which Degree (regularly updated). *VNU Business Publications*
Five volumes. Provide information about all full-time and
sandwich degree courses taught by universities, polytechnics
and colleges in the UK.

Geography Studies

A directory of Geography Courses (12th edn), Weber, M (ed.)
(1984). *Geo Books*

Handicapped Students' Studies

**Applying to Higher Education: some notes for disabled
students.** *National Bureau for Handicapped Students (NBHS)* (1985)

**Compendium of Post-16 Education in Residential Estab-
lishments for Handicapped Young People.** *National Bureau for
Handicapped Students (NBHS)* (1985)
A directory of residential establishments offering further
education and training to young people.

Directory for the Disabled (compiled by Ann Darnborough and
Derek Kinrade). *Woodhead Faulkner* (1979)
Contains a useful chapter on education.

**A Guide to Specialist Facilities and Courses for Handicapped
People in Post-school Educational Institutions in the Region.**
*London & Home Counties Regional Advisory Council for Tech-
nological Education*

Language Studies

**Part-time and Intensive Language Study – a guide for adult
learners,** *Centre for Information on Language Teaching (CILT)*
(1982)
Contains details of types of language study courses available and
guidance on how to chose an appropriate couse.

Law Studies

University Entrance Requirements for Law. *Secondary Heads
Association*

Medical Studies

Careers in Medicine, Dentistry and Mental health, Humpries, J
(1981). *Kogan Page*

Directory of Schools of Medicine and Nursing (2nd edn). *Kegan Paul*
The directory is divided into four parts: (1) Consists of an introductory section with articles on various aspects of health-care training; (2) Provides careers information on medicine and surgery, dentistry, nursing and midwifery, professions supplementary to medicine, professions related to medicine, alternative medicine professions, medical technicians; (3) Directory of medical schools, schools of nursing, etc. The final section consists of addresses, bibliography, etc.

Directory of Schools of Nursing (4th edn), Department of Health and Social Security (1980). *HMSO*

Directory of Postgraduate Medical Centres, Council for Postgraduate Medical Education in England and Wales (1982). *CPME*

A Doctor ... Or Else, Thurman, J (1983). *Yare Valley Publications*

Entrance Requirements for Medical Schools. *Secondary Heads Association*

Entry to Schools of Medicine for Mature Students, prepared by P. Quinn. *Leeds Careers Service* (1979)

How To Obtain a Place in Medical School, Westall, W G (1984). *Published privately, available from the author at 2 St Edeyrns Road, Cardiff CF2 6TB*
Aimed chiefly at sixth formers desiring to go to medical school. Consists of general advice on choosing 'A'-level subjects, UCCA applications and interviews.

Learning Medicine, Richards, P (1983). *BMA*

Summary of Postgraduate Degrees, Diplomas and Courses in Dentistry,Council for Postgraduate Medical Education (1980). *National Advice Centre, CPME*

Summary of Postgraduate Diplomas and Courses in Medicine, Council for Postgraduate Medical Education (1982). *National Advice Centre, CPME*

Survey of Attitudes to Mature Applicants for Training in Professions Supplementary to Medicine, Martin, J and Wood, A (1984). *Sheffield Careers Service*
A specialised work for mature students interested in the paramedical professions. It reviews the present position with relation to the recruitment of mature students. The appendices give information relating to the individual training estab-

lishments. Obtainable from Mrs A Wood, Sheffield Careers Service, AUEW House, Furnivale Gate, Sheffield S1 3SL (Tel. 0742 735491) price 50p. Cheques payable to Sheffield Education Authority.

Photographic Studies

Where to Study, The BJ Directory of photographic education, Martin, E (1981). *Henry Greenwood*
Lists, with details, courses in photography, film and television available throughout the United Kingdom.

Social Work Studies

Education and Training in Social Work Including the Probation Service, Central Council for Education and Training in Social Work (CCETSW). *Obtainable from CCETSW Information Service, Derbyshire House, St Chad's Street, London WC1H 8AD*

Social Services Year Book (annual). *Councils and Education Press Ltd*
A standard reference book giving local authority addresses. It includes information on health services, charities, voluntary organisations and bodies concerned with welfare and information/advice. Useful for the mature student who may need to call upon such services.

Social Work Directory and Charities' Year Book.
Belfast Voluntary Welfare Society, Bryson House, 28 Bedford Street, Belfast BT2 7FE

Professional Training for Social Work. *Central Council for Education and Training in Social Work (CCETSW)*
Gives information about CQSW courses and entry requirements.

Technological/Technical Studies

Alternatives to 'A' levels, 1983-85. *London and Home Counties Regional Advisory Council for Technological Education*

Compendium of Advanced Courses in Colleges of Further and Higher Education, Edited by R. Eberhard. *London and Home Counties Regional Advisory Council for Technological Education*
An annual publication which describes both full-time and sandwich courses in polytechnics and other institutions outside the university sector. Straightforward and simple to use. Lists courses with details of college, title, duration of course

and entry requirements. Basic information only as entries are brief. Courses are listed by subject.

Directory of Technical and Further Education (annual). *Goodwin*

Guide to IEE accredited degree courses, Institution of Electrical Engineers (1984). *New Opportunity Press*
Lists the courses in electrical engineering and related subjects at universities, polytechnics and colleges, which are currently accredited by IEE. Gives details of title of course, department offering it, length, entry requirement structure of the course, industrial sponsorship linked to the course, etc. Special emphasis is made of the career prospects for women.

Training Opportunities (published June/July annually), *Institution of Mechanical Engineers*
Gives details of undergraduate sponsorship and graduate training places provided by engineering companies. Available to schools and colleges through the Careers and Occupational Information Centre or free on request from the Schools Liaison Service, Institution of Mechanical Engineers, PO Box 23, Northgate Avenue, Bury St Edmunds, Suffolk IP32 6BN, Tel. 0284 63277

Veterinary Studies

A Career as a Veterinary Surgeon. *Royal College of Veterinary Surgeons (RCVS)*
Obtainable from RCVS, 32 Belgrave Square, London, SW1X 8QP. Price £2, post free.

General

Access/Preparatory Courses: some data collected by CNAA. *Council For National Academic Awards* (1984)

Alternative Prospectuses. These are produced by some Students' Unions on an annual basis to provide prospective students with an alternative view of life at their university. They describe both the academic and social life of university. Obviously the contents will vary between university and often from department to department, within an institution. Availability for a particular university can be checked by contacting the relevant Students Union.

A Bibliography of Reference Materials for Educational Guidance Services. *London Educational Advice and Counselling Services for Adults (LEACSA)* (1983)

Concerned primarily with educational information and advice for the London area and this is reflected in its contents. It is however a useful starting point listing: course compendiums – national, regional and Inner London; course choice; careers, money and general reference.

British Qualifications: A comprehensive guide to educational, technical professional and academic qualifications in Britain (ed. B Priestly). *Kogan Page*
Lists awards made by universities, polytechnics and other institutions as well as qualifications listed in alphabetical order of trade and profession. Outlines the professional bodies and their qualification requirements as well as the institutions awarding degrees in the subject. Contains information on age limits for entry to various professions and careers, although this can be difficult to locate. Contains a useful index.

Choose Your Course. *Department of Education and Science*
A series of leaflets as follows:
1. After 'O' levels
2. Agriculture, horticulture and forestry
3. Becoming an engineer
4. Business studies
5. Languages at work
6. Looking after people
7. On from 'A' levels
8. Science at work
9. Using your maths
10. What next after school?
The DES also publish a range of other booklets (all obtainable from the DES, Room 2/11, Elizabeth House, York Road, London SE1 7PH), such as: **A Career in Teaching: Teaching in Primary Schools; Teaching Mathematics and Science; Teaching Craft, Design and Technology; Teacher-Training Awards in Craft Design and Technology; Schoolteacher's Pay and Pensions; Salaries for Teachers in Further Education.**

A Dictionary of British Qualifications: Abbreviations and Qualifications (1985). *Kogan Page*
Information is provided in three columns. The first gives abbreviations, the second gives the full qualifications and the third the name and address of the qualifying body. A useful reference book.

Directory of Independent Training and Tutorial Organisations (2nd edn), (ed. E Summerson and M Davies) (1985).*Careers Consultants*
Deals with educational opportunities available in the private sector, listing courses and facilities available.

A Directory of Open Learning Opportunities in Scotland (annual). *Glasgow Network*

Education Authorities Directory and Annual. *The School Government Publishing Company*
Published annually, a reference work listing government departments, LEA's secondary and middle schools, teachers centres, further education colleges, polytechnics, Scottish central institutions, institutes/colleges of higher education, teacher training establishments, universities, special schools, special community homes, directors of social services, careers offices, public library authorities. Gives addresses and officials responsible. Has indexes to LEAs and place names, in addition to the general index.

The Education Fact Book: an A – Z guide to education and training in Britain, Pates, A and Good, M (1983). *Macmillan Press*
Basically a dictionary of educational terms, although the definitions are substantial and useful. Contains an extensive and valuable address list of educational and related organisations. Brief book list.

Information Sheets, Educational Guidance for Adults (1985). *EGA, Hatfield Polytechnic*
A series of information sheets which despite having bias for the Hatfield area do contain some generally applicable and useful information. The sheets are:
Educational opportunities for adults
Sources of help (books)
Small businesses
Grants
Training Opportunities Scheme
Teacher training
Social work
Preparatory courses
Postgraduate study
Computing
Book-keeping and accounting
Studying with the Open University
Psychology
Studying whilst unemployed

These sheets are free to local enquirers but a charge is made to outside organisations. Enquiries to: EGA Centre, Hatfield Polytechnic, P.O. Box 109, College Lane, Hatfield, Herts.

Education Year Book (1985). *Longman*
The standard education reference work. Lists adult education associations, residential colleges etc. Useful for addresses for universities, professional bodies, charitable trusts, etc. as well as all educational and allied organisations. Can be difficult to use if one is unfamiliar with the work. Tries to include all there is to know about the British education system.

International Guide to Qualifications in Education (1984). *Mansell for British Council*
Replaces *Guide to Overseas Qualifications*. It explains the education system for each country for schools, further and higher education. Usually includes marking systems and comparisons are made with British GCE, degrees, etc. An authoritive work.

A Simple Guide to British Qualifications, Austin, M & Ashcroft, F (1983). *Great Ouse Press*

Student Welfare Manual (annual). *National Union of Students*
Designed for counsellors, student union officers, careers officers, students, etc. Consists of eighteen bound leaflets which explain in detail regulations relating to grants, rents, etc. Very comprehensive.

Women's studies courses in the United Kingdom. *Women's Research and Resources Centre* (1982)

Books and articles relating to mature students

Access to Higher Education: non-standard entry to CNAA first degree and Dip HE courses, CNAA Development Services Publication 6 (1984). *Council for National Academic Awards (CNAA)*

Chapters on: (1) The enquiry; (2) Profile of Non-standard entry; (3) Criteria and procedures for non-standard entry etc. A policy statement and includes the relevant part of the CNAA's Principles and Regulations regarding admission of students who do not meet formal minimum entry requirements.

The Adult as a Developing Person, Hopson, B and Scally, M (1980). *Counselling and Career Development Unit, Department of Psychology, University of Leeds*

Adult Students and Higher Education, Jones, H A & Williams, K E (1979). *Advisory Council for Adult and Continuing Education/ National Institute of Adult Continuing Education*

Adult Students at the University, Smith, H P (1945). *Rawley House Papers,* Vol 2, No. 8, March 1945, pp. 310 – 20.

Adult Students: education, selection and social control, Hopper, C and Osborn, M (1985). *Francis Pinter*

Adult Students, work experience and academic studies, Usher, R (1982). **Stud. Adult Educ., 14,** Sept 1982, pp 78 – 84.

Adults: their educational experience and needs, report of a national survey, (Leicester, ACACE/NIACE) (1982). *Advisory Council for Adult and Continuing Education (ACACE)*

An alternative entrance system for adults, Smith, B (1977). *Adult Educ.,* **50** (4), Nov 1977, pp. 233 – 7.

Annotated bibliography of university publications on adult education, 1970–77, Macoun, D and Van Ments, M (1977). *Centre of Extension Studies, Loughborough University of Technology*
The aim of the bibliography is to fill the gap between unpublished student project work and the well indexed journal articles. It lists the relevant publications from university departments which should be readily available.

BEC goes for the mature student, Sellars, J E (1981). **Educ. and Training, 23** (5), May 1981, pp. 135–7.
Reviews the post-experience courses and awards designed for mature students by the Business Education Council. (BEC)

Conflicts between student/professional, parental and self-development roles, Gilbert, L A (1982). **Human Relations, 35** (8), Aug. 1982, pp 635–48.
This study investigated the way in which those adults returning to university dealt with the conflicts arising from their roles as students and as parents or between the student role and their 'self'. The investigators developed nine scales to describe strategies for coping, and both they and the subjects themselves rated their strategies for coping. It was found that women reported higher role conflict than men.
Although an American study with the consequent jargon it is a useful reference for the problems experienced by mature students in coping with dual jobs.

A Degree of Difference: A study of the first year's intake of the Open University, McIntosh, N E *et al.* (1976). *Society for Research into Higher Education*
A study, based on a one-in-four sample of all students who started with the Open University in its first year in 1971. The basic statistical tables (volume II) are obtainable in mimeographed form from the Open University. Additional tables in the printed volume show some of the relevant changes in the student body up to 1975 and the charac-teristics of the Open University and its teaching system are summarised. The methodology of the research is considered, as are some of the implications of the research, for future development. Bibliographical references are included.

Educating Older People, Cleugh, M F (1970). *Tavistock Publications*
An account of methods of teaching older students in general with personal reference to experience in mature teacher training. Much attention is paid to the learning difficulties which such students experience and to methods of overcom-ing them.

Education for mature women: the uses of 'O'-level English Language, Nashashibi, P (1980). **Adult Educ. 52** (5), Jan, pp 333–6

Courses for Mature Students Without Previous University Education, Perry, W (1974). Information No. 25, pp 21–30. *The University of Geneva.*
Summarises research which suggests that maturity is a posi-tive predictor of success in such subjects as philosophy, law, psychology, history and economics. University of Sussex ex-perience suggests lack of preliminary qualification is a hand-icap for science studies, and Open University experience confirms this also in mathematics. Experience suggests that lack of previous qualification is of little importance as a factor inhibiting success, but previous experience of part-time study, and especially institutional impetus stemming from the obtaining of some credit exemption, is a useful aid to continu-ing study.

A Custom-built degree for mature students, Michaels, R (1979). **Studies in Higher Education, 4** (1), Mar. 1979, pp. 103–11.
Describes a 'custom-built' CNAA degree in Contemporary Studies for mature students devised by Hatfield Polytechnic. The four year degree course has a flexible structure to allow for an adjustable rate of study. It has proved to be attractive particularly to married women. The intake was limited to those

235

over 23 and the article describes both the intake and fall-out levels. It attributes some of the fall-out level to the lack of educational guidance available for adults. It also notes that mature students (and particularly women) need to be highly motivated in order to overcome the difficulties inherent in their position and so to succeed. Overall the course was seen as a rewarding experience for those involved with it.

The Education of Adults in Britain, Legge, D (1982). *Open University Press*

The Experience of mature students, Challis, R (1976). **Studies Higher Educ.,** 1 Oct, 1976, pp. 209–22.

Forty to Sixty – How We Waste the Middle Aged, Fogarty, M P (1975). *Bedford Square Co.*
A review of situation and requirements of those aged 40 to 60. Concludes that their potential is under-utilised and that social policies are required to rectify this. Useful bibliography.

Fresh Start: a guide to training opportunities. *Equal Opportunities Commission*
A guide for women on how and where to train for a new job.

Higher Education: a brief guide for adults, Association of Graduate Careers Advisory Services/Central Services Unit (AGCAS/CSU). *(Available from CSU, Crawford House Precinct Centre, Manchester M13 9EP)*

Higher Education for Adults: where more means better, Perry, W (1974). *Cambridge University Press*
The address made in the form of the Reed lecture 1974 by the Vice-Chancellor of the Open University on the need for higher education for adults.

Independent second chance study, Baum, T (1984). **Adult Educ. 56** (1), pp. 36–8.
A brief description of a course in communications skills. Suggests that this co-operative learning approach could be used to help those unable to or unwilling to attend Second Chance courses.

Invisible Students: survey of National Extension College students, Freeman, R (1976). *National Extension College*

It's Never Too Late . . . A Practical Guide to Continuing Education for Women of All Ages, Perkin, J (1984). *Impact Books*
Designed to give practical help to women contemplating a return to education. Includes sections on 'Finding the money',

'Fitting in at college', 'Getting down to study', as well as a chapter devoted to special opportunities for mature students. Describes courses including New Opportunities for Women (NOW) and Wider Opportunities for Women (WOW), TOPS, BTEC, etc. as well as institutions and methods of application. Includes case studies. A practical and useful work for mature women.

Late but in earnest: a case study of mature women students at university, Morgan, V. **Collected Original Research in Education** (CORE), **5** (2) fr.F9 on No. 6 to E3 on No 7 at 10 microfiches.

Learning difficulties of part-time mature students, Smith, Barbara R (1983). **Furth. Higher Educ.**, **7** (3), Autumn 1983, pp. 81–5. A survey of 162 part-time students at a college of higher education and their lecturers. It would appear that mature students spend on average more time in private study than younger students. The perceived difficulties in learning of mature students could be eased by lecturers being more aware of the lack of communication skills of some mature students. It would also appear that greater feedback and tutorial contact would greatly aid mature students.

Learning Later – Fresh Horizons in English Adult Education, Hutchinson, E and Hutchinson E (1978). *Routledge & Kegan Paul*
Describes and analyses the 'Fresh Horizons' courses at the City Literary Institute in London.

Married women students in further education: the meaning of coming to college, Burwood L R V and Brady, C A (1980). **J Furth. Higher Educ. 4** (2), Summer, pp. 21–3.
Report of a study of married women full-time students at Barnfield College, Luton.

Mature age unmatriculated students and the justification of a more liberal admissions policy, Barrett, E (July 1980). **Higher Educ. 9** (4), pp. 365–83.

A Mature Applicant's Guide to Scottish Degree Courses. *Careers Information Unit, Fife* (1984)
Based on a questionnaire, sent out by the Fife Careers Service, to Scottish educational establishments offering degree courses. Covers details of admission and selection procedures. Available (limited number only) on receipt of large stamped addressed envelope to:

Careers Information Unit, Albany House, Glenrothes, Fife KY7 5NZ

The mature student, Nisbet, J and Welsh, J (1972). **Educational Research, 14** (3), June 1972, pp. 204–7
A study of mature students at Aberdeen University who have a break of two years or more between leaving school and re-entering full-time education. The characteristics of the mature students are considered in terms of age and length of break in study, school and employment records education of parents and spouses. Their failure and withdrawal rates, and performance were shown to be broadly the same as for younger students.

Mature Students, Charnley A, Osborn M and Withnall A (1980). *National Institute of Adult Education (England and Wales)*
A review of existing research in adult and continuing education. *Mature Students* is Volume 1 in a series of reviews of research. Publications are reviewed under the headings of: 'Introduction'; 'Where do you find mature students?'; 'Who are the mature students?'; 'The courses students take, transferability, careers and special needs'; 'Motivation, learning patterns and achievements'; and 'Jumping the hurdles'.

Mature Students: a brief guide to university entrance. *Committee of Vice-chancellors and Principals* and *TUC* (1979)
Leaflet giving advice to mature students considering undertaking a degree course. Available free from: Committee of Vice-Chancellors and Principals of the Universities of the UK, 29 Tavistock Square, London, WC1H 9EZ

Mature students' experiences of university, Elsey, B (1982). **Studies in Adult Educ. 14,** Sept. 1982), pp. 69–77.

Mature Students in Further and Higher Education: a study in Sheffield, Roderick, G W, Bell, J M, Dickinson, R., Turner, R. and Wellings, A. (1981). *University of Sheffield*
Covers the experience of mature students in Sheffield University and Polytechnic in great detail covering the routes they followed, obstacles encountered and help received.
Obtainable from the Division of Continuing Education, University of Sheffield, Broomspring House, Wilkinson Street, Sheffield 10

Mature students in higher education, Wood, B (1983). **Assess. and Eval. in Higher Education, 8** (3), Winter 1983, pp 210–17.
Considers the performance by matriculated and non-matriculated students undertaking two DipHE courses at Doncaster Metropolitan Institute of Higher Education. Although prior studying experience was not found to affect overall

performance, it did appear that there was a difference in performance in the first year between matriculated and non-matriculated students. This difference disappears when examination techniques are taught.

Mature Students: perception and experiences of full-time and part-time higher education, Johnson, R and Bailey, R (1984). *PAVIC Publications*

Mature Students in the Strathclyde Region. Report of a Survey of Mature Students, MacDonald, C (1982). *Department of Adult and Continuing Education, University of Glasgow*

Meeting the needs of mature students; an evaluation of the Dip HE at Humberside College of Higher Education, Bremmer, K and Wells J H (1983). **Assess and Eval. in Higher Educ. 8** (12), Summer 1983, pp. 130–9.

A case study of the intake at Humberside College of Higher Education which has attracted increasing numbers of mature applicants.

Reviews the teaching and learning methods applied to mature students, including the DipHE Workshop Programmes. These cover communication skills and quantitative methods. Also analyses the role played by staff on the course in academic and personal counselling.

The examination results illustrate the effectiveness of the techniques used with mature students both with and without 'A' level on entry.

Never Too Late to Learn: the complete guide to adult education, Bell, Judith and Roderick, Gordon (1982). *Longman*
Is, as its title suggests, a guide to educational opportunities for adults. Contains lists of addresses and a short bibliography.

New horizons: an introduction to university studies, Jones, B (1983). **Adult Educ. 56** (3), Dec. 1983, pp. 218–26.

New Opportunities For Women: a survey of mature women students, Michaels, R (1973). *Hatfield Polytechnic, Occasional Papers, No. 1*

Notes for Mature Students Entering Higher Education. *Association of Graduate Careers Advisory Services/Central Services Unit* (1983)

Older Learners – The Challenge of Adult Education, Johnston, S and Phillipson, C (eds,) (1983). *Bedford Square Press*

A part-time psychology degree course for mature students: an empirical study, Vinegrad, M (1979). **Psycol. Teach.,** **7** (2), Nov. 1979, pp. 163–9.
A review of the mature students undertaking a part-time psychology degree course for mature students.

Polymaths for the mature. Kellaway, F W (1978). **Educ. Suppl.,** No. 3287, 7 July 1978, p. 27.

Problems in Adult Training. Belbin, E and Belbin, R M (1972). *Heinemann*
Based on a large number of case studies. Contains suggestions on the do's and dont's for trainers.

Recent Developments in New Opportunities for Women in Scotland, Wilson, V (1981). *Scottish Institute of Adult Education, Edinburgh, £1.50*
A booklet intended to act as a handbook for course providers. Deals with questions of syllabuses, teaching methods, and resources. Also discusses the problems of women and education in Scotland where women are at a greater disadvantage than their counterparts in England. Contains an essay on 'Issues in women's education in Scotland'.

Report of the Committee on continuing education (The Venables Report 1976). *The Open University*

Report of the one-day conference on continuing education for women at the Hatfield Polytechnic 10 March 1976, Michaels, R (1976) **Adult Educ. 49,** (2).

Return to study: provision for women, Kirk, P (1983) **Adult Educ., 55** (3), pp. 241–8.
A review of return to study classes for women in the Leeds area. Discusses the factors affecting enrolment and attendance. It suggests that there is room within cities for many types of return-to-study classes providing opportunities for formal education leading to qualifications, intellectually stimulating courses without academic examinations and hobby and craft courses.

Returners, Dobbie, E (1982). *National Advisory Centre on Careers for Women*
Intended mainly for women as a handbook for those intending to return to work after a break, or for those intending to change their career.

21+ – Returning to Learning. *Joint Matriculation Board*
Leaflet which describes the JMB special scheme for mature students. Available free from the JMB, Manchester M15 6EU

Returning to study: the mature age student, McDonald, R (1979). **Program. Learn. Educ. Technol. 16** (2), May 1979, p. 101–5.
Report of a conference held in Australia on mature students. Provides a summary of current research against a background of a dramatic increase in the number of mature students returning to higher education.

Review of Existing Research in Adult and Continuing Education. Vol 1 – **Mature Students,** Charnley, A, Osborn, M and Withnal, A (1980). *National Institute of Adult Continuing Education*
Provides abstracts and commentary on research relating to mature students. Very useful publication.

The Second Time Around, Levene, M (1976). *Davis Poynton*

Start Again: make a fresh start through education and training. *Equal Opportunities Commission in Northern Ireland* (n.d.)

Staying the Course (2nd edn), Gilbert, J (1985). *Kegan Paul*
How to survive higher education. Covers application procedures, how to fill in forms, interviews. Includes chapters on settling in, coping with problems such as housing, grants, etc. Includes descriptions of different methods of study and explanations. Useful and relevant for those contemplating higher education.

Stresses of mature students, Cleugh, M F (1972). **Brit. J. Educ. Studies,** Feb. 1972, pp. 76–90.
This article discusses factors causing stress to teachers (Twenty-nine in number) attending one-year courses at the University of London Institute of Education.

Student support and advisory services in distance and adult education, Mills, R (1978). **Teaching at a Distance,** May 1978, (11), p. 73–9.
Covers the student support services operated by distance teaching institutions in a number of countries. Suggests cooperation between the Open University and other institutions, and a general advisory service.

Supply and demand: mature students at British Universities, Roderick, G W, Bilham, T and Bell, J M (1982). **High. Educ. Rev., 15** (1), Autumn 1982,, pp. 29–45.
Discusses, with detailed statistical tables both the supply and demand of mature students for places at British universities in

241

the wake of the DES discussion paper *Higher Education into the 1990s*. Considers how well the demand that exists has been met and how students can maximise their chances of acceptance by considering less popular courses. Considers there is a need for proper client centred agencies of advice and guidance for adult students.

A Survey of 'Access' Courses in England, Lucas, S and Ward, P (1985). *School of Education, University of Lancaster*
A survey of courses which offer adults opportunities without 'A' levels to qualify for entry to higher education. This is a revised edition and reflects the increasing number of courses of this kind.
　　Includes detailed information on each scheme, its structure, content, etc., and is intended to be of use both to potential students and those assisting them.

Survey of Attitudes to Mature Applicants for Training in Professions Supplementary to Medicine, Martin, J and Wood, A (1984). *Sheffield Careers Service*

The universities and mature student entry, Liggett, E (1982). **Adult Educ, 55** (2), Sept. 1982, pp. 125–36.

The university education of mature students, MacKay, A L (1968). **Universities Quarterly 22** (2), Mar. 1968, pp. 197–216.

A University introduction course, MacDonald, C (1982). **Scottish J. Adult Educ., 5** (5) Autumn 1982, pp. 7–11.
　　Describes the students who enrolled on the course run by the Department of Adult and Continuing Education, University of Glasgow, which was designed to provide opportunities for adults who had not previously had the chance to study at university level. Concludes that the course has now been running for three years and has been justified in terms of student numbers.

The University performance of mature students, Walker, P (1975). **Research in Education,** No. 14, Nov. 1975, pp. 1–13.
　　Analyses the performance of mature students on undergraduate courses at the University of Warwick. Performance, judged by class of degree obtained, is better than average in arts, but less good in science. Age group 26–30 performed best of all, and of the mature students, those without general qualifications for entry to the University did best.

Unqualified mature students at the University of Sheffield, Roderick, G W, Bell, J M, and Hamilton, S (1982). **Stud. Higher Educ, 6** (2), pp. 123–9.
　　A study of 'unqualified' mature applicants to the University of

Sheffield. These students obtained a place under the JMB special scheme from 1975–77. Compares with similar applicants at Birmingham, Leeds, Liverpool and Manchester. Discusses subjects chosen, withdrawal rates, dropout, final degree results and the problems experienced by mature students.

Women in engineering, Swarbrick, A (1981). **Energy World,** Aug /Sept, p 16

Women in Industry (ed A. Bridgewater), Careers Research and Advisory Centre (CRAC) (1983). *Hobsons Press*
A paperback in which women talk about the problems and challenges they have encountered in their role as engineers, technicians, managers, etc.

Women in Universities. Equal Opportunities Commission (1982). *(leaflet available free from EOC)*

'**Taking Account of Mature Students**' (Woodley, A.), in **The Future of Higher Education**, Jacques, D and Richardson, J (1985). *SHRE and NFER/Nelson*

Grants and Awards

Adult Education Bursaries (annual). (replaces **Guides to State Bursaries for Adult Education)**
Gives full information about Adult Education Bursaries available for 1985–86 for students attending one-year and two-year full-time courses of liberal and adult education at the eight long-term residential adult colleges.
Obtainable free from the Awards Officer, Adult Education Bursaries, c/o Ruskin College, or the Welsh Office, Education Department.

Awards For Commonwealth University Academic Staff. *Association of Commonwealth Universities (ACU)*
Published every three years (most recent publication 1986), contains details of over 600 fellowships, visiting professorships, grants, etc. open to university staff in one Commonwealth country for research, etc. in another.

Awards Regulations (1981). England and Wales statutory instrument (No. 943). *HMSO*

Bursary Handbook – for students in business and management studies. *Economic and Social Research Council (ESRC)*

Available free from: Economic and Social Research Council, Postgraduate Training Division.
Intended for post-graduate study on diploma or certificate courses of a vocational nature in business and management study.

Charities Digest. *Family Welfare Association* (1980)
Has a chapter on education and includes details of exhibitions and scholarships.

Covenants for students. *National Union of Students (NUS)*
Leaflet produced by NUS explaining what a covenant is and how it works.

Deed of Covenant by Parent to Adult Student. Inland Revenue Income Tax, (Leaflet 1R47) *HMSO*

Directory of Grant-Making Trusts. Charities Aid Foundation.
Updated periodically
A comprehensive guide to sources of charitable funds.

Disability Rights Handbook: a guide to income benefits and certain aids and services for handicapped people of all ages (ed. T. Loach *et al.*). *The Disability Alliance* (1981)
Contains in the educational and training section information on grants and allowances for those staying on at school and financing further study.

Educational Charities: a guide to educational trust funds. *National Union of Students* (1979)
A selected list of the larger national and regional trusts offering grants and loans to students. Most of the trusts will consider applications from postgraduate students. Many do however have geographical conditions for eligibility as well as other sometimes strange conditions typical of many educational trust funds.

Educational Grants Advisory Service. Free leaflet explaining the work of the service

Fee Status and Award Eligibility. *United Kingdom Council for Overseas Student Affairs* (1985)
A guide to the current situation regarding fees, mandatory award and discretionary award regulations with notes on ordinary residence and retrospection. Intended for advisers of overseas students.

Financial Aid for First Degree Study at Commonwealth Universities. *Association of Commonwealth Universities (ACU)*
Published every three years most recent (publication 1986), contains details of about 100 scholarships, bursaries, grants, etc,

244

for Commonwealth students wishing to study for a first degree at a Commonwealth university outside their own country. Majority are for students from developing countries.

Financial Assistance for Disabled Students *(annual). National Bureau for Handicapped Students*
Contains a brief guide to the main sources of finance for disabled students for further or higher education.
Revised annually, single copies are available to disabled students from the National Bureau.

Grant-Awarding Bodies. *Open University Students Association* (1980)
Aimed specifically at those who have completed Open University degrees. Lists those charitable bodies and organisations whose terms of reference permit financial assistance to part-time students over the age of 21 who are prepared to consider applications from Open University students.
Copies available from OUSA at The Open University.

Grants and Awards: a guide for mature students and their advisers, Open University, North West Region (1982). *Open University*
Primarily a guide for mature students, contains information on local authority grants, and other awards available. Also has a useful section on references and vital addresses. Rather out of date now, but still useful. Obtainable free (as long as stocks last) from the OU, NW Region.

Grants Survey: a reference work for advisers (annual). *National Union of Students*
This is annually updated and includes details of the LEA Awards Regulations plus Regulations for Scotland and notes on Northern Ireland. Includes details of LEA's discretionary award policies and practices. A useful publication but the information can quickly become outdated.

Grants to Students (annual). *Inner London Education Authority.*
Free and published annually. It contains details and information on mandatory and discretionary awards available from the ILEA. Students should check to see if their local authority produces a similar publication.

Grants to Students: a brief guide. *Department of Education and Science*
A free booklet which is revised regularly containing basic information on mandatory and discretionary awards. Should

245

be read in conjunction with **Designated Awards** which is also free and revised regularly. Contains details of courses carrying mandatory awards. Available from: Room 2/11, Department of Education and Science, Elizabeth House, York Road, London SE1 7PH.

The Grants Register. *Macmillan*
Published every two years. It is aimed at people at or above graduate level, and those requiring further professional or advanced vocational training. It lists scholarships and fellowships from sources worldwide.

It has a subject index to the main alphabetical sequence as well as an index of awards and awarding bodies. Contains some indication of other sources. Includes information on exchange opportunities, grants for projects, competitions, professional and vocational awards, scholarships and special cases. The first stop for those searching for grants.

Guide to Student Allowances. *Scottish Education Department (SED)*
Available free from Scottish Education Department, Awards Branch.

Money Which?, Sept. 1982. A Guide to Student Finance (1982).

Music Competitions, Awards and Scholarships. *Arts Council*
Revised regularly, it contains details of awards available to music students. Available free from the Arts Council Shop.

NUS Welfare Manual. *National Union of Students (NUS)*
A number of the leaflets making up this manual relate to grants and financial matters.

Paid Educational Leave, Educational Leave, Grants and Awards (A Working Party Report). *Association for Recurrent Education (ARE)* (1979)
A report outlining the, then, present provision for training and education and grants and awards. It outlines the problems and makes recommendations including the establishment of minimum rights to education and training grants for the whole population.

Postgraduate Awards. *Department of Education and Science*
Revised regularly and available free from: Department of Education and Science, HFE3 (Awards 2, Government Buildings, Honeypot Lane, Stanmore Middlesex HA7 1AZ.)

246

Four titles available: (1) State bursaries for post-graduate study in the humanities; (2) State bursaries for post-graduate study in the sciences; (3) Information science studentship and fellowships; (4) Postgraduate awards for librarianship and information science.

Regulations Governing Postgraduate Awards. *Agricultural Research Council (ARC)*
Available free from the Agricultural Research Council.

Research Studentships and Advanced Course Studentships.
Medical Research Council
Available free from the Medical Research Council

Scholarships Abroad. *British Council*
Published annually, lists scholarships offered to British students by overseas governments and universities.

Scholarships Guide for Commonwealth Postgraduate Students 1985–6.
Gives information about international awards and country of tenure. Arranged by subject order within each country. Only postgraduate courses. Includes scholarships, grants, loans, etc.

Sponsorships Offered to Students by Employers and Professional Bodies for First Degrees, BTEC Higher Awards, or Comparable Courses Beginning in 1986 (annual). *Careers and Occupational Information Centre*
Published annually. Lists employers and professional bodies offering sponsorships and supplementary awards.
Intended mainly for school leavers, the amounts on offer vary and some kind of commitment to the industry or awarding body on completion of course is sometimes expected.

Sources of Funding for Retraining. *Sheffield Careers Service*

Studentship Handbook. *Economic and Social Research Council (ESRC)*
Available free from the Economic and Social Council. Intended for postgraduate students in the social sciences.

Studentships and Fellowships. *Science and Engineering Research Council (SERC)*
Available free from the Science and Engineering Research Council.

Study abroad. UNESCO

Published every two years and contains detailed information on awards for graduate and post-graduate study tenable in the majority of countries including the United Kingdom.

Training Awards. *Natural Environment Research Council (NERC)*
Available free from the Natural Environment Research Council.

Trusts and Foundations, Keeling, G W (1953). *Bowes & Bowes*
Although now dated, and addresses would need to be verified elsewhere, it would probably be worth consulting particularly for the subject index.

United Kingdom Engineering Awards. *The Fellowship of Engineering* (1983)
A comprehensive list of awards and grants available in the United Kingdom. Covers those from industry, institutions and the educational sector. Divided into two main sections: (1) General; (2) Education. Also has an index to both subjects and award titles.

Guidance and Counselling

Back to Work: a practical guide for women, Moulder, C and Sheldon, P (1979). *Kogan Page*
As the title suggests it's a guide for women intending to return to paid employment. Includes how to apply for jobs, qualifications, etc.

Bibliography of Educational Information, Advisory and Councelling Services for Adults (ed. H. Marks) (1970).
Gathers together brief details of publications on adult services and related research on developments on guidance, methods of teaching courses specifically for women, counselling and problems faced by mature students and adults being retrained in work situations.

Opportunities in the professions, industry, commerce and the public service. Careers guide (annual). *Careers and Occupational Information Centre*

Careers Information Booklets. *Association of Graduate Careers Advisory Services/Central Services Unit (AGCAS/CSU)*
These booklets cover a wide range of careers and are obtainable from the Central Services Unit.

Changing Your Job After 35 (5th edn), Golzen, Godfrey and Plumbley, Philip (1985). *Kogan Page*
Deals with ways of coping with job change and discusses ways of constructing a curriculum vitae, preparing for interviews, branching out with self employment, franchising and working abroad.

Concepts of Counselling, Vaughan, T (1976). *Bedford Square Press*

Counselling the adult learner in the Open University, Nicholson, N (1977). **Teaching at a Distance,** Mar. 1977 No. 8, pp. 62–9.

Counselling and Advisory Services – England and Wales Directory. *Standing Conference for the Advancement of Counselling (SCAC)* (1976)

Counselling for Special Groups, Williams, Lady, G (1969). *OECD Paris*
A report of a study in five countries, the Federal Republic of Germany, the Netherlands, Sweden, the UK and the USA, of experiments designed to test the value of special counselling techniques in assisting long-term unemployed and frequent job-changers to become more productive workers. The results were generally positive. Not specifically relevant to mature students.

Counselling for tutors in adult education, Goodman, S (1977). **Educ. and Trng, 19** No. 6. June 1977.
Describes a course for part-time adult education tutors developed to meet their need for help in their general counselling function with mature students in an FE college, some of the problems encountered and techniques adopted. Help with students' educational problems is included though main weight is given to their general personal problems.

Counselling in continuing education, Murgatroyd, S (1976). **Teaching at a Distance** No. 6, 1976, pp. 40–45.
This article considers the function of adult and continuing education in aiding personal growth as well as in the context of preparation for work and leisure. Helping others to learn about themselves is possible within situations specially set up for the purpose, such as T groups and other sensitivity training arrangements, but is also possible in teaching situations primarily concerned with other content. In Open University experience, the personal development of students has been assisted by the choice of study methods, by the physical conditions in group sessions, by the design of courses (e.g.

249

involving students in selection of options, and in discovering new learning skills) and through the use of feed-back from assessment which could take the form of tutor/student negotiations of acceptable grades for pieces of work.

Counselling in continuing education. Watkins, R (1976). **Teaching at a Distance** No. 6, 1976, pp. 35–9.
The article argues briefly the importance of a guidance and information service for the development of adult and continuing education. Such a service might properly be based on Local Development Councils for Adult Education, but it is important that the careers service should be closely associated with whatever facility is established, as requirements will sometimes be vocationally motivated and studies will commonly have some vocational significance.

Counselling In London. *London Voluntary Service Council* (1983)
A directory of counselling services for the London area. Has information on 130 agencies.

The counselling needs of mature students, Redmond, M A. *(Unpublished article, available from M A Redmond, Open University, Yorkshire Region)*

A counselling service as a growth centre, Thorne, D and Da Costa M (1974) **Counselling and Guidance, 2,** July 1974, pp. 211–17.
Describes the setting up, the scheme adopted, and some of the results of a Counselling Associates' Programme at the University of East Anglia. Potential associates join in a programme of five weekly sessions and a week-end held over a period of five weeks. At the time of writing, 100 persons recruited by advertisement from the university and outside had participated and in consequence developed a variety of helping and developmental roles. (Of possible interest in developing plans for volunteer participation in adult educational/ vocational guidance counselling.)

A counselling service for nurses in training, Gilbert, G (1976). **Guidance and Counselling** No. 4 July 1976, pp. 224–31.
Describes the setting up and operation from 1973 of a general counselling service in a London teaching hospital (Guy's). Primarily concerned with problems arising from the work situation and the personal problems of clients. The need for educational and occupational information, general as well as concerned with nursing, has been noted and met.

Counselling training for tutors in higher education, Ratigan, D (1977). **Br. J. Guidance and Counselling, 5**, No. 1, Jan. 1977, pp. 98–101.
Describes the organisation and content and comments on the success of a short course of eight sessions of 2½ hours designed to help teachers in institutions of further education to operate more effectively as personal tutors. The method adopted involved a number of practical exercises; for instance, in the development of empathy, the realisation of client problems and the need to develop study and social skills, etc. Use was made both of exercises and of video tapes in enabling participants to consider their own and their colleagues' efforts, thus taking in perspective the roles of experts and non-experts in human relationships and the counselling process. (Helpful towards planning short training courses for volunteer and part-time educational counsellors.)

Directory of Educational Guidance Services for Adults. Compiled by Linda Butler, *Educational Counselling and Credit Transfer Information Service (ECCTIS)* and *National Association of Educational Guidance Services for Adults (NAEGS)*
Updated periodically. Gives information about educational guidance services for adults in existence at the time of going to print.

Education and the aims of counselling, Vaughan, T (1975). *Basil Blackwell*
A review of guidance and counselling techniques and comparisons between the techniques used in various European countries. Contains a useful bibliography.

Education guidance for adults, Eagleson, D (1977). **Educ. and Trng, 19**, No. 8, Sept. 1977.
Dorothy Eagleson, who is the organiser of the Educational Guidance Service for Adults in Belfast, describes the role of the guidance service, and the enquiries dealt with.

Educational advice for adults, Brookfield, S **Educ. and Trng, 19** , No. 5 pp 137–139.
Steve Brookfield describes the educational advisory service at Malvern Hills College and discusses categories of mature student need.

Educational counselling of adults, Eagleson, D (1978). **Guidance and Counselling, 6** (2) July 1978, pp. 225–8.
Gives an account of the UNESCO symposium on counselling and reviews the Belfast Educational Guidance Service.

251

An educational counselling seminar for adults, Harding, C (1978). **Adult Educ. 50**, No. 5, Jan. 1978, pp. 305–8.
Describes a seminar held at the Rochdale College of Adult Education for adult students on GCE courses in Rochdale Technical College.

Educational Guidance: a new service for adult learners, Butler, Linda (ed.) (1983). *Open University, Yorkshire region*
Has chapters on planning a service, types of EGSA structure, securing funding, information, assessment, advice and counselling, implementation, outreach, training and record keeping.

Educational Information and Guidance for Adults, Mercer, R (ed.) (1981). *Sheffield City Polytechnic, Department of Education Management* (Sheffield Papers in Education Management No. 16)

Equal At Work? Women in Men's Jobs, Coote, Anna and Phillips, Angela (1979). *Collins*

Equal Opportunities: a careers guide for women and men, Miller, R 1984). *Penguin*
Includes checklists for grants, pay and prospects, etc. Has chapters on sex discrimination legislation, entrance qualifications, etc. Although about opportunities for all its emphasis is on the needs of women and returners.

Ethical Standards in Counselling, Blackham, H J (ed.) (1974). *Bedford Square Press*

Examination anxiety: what the student counsellor can do, Dryden, W (1978). **Br. J. Guidance and Counselling, G** (2) July 1978, p. 175–82.

Guidance and counselling: a select list of articles, Maguire, G. **Educ. Rev, 36** (3), pp. 321–23.

Guidance and Counselling Services for Adults in the U.K., Stock, A K (1977). (Learning Opportunities for Adults, Vol. 2, New structures and programmes). *OECD*
Gives a review of the then recent growth in counselling and guidance services in the United Kingdom.

Handbook of Counselling in Higher Education, Gallagher, P J and Demas, E (eds) (1983), *Praeger*

Links to Learning – A Report on Educational Information Advisory and Counselling Services for Adults. *Advisory Council for Adult and Continuing Education (ACACE)* (1979)

Describes the provision of counselling services and hoped for future developments as they stood in 1979. Now somewhat out-dated.

Nightline: a student self-help organisation. Thompson, D and Thompson, J. (1974). **Guidance and Counselling, 2**, No. 2, July 1974, pp. 200–11.
The text describes the organisation and functioning of a student counselling organisation established in 1971. Selection of student volunteers is based on discussion following the completion of two personality inventories, and preparation involves attendance at a series of lectures and discussions including some telephone techniques.

Peer Counselling and Self-help Groups on Campus, Austin, M J and Giddan, N S (1982). *Charles C Thomas*

Personal Counselling in the Open University. Watts, G. **Teaching at a Distance, 15** , pp. 21–6.
Notes that the boundary between academic and personal counselling is hard to establish and suggests that even academic counselling is unlikely to be taken up unless there has been personal contact with the academic involved. The article tries to air these points and to contribute to the ongoing discussion of personal and crisis counselling as exercised by the Open University.

Personal Tutoring in Higher Education, Bramley, W (1977). *Society for Research into Higher Education*
Although the article deals predominantly with the 17–25 years age group it includes some case studies dealing with mature students. It aims to assist those concerned in counselling students in higher education whether full or part time.

Register of Graduate Employment and Training (Roget) (annual). *Central Services Unit*
Lists 1,341 organisations and the recruitment and training practices they adopt. Chapters on 'Your final year programme', 'The chemistry of career choice', 'How relevant is your degree?' and 'If at first you don't succeed'.

Student Counselling in Practice, Newsome, A *et al.* (1973). *University of London Press*
Intended for both students of counselling and educational counsellors. A review of both counselling techniques and the role of counselling in the university. Includes examples of

techniques and case studies from Keele University, one of the first universities to establish a counselling service.

Theory and Practice of Vocational Guidance, Hopson, B and Hayes, J (1969). *Pergamon Press*

Training in Counselling: a directory. *British Association of Counselling* (1981)
A comprehensive directory of counselling courses available. It contains summaries of each course, and is therefore useful for course selection.

We'll all collaborate together when we go, Fothergill, R (1978) **Teaching at a Distance,** May 1978, 11, pp. 37–9.
Describes an Open University sponsored conference on the development of collaborative educational advisory services for adults. Emphasis on the role of the Open University in the development of local services.

What do graduates do? (annual), Association of Graduate Careers Advisory Services. *Hobson Press*
This annual publication provides information about the graduate labour market. The 1985 edition reports an encouraging improvement in graduate job prospects.

Study and examination skills

Brain Train: studying for success, Palmer, R and Pope, C (1984). *E & F N Spon*
A useful and sometimes irreverent approach to studying and its techniques. Aimed at all 'voluntary' students. Chapters on approaches and attitudes, skills and techniques, examinations. Sensible approach to studying, suitable for mature students returning to study after a gap.

The complete plain words, Gowers, E (revised by Fraser, B). (1977). *Penguin*

Effective Study, Ewing, J M (1977). *Dundee College of Education*

Encouraging Effective Learning – An approach to Study Counselling, Main, A (1980). *Scottish Academic Press*

A Guide to Study. Baker, E (1980). *British Association for Commercial and Industrial Education*

How To Pass Examinations, Kemble, B. *Orbach & Chambers*

How To Pass Examinations, Erasmus, J (1979). *Oriel Press*

How To Prepare For Examinations, Nixon, D. *Harrop*

How To Study, Bowles, J H. Available from the author, Bagmere Bank Cottage, Brereton, Sandbach, Cheshire.

How To Study, Maddox, H (1967). *Pan Books*

How To Study Effectively, Parsons, C J (1976). *Arrow Books*

Learn How To Study, Rowntree, D (1976). *MacDonald & Co.*

Passing Examinations, Allen, C (1966). *Pan Books*

Preparing To Study, The Open University. *Open University Press*

The Road To Effective Reading, Latham, W (ed.) (1975). *Ward Lock*

Student Note-Taking as an Aid To Learning, Howe, M J A and Godfrey, J (1977). *Exeter University Teaching Services*

A Student's Guide To Effective Study. James, D E (1967). *Pergamon*

Study: a guide for effective study revision and examination techniques, Barras, R (1984). *Chapman & Hall*
A useful guide on study and examination techniques, also includes chapters on 'Looking after yourself', 'Friendship', 'Making good use of your time'. These supplement information on making good lecture notes, expressing yourself and preparing for and taking examinations. Useful for mature students as well as 'normal' undergraduates.

Study Hints for Students, Whyman, J and Farnell, P G (1976). *University of Kent*

Study skills sessions with mature students or can wastage rates be wasted by wasting time, Clinton, M (1983). **Bull. Educ. Dev. Res.,** No. 26, Summer 1983, pp. 13–18.
Case study of the effects of study skill sessions and their possible relationship to wastage rates from part-time degree course in Health Studies. Concludes that study skill sessions may help students to learn effectively and secondly may 'promote feelings of solidarity'. It is thought that the second may be as beneficial as the first.

Study Skills: A Students' guide for survival, Carman, R (1976). *Wiley.*

Teaching mature students to study, Rickwood, P. **Adult Educ., 54** (1), pp. 6–11.

255

Discusses the benefits of teaching mature students about to enter continuing education the study skills that they may lack. The article covers some of the theoretical points involved and describes one approach that has been used with mixed ability students.

Teaching Students To Learn – A Student-centred Approach, Gibbs, G (1981). *Open University Press*

Use Your Head, Buzan, T (1974). *BBC*
Although prepared initially to be used in conjunction with a series of BBC television programmes it can be used independently. Contains useful suggestions for making studying more effective.

Writing Research Papers, Bailey, E P (1981). *R & W Molt*

Writing the Research Paper, Winkler, A C and McCuen, J R (1979). *New York: Harcourt Brace*

PART FOUR

Appendices

Universities

University of Aberdeen,
Aberdeen AB9 1FX (Tel. 0224
40241)

**University of Aston in
Birmingham,** Gosta Green,
Birmingham B4 7ET (Tel. 021
359 3611)

University of Bath, Claverton
Down, Bath BA2 7AY (Tel. 0225
61244)

Queen's University of Belfast,
Belfast, N. Ireland BT7 1NN (Tel.
0232 245133)

University of Birmingham, PO
Box 363, Birmingham B15 2TT
(Tel. 021 472 1301)

University of Bradford,
Bradford, West Yorkshire BD7
1DP (Tel. 0274 733466)

University of Bristol, Senate
House, Bristol BS8 1TH (Tel.
0272 24161)

Brunel University, Uxbridge,
Middlesex UB8 3PH (Tel. 0895
37188)

The University of Buckingham,
Hunter Street, Buckingham MK18
1EG (Tel. 0280 814080)

University of Cambridge,
University Registry, The Old
Schools, Cambridge CB2 1TN
(Tel. 0223 358933)

City University, Northampton
Square, London EC1V 0HB (Tel.
01 253 4399)

**Cranfield Institute of
Technology,** Cranfield, Bedford
MK43 0AL (Tel. 0234 750111)

University of Dundee, Dundee
DD1 4HN (Tel. 0382 23181)

University of Durham, Old Shire
Hall, Durham DH1 3HP (Tel. 0385
64466)

University of East Anglia,
Norwich NR4 7TJ (Tel. 0603
56161)

University of Edinburgh,
Old College, South Bridge,
Edinburgh EH8 9YL (Tel. 031 667
1011)

University of Essex, Wivenhoe Park, Colchester CO4 3SQ (Tel. 0206 862286)

University of Exeter, Admissions Office, Northcote House, The Queen's Drive, Exeter EX4 4QJ (Tel. 0392 77911)

University of Glasgow, Glasgow G12 8QQ (Tel. 041 339 8855)

Heriot-Watt University, Chambers Street, Edinburgh EH1 1HX (Tel. 031 225 8432)

University of Hull, Hull HU6 7RX (Tel. 0482 46311)

University of Keele, Keele, Staffordshire ST5 5BG (Tel. 0782 621111)

University of Kent at Canterbury, Canterbury, Kent CT2 7NZ (Tel. 0227 66822)

University of Lancaster, University House, Lancaster LA1 4YW (Tel. 0524 65201)

University of Leeds, Leeds LS2 9JT (Tel. 0532 431751)

University of Leicester, University Road, Leicester LE1 7RH (Tel. 0533 554455)

University of Liverpool, PO Box 147, Liverpool L69 3BX (Tel. 051 709 6022)

University of London, Senate House, London WC1E 7HU (Tel. 01 636 8000)

Loughborough University of Technology, Loughborough, Leicestershire LE11 3TU (Tel. 0509 263171)

University of Manchester, Oxford Road, Manchester M13 9PL (Tel. 061 273 3333)

University of Manchester Institute of Science and Technology (UMIST), PO Box 88, Sackville Street, Manchester M60 1QD (Tel. 061 236 3311)

University of Newcastle upon Tyne, 6 Kensington Terrace, Newcastle upon Tyne, NE1 7RU (Tel. 0632 328511)

University of Nottingham, University Park, Nottingham NG7 2RD (Tel. 0602 506101)

The Open University, Walton Hall, Milton Keynes MK7 6AA (Tel. 0908 74066)

University of Oxford, University Offices, Wellington Square, Oxford OX1 2JD (Tel. 0865 56747)

University of Reading, Whiteknights, Reading RG6 2AH (Tel. 0734 875123)

Royal College of Art, Kensington Gore, London SW7 2EU (Tel. 01 584 5020)

University of St Andrews, College Gate, St Andrews KY16 9AJ (Tel. 0334 76161)

University of Salford, Salford M5 4WT (Tel. 061 736 5843)

University of Sheffield, Western Bank, Sheffield S10 2TN (Tel. 0742 78555)

University of Southampton, Highfield, Southampton SO9 5NH (Tel. 0703 559122)

University of Stirling, Stirling FK9 4LA (Tel. 0786 73171)

University of Strathclyde, George Street, Glasgow G1 1XW (Tel. 041 552 4400)

University of Surrey, Guildford, Surrey GU2 5XH (Tel. 0483 571281)

260

University of Sussex, Sussex House, Falmer, Brighton BN1 9RH (Tel. 0273 606755)

University of Ulster, University House, Cromure Road, Coleraine, Co. Londonderry, N. Ireland BT52 1SA (Tel. 0265 4141)

University of Warwick, Coventry CV4 7AL (Tel. 0203 24011)

University of York, Heslington, York YO1 5DD (Tel. 0904 59861)

University addresses in Wales

University of Wales, Cathays Park, Cardiff CF1 3NS (Tel. 0222 382656)

University College of Wales, Old College, King Street, Aberystwyth, Dyfed SY23 2AX (Tel. 0970 3177)

University College of North Wales, Bangor, Gwynedd LL57 2DG (Tel. 0248 351151)

University College, PO Box 78, Cardiff CF1 1XL (Tel. 0222 44211)

University College of Swansea, Singleton Park, Swansea SA2 8PP (Tel. 0792 205678)

University of Wales Institute of Science and Technology (UWIST), PO Box 68, Cardiff CF1 3XA (Tel. 0222 42588)

St David's University College, Lampeter, Dyfed SA48 7ED (Tel. 0570 422351)

London University non-medical constituent schools and institutes

Birkbeck College, Malet Street, WC1E 7HX (Tel. 01 831 6222)

Imperial College of Science and Technology, South Kensington, SW7 2AZ (Tel. 01 589 5111)

King's College London (incorporating King's College, Queen Elizabeth College and Chelsea College), Strand, WC2R 2LS (Tel. 01 836 5454)

Chelsea Campus: 552 King's Road, SW10 0UA (Tel. 01 351 2488)

Kensington Campus: Campden Hill Road, Kensington W8 7AH (Tel. 01 937 5411)

London School of Economics and Political Science, Houghton Street, WC2A 2AE (Tel. 01 405 7686)

Queen Mary College (in association with Westfield College), Mile End Road, E1 4NS (Tel. 01 980 4811)

Royal Holloway and Bedford New College, Egham Hill, Egham, Surrey TW20 0EX (Tel. 0784 34455)

Royal Veterinary College, Royal College Street, NW1 0TU (Tel. 01 387 2898)

School of Oriental and African Studies, Malet Street, WC11 7HP (Tel. 01 637 2388)

School of Pharmacy, 29–39 Brunswick Square, WC1N 1AX (Tel. 01 837 7651)

University College London, Gower Street, WC1E 6BT (Tel. 01 387 7050)

Westfield College, Kidderpore Avenue, Hampstead NW3 7ST (Tel. 01 435 7141)

Wye College, Wye, Ashford, Kent TN25 5AH. (Tel. 0233 812401)

Other institutions in London University

Heythrop College, 11–13 Cavendish Square, W1M 0AN (01 580 6941)

British Institute in Paris. *London*: 15 Woburn Square, WC1H 0NS (Tel. 01 636 8000) *Paris*: 11 rue de Constantine, 75007 Paris

Courtauld Institute of Art, 20 Portman Square, W1H 0BE (Tel. 01 935 9292–5; 01 486 5913–4)

Institute of Advanced Legal Studies, 17 Russell Square, WC1B 5DR (Tel. 01 637 1731)

Institute of Archaeology, 31–34 Gordon Square, WC1H 0PY (Tel. 01 387 6052)

Institute of Classical Studies, 31–34 Gordon Square, WC1H 0PY (Tel. 01 387 7696–7)

Institute of Commonwealth Studies, 27–28 Russell Square, WC1B 5DS (Tel. 01 580 5876)

Institute of Education, 20 Bedford Way, WC1H 0AL (Tel. 01 636 1500; *Library*: 01 637 0846)

Institute of Germanic Studies, 29 Russell Square, WC1B 5DP (Tel. 01 580 2711; 01 580 3480)

Institute of Historical Research, Senate House, Malet Street, WC1E 7HU (Tel. 01 636 0272–3)

Institute of Latin American Studies, 31 Tavistock Square, WC1H 9HA (Tel. 01 387 5671; *Library:* 01 387 4055)

Institute of United States Studies, 31 Tavistock Square, WC1H 9EZ (Tel. 01 387 5534)

School of Slavonic and East European Studies, Senate House, Malet Street, WC1E 7HU (Tel. 01 637 4934–9)

Warburg Institute, Woburn Square, WC1H 0AB (Tel. 01 580 9663)

Goldsmith's College, Lewisham Way, New Cross, SE14 6NW (Tel. 01 692 7171)

Jews' College, 44A Albert Road, NW4 2SJ (Tel. 01 203 6427/8/9/0)

London Graduate School of Business Studies, Sussex Place, Regent's Park, NW1 4SA (Tel. 01 262 5050)

Royal Academy of Music, Marylebone Road, NW1 5HT (Tel. 01 935 5461)

Royal College of Music, Prince Consort Road, SW7 2BS (Tel. 01 589 3643)

Trinity College of Music, Mandeville Place, W1M 6AQ (Tel. 01 935 5773)

Appendix 1.2

The Open University –
Regional Centres

Headquarters: Walton Hall, Milton Keynes MK7 6AA (0908 74066)

Regional Centres:

Region 01 London, The Open University, London Region, Parsifal College, 527 Finchley Road, LONDON NW3 7BG (Tel. 01 794 0575)
Area covered: Greater London

Region 02 South, The Open University, Southern Region, Foxcombe Hall, Boars Hill, OXFORD OX1 5HR (Tel. 0865 730731)
Area covered: Berkshire, Buckinghamshire, Channel Islands, Dorset, Hampshire, Isle of Wight, Oxfordshire, part of Wiltshire

The sub-office in Winchester may also be contacted for advice and information:
The Open University, Medecroft, Sparkford Road, Winchester, SO22 4NJ (Tel. 0962 67969)

Region 03 South West, The Open University, South West Region, 41 Broad Street, BRISTOL BS1 2EP (Tel. 0272 299641)
Area Covered: Avon, Cornwall, Devon, Gloucestershire, Somerset, Scilly Isles, most of Wiltshire

The sub-office in Plymouth may also be contacted for advice and information:
59 Southside Street, The Barbican, Plymouth PL1 2LA (Tel. 0752 28321)

Region 04 West Midlands, The Open University, West Midlands Region, 66 High Street, Harborne, BIRMINGHAM B17 9NB (Tel. 021 426 1661)
Area covered: Hereford and Worcester, Shropshire, most of Staffordshire, Warwickshire, West Midlands

Region 05 East Midlands, The Open University, East Midlands Region, The Octagon, 143 Derby Road, NOTTINGHAM NG7 1PH (Tel. 0602 473072)

Area covered: Most of Derbyshire, Leicestershire, Lincolnshire, Northamptonshire, Nottinghamshire, South Humberside, part of Staffordshire (Burton-on-Trent)

Region 06 East Anglia, The Open University, East Anglian Region, Cintra House, 12 Hills Road, CAMBRIDGE CB2 1PF (Tel. 0223 64721)
Area covered: Bedfordshire, Cambridgeshire, Essex, Hertfordshire, Norfolk, Suffolk

Region 07 Yorkshire, The Open University, Yorkshire Region, Fairfax House, Merrion Street, LEEDS LS2 8JU (Tel. 0532 444431)
Area covered: North Humberside, North Yorkshire, South Yorkshire, West Yorkshire

Region 08 North West, The Open University, North Western Region, Chorlton House, 70 Manchester Road, Chorlton-cum-Hardy, MANCHESTER M21 1PQ (Tel. 061 861 9823)
Area Covered: Cheshire, part of Derbyshire (High Peak area), Isle of Man, Lancashire, Greater Manchester, Merseyside

Region 09 North, The Open University, North Region, Eldon House, Regent Centre, Gosforth, NEWCASTLE UPON TYNE NE3 3PW (Tel. 091 284 1611)
Area covered: Cleveland, Cumbria, Durham, Northumberland, Tyne and Wear

The regional sub-offices may also be contacted for local advice and information. They are:
Cumbria: 2 Sandgate, PENRITH CA11 7LX (Tel. 0768 64720)
Cleveland: 37 Harrow Road, MIDDLESBROUGH TS5 5NT (Tel. 0642 816227)

Region 10 Wales, The Open University in Wales, 24 Cathedral Road, CARDIFF CF1 9SA (Tel. 0222 397911)
Area covered: Wales

Region 11 Scotland, The Open University in Scotland, 60 Melville Street, EDINBURGH EH3 7HF (Tel. 031 226 3851)
Area covered: Scotland

The sub-office in Glasgow may also be contacted for advice and information:
2 Park Gardens, Glasgow G3 7XE (Tel. 041 332 4364)

Region 12 Northern Ireland, The Open University in Northern Ireland, 40 University Road, BELFAST BT7 1SU (Tel. 0232 245025)
Area covered: Northern Ireland

Region 13 South East, The Open University, South East Region, Wyvern House, 230/232 London Road, EAST GRINSTEAD RH19 ILA (Tel. 0342 27821)

Answering service: (Tel. 0342 26509)
Area Covered: Kent, Surrey, East Sussex, West Sussex

Appendix 2

Polytechnics

City of Birmingham Polytechnic, Franchise Street, Perry Parr, Birmingham B42 2SU (Tel. 021 356 6911)

Brighton Polytechnic, Lewes Rd, Moulsecoomb, Brighton BN2 4AT (Tel. 0273 693655)

Bristol Polytechnic, Coldharbour Lane, Frenchay, Bristol BS16 1QY (Tel. 0272 656261)

Coventry (Lanchester) Polytechnic, Priory Street, Coventry CV1 5FB (Tel. 0203 24166)

The Hatfield Polytechnic, P.O. Box 109, College Lane, Hatfield, Herts AL10 9AB (Tel. 07072 79000)

The Polytechnic, Queensgate, Huddersfield HD1 3DH (Tel. 0484 22288)

Kingston Polytechnic, Penrhyn Road, Kingston-upon-Thames, Surrey KT1 2EE (Tel. 01 549 1366)

Lancashire Polytechnic, Preston, Lancs PR2 2TQ (Tel. 0772 22141)

Leeds Polytechnic, Calverley Street, Leeds LS1 3HE (Tel. 0532 462329)

Leicester Polytechnic, P.O. Box 143, Leicester LE1 9BH (Tel. 0533 551551)

Liverpool Polytechnic, Rodney House, 70 Mount Pleasant, Liverpool L3 5UX (Tel. 051 207 3581)

London Polytechnics

The Polytechnic of Central London, 309 Regent Street, London, W1R 8AL (Tel. 01 580 2020)

City of London Polytechnic, 177 Houndsditch, London EC3A 7BU (Tel. 01 283 1030)

Middlesex Polytechnic, The Admissions Office, 114 Chase Side, Southgate, London N14 5PN (Tel. 01 886 6599)

The Polytechnic of North London, Holloway Road, London N7 8DB (Tel. 01 607 2789)

265

North East London Polytechnic, Longbridge Road, Dagenham, Essex, RM8 2AS (Tel. 01 590 7722)

Polytechnic of the South Bank, Borough Road, London SE1 0AA (Tel. 01–928 8989)

Thames Polytechnic, Wellington Street, Woolwich, London SE18 6PF (Tel. 01 854 2030)

Manchester Polytechnic, All Saints, Manchester M15 6BH (Tel. 061 228 6171)

Newcastle upon Tyne Polytechnic, Ellison Building, Ellison Place, Newcastle upon Tyne NE1 8ST (Tel. 0632 326002)

North Staffordshire Polytechnic, College Road, Stoke-on-Trent ST4 2DE (Tel. 0782 45531)

Oxford Polytechnic, Headington, Oxford OX3 0BP (Tel. 0865 64777)

Plymouth Polytechnic, Drake Circus, Plymouth PL4 8AA (Tel. 0752 21312

Portsmouth Polytechnic, Alexandra House, Museum Road, Portsmouth, PO1 2QQ (Tel. 0705 827681)

Sheffield City Polytechnic, Pond Street, Sheffield S1 1WB (Tel. 0742 20911)

Sunderland Polytechnic, Langham Tower, Ryhope Road, Sunderland SR2 7EE (Tel. 0783 76231)

Teesside Polytechnic, Borough Road, Middlesborough, Cleveland TS1 2BA (Tel. 0642 218121)

Trent Polytechnic, Burton Street, Nottingham NG1 4BU (Tel. 0602 418248)

The Polytechnic of Wales, Llantwit Road, Treforest, Pontypridd, Mid-Glamorgan CF37 1DL (Tel. 0443 405133)

The Polytechnic, Wolverhampton, The Molineux, Molineux Street, Wolverhampton, WV1 1SB (Tel: 0902 710654)

266

Colleges of Education and Colleges/Institutes of Higher Education

Aberdeen College of Education, Hilton Place, Aberdeen AB9 1FA (Tel. 0224 42341)

Avery Hill College, Bexley Road, Eltham, London SE9 2PQ (Tel. 01 850 0081)

Bath College of Higher Education, Newton Park, Bath BA2 9BN (Tel. 02217 3701)

Bedford College of Higher Education, 37 Lansdowne Road, Bedford (Tel. 0234 51966)

Bishop Grosseteste College, Newport, Lincoln LN1 3DY (Tel. 0522 27347)

Bolton Institute of Higher Education, Deane Road, Bolton BL3 5AB (Tel. 0204 28851)

Bradford and Ilkley Community College, Great Horton Road, Bradford BD7 1AY (Tel. 0274 753111)

Bretton Hall College of Higher Education, West Bretton, Wakefield WF4 4LG (Tel. 092 485 261)

Buckinghamshire College of Higher Education, Queen Alexandra Road, High Wycombe HP11 2JZ (Tel. 0494 22141/7)

Bulmershe College of Higher Education, Woodlands Avenue, Earley, Reading RG6 1HY (Tel. 0734 663387)

Camborne School of Mines, Trevenson, Pool near Redruth, Cornwall (Tel. 0209 714866)

Cambridgeshire College of Arts and Technology, East Road, Cambridge CB1 1PT (Tel. 0223 63271)

Canterbury College of Arts, New Dover Road, Canterbury CT1 3AN (Tel. 0277 69371)

Christ Church College Canterbury, North Holmes Road, Canterbury CT1 1QU (Tel. 0227 65548)

Charlotte Mason College of Education, Ambleside, Cumbria LA22 9BB (Tel. 096 63 3066)

Chelmer Institute of Higher Education, Victoria Road South, Chelmsford CM1 1LL (Tel. 0245 354491)

Chester College, Cheyney Road, Chester CH1 4BJ (Tel. 0244 375444)

The College of Ripon and York St John, The College, Lord Mayor's Walk, York YO3 7EX (Tel. 0904 56771)

College of St Mark and St John, Derriford Road, Plymouth PL6 8BH (Tel. 0752 777188)

College of St Paul and St Mary, The Park, Cheltenham GL50 2RH (Tel. 0242 513836)

Craigie College of Education, Ayr KA8 0SR (Tel. 0292 260321)

Crewe and Alsager College of Higher Education, Crewe Road, Crewe CW1 1DU (Tel. 0270 583661)

Colchester Institute, Sheepen Road, Colchester CO3 3LL (Tel. 0206 570271)

De la Salle College of Higher Education, Hopwood Hall, Middleton, Manchester M24 3XH (Tel. 061 643 5331)

Derbyshire College of Higher Education, Kedleston Road, Derby DE3 1GB (Tel. 0332 47181)

Dorset Institute of Higher Education, Wallisdown Road, Poole BH12 5BB (Tel. 0202 524111)

Duncan of Jordanstone College of Art, Perth Road, Dundee DD1 4HT (Tel. 0382 23261)

Dundee College of Education, Gardyne Road, Broughty Ferry DD5 1NY (Tel. 0382 453433)

Dundee College of Technology, Bell Street, Dundee DD1 1HG (Tel. 0382 27225)

Dunfermline College of Physical Education, Cramond Road North, Edinburgh EH4 6JD (Tel. 031 336 6001)

Ealing College of Higher Education, St Mary's Road, Ealing, London W5 5RF (Tel. 01 579 4111)

Edinburgh College of Art, Lauriston Place, Edinburgh EH3 9DF (Tel. 031 229 9311)

Edge Hill College of Higher Education, St Helen's Road, Ormskirk L39 4QP (Tel. 0695 75171)

Essex Institute of Higher Education, Victoria Road South, Chelmsford, Essex CM1 1LL (Tel. 0245 354491)

Glasgow College of Technology, Cowcaddens Road, Glasgow G4 0BA (Tel. 041 332 7090)

Gloucestershire College of Arts and Technology, Oxstalls Campus, Gloucester (Tel. 0242 26321)

Gwent College of Higher Education, College Crescent, Caerleon, Newport NP6 1XJ (Tel. 0633 421292)

Harrow College of Higher Education, Northwick Park, Harrow, HA1 3TP (Tel. 09276 2511)

Hertfordshire College of Higher Education, Wall Hall, Aldenham, Watford WD2 8AT (Tel. 09276 2511)

Homerton College, Hills Road, Cambridge CB2 2PH (Tel. 0223 245931)

268

Humberside College of Higher Education, Cottingham Road, Hull HU6 7RT (Tel. 0482 41451)

Jordanhill College of Education, Southbrae Drive, Glasgow G13 1PP (Tel. 041 959 1232)

King Alfred's College of Higher Education, Sparkford Road, Winchester SO22 4NR (Tel. 0962 62281)

La Sainte Union College of Higher Education, The Avenue, Southampton SO9 5HB (Tel. 0703 228761)

Liverpool Institute of Higher Education, Woolton Road, Liverpool L16 8ND (Tel. 051 722 7331)

Liverpool Polytechnic, C.F. Mott Campus, Liverpool Road, Prescot L34 1NP (Tel. 051 489 6201)

Luton College of Higher Education, Park Square, Luton LU1 3JU (Tel. 0582 34111)

Moray House College of Education, Holyrood Road, Edinburgh EH8 8AQ (Tel. 031 556 8455)

Napier College, Admissions Section, Craig Lockhard Site, 219 Colinton Road, Edinburgh EH14 1DJ (Tel. 031 447 7070, Ext. 246)

Nene College, Moulton Park, Northampton NN2 7AL (Tel. 0604 715000)

New College, Framwell Gate Moor Centre, Durham DH1 5ES (Tel. 0385 62421)

Newman College, Genners Lane, Bartley Green, Birmingham B32 3BT (Tel. 021 476 1181)

Nonington College, Nonington, Dover CT15 4HH (Tel. 0304 840671)

North Cheshire College, Padgate Campus, Fearnhead, Warrington WA2 0DB (Tel. 0925 814343)

North East Wales Institute of Higher Education, Aston College, Mold Road, Wrexham (Tel. 0978 56601)

North Riding College of Education, Filey Road, Scarborough YO11 3AZ (Tel. 0723 362392)

Paisley College of Technology, High Street, Paisley PA1 2BE (Tel. 041 887 1241)

The Queen's College Glasgow, 1 Park Drive, Glasgow G3 6LP (Tel. 041 334 8141)

Robert Gordons Institute of Technology, Schoolhill, Aberdeen AB9 1FR (Tel. 0224 633611)

Roehampton Institute of Higher Education, Roehampton Lane, London SW15 5PJ (Tel. 01 878 5751)

Rolle College, Exmouth EX8 2AT (Tel. 0395 265344)

Royal Scottish Academy of Music and Drama, St George's Place, Glasgow G2 1BS (Tel. 041 332 4101)

Slough College of Higher Education, Wellington Street, Slough, Berkshire SL1 1YG (Tel. 0753 34585)

St Andrews College of Education, Bearsden, Glasgow G61 4QA (Tel. 041 943 1424)

St Martin's College of Education, Bowerham, Lancaster LA1 3JD (Tel. 0524 63446)

St Mary's College, 191 Falls Road, Belfast BT12 6FE (Tel. 0232 227678)

269

St Mary's College, Strawberry Hill, Twickenham, Middlesex TW1 4SX (Tel. 01 892 0051)

South Glamorgan Institute of Higher Education, Cyncoed Road, Cyncoed, Cardiff CF2 6XD (Tel. 0222 755755)

Southampton Institute of Higher Education, East Park Terrace, Southampton SO9 4WW (Tel. 0703 29381)

Stranmillis College, Stranmillis Road, Belfast BT9 5DY (Tel. 0232 665271)

Trinity and All Saints' College, Brownberrie Lane, Horsforth, Leeds LS18 5HD (Tel. 0532 584341)

Trinity College, Carmarthen, Dyfed SA31 3EP (Tel. 0267 237971/2/3)

West Glamorgan Institute of Higher Education, Townhill Road, Townhill, Swansea SA2 0UT (Tel. 0792 203482)

Westhill College, Wesley Park Road, Selly Oak, Birmingham, B29 6LL (Tel. 021 472 7245/8)

West London Institute of Higher Education, Gordon House, St Margaret's Road, Twickenham TW1 1PT (Tel. 01 891 0121)

West Midlands College of Higher Education, Gorway Road, Walsall WS1 3BD (Tel. 0922 29141)

Westminster College, Oxford, North Hinskey, Oxford OX2 9AT (Tel. 0865 247644)

West Sussex Institute of Higher Education, The Dome, Upper Bognor Road, Bognor Regis, West Sussex PO21 1HR (Tel. 0243 865581)

Worcester College of Higher Education, Henwick Grove, Worcester WR2 6AJ (Tel. 0905 428080)

Appendix 4

Colleges of Education (Technical)

Bolton College of Education (Technical), Bolton Institute of Higher Education, Chadwick Street, Bolton, Lancashire BL2 1JW (Tel. 0204 22132)

Garnett College, Downshire House, Roehampton Lane, London SW15 4HR (Tel. 01 789 6533)

Huddersfield Polytechnic (formerly Huddersfield College of Education (Technical)), Holly Bank Campus, Lindley, Huddersfield HD3 3BP (Tel. 0484 25611)

Wolverhampton Polytechnic (incorporating Wolverhampton Technical Teachers' College, Dudley College of Education and Wolverhampton Teachers' College for Day Students), Castle View, Dudley DY1 3HR (Tel. 0902 710654)

271

The Scottish Central Institutions

Duncan of Jordanstone College of Art, Perth Road, DUNDEE DD1 4HT (Tel. 0382 23261)

Dundee College of Technology, Bell Street, DUNDEE DD1 1HG (Tel. 0382 27225)

East of Scotland College of Agriculture, West Mains Road, EDINBURGH EH9 3JG (Tel. 031 667 1041)

Edinburgh College of Art, Lauriston Place, EDINBURGH EH3 9DF (Tel. 031 229 9311, Ext. 235)

Glasgow College of Technology, 70 Cowcaddens Road, Glasgow G4 0BA (Tel. 041 332 7090)

Glasgow School of Art, 167 Renfrew Street, GLASGOW G3 6RQ (Tel. 041 332 9797)

The Queen's College, Glasgow, 1 Park Drive, GLASGOW G3 6LP (Tel. 041 334 8141)

Leith Nautical College, 24 Milton Road East, EDINBURGH EH15 2PP (Tel. 031 669 8461)

Napier College of Commerce and Technology, Craig Lockhard Site, 219 Colinton Road, Edinburgh EH14 1DJ (Tel. 031 447 7070)

North of Scotland College of Agriculture, 581 King Street, ABERDEEN AB9 1UD (Tel. 0224 40291)

Paisley College of Technology, High Street, PAISLEY PA1 2BE (Tel. 041 887 1241)

Queen Margaret College, Clerwood Terrace, EDINBURGH EH12 8TS (Tel. 031 339 8111)

Robert Gordon's Institute of Technology, Schoolhill, ABERDEEN AB9 1FR (Tel. 0224 633611)

Royal Scottish Academy of Music and Drama, St George's Place, GLASGOW G2 1BS (Tel. 041 332 4101 (Music and General) Tel. 041 332 5294 (Drama)

Scottish College of Textiles, Netherdale, GALASHIELS TD1 3HF (Tel. 0896 3351)

The West of Scotland Agricultural College, Auchincruive, AYR KA6 5HW (Tel. 0292 520331)

Colleges of Art and Design

Bath College of Higher Education, Incorporating Bath Academy of Art, Corsham, Wiltshire SN13 0DB (Tel. 0249 712571)

City of Birmingham Polytechnic, Art and Design Centre, Corporation Street, Birmingham B4 7DX (Tel. 021 359 6721)

Bradford College, Great Horton Road, Bradford BD7 1AY (Tel. 0274 734844)

Brighton Polytechnic, Faculty of Art and Design, Grand Parade, Brighton BN2 2JY (Tel. 0273 604141)

Bristol Polytechnic, Faculty of Art and Design, Clanage Road, Bower Ashton, Bristol BS3 2JU (Tel. 0272 660222)

Buckinghamshire College of Higher Education, Queen Alexandra Road, High Wycombe, Buckinghamshire HP11 2JZ (Tel. 0494 22141)

Camberwell School of Art and Crafts, Peckham Road, London SE5 8UF (Tel. 01 703 0987)

Canterbury College of Art, New Dover Road, Canterbury, Kent (Tel. 0227 69371)

Central School of Art and Design, Southampton Row, London WC1B 4AP (Tel. 01 405 1825)

Chelsea School of Art, Manresa Road, London SW3 6LS (Tel. 01 351 3844)

Cornwall College of Further and Higher Education, Redruth, Cornwall TR15 3RD (Tel. 0209 721911)

Coventry (Lanchester) Polytechnic, Registrar and Secretary (Admissions), Priory Street, Coventry CV1 5FB (Tel. 0203 24166)

Crewe & Alsager College of Higher Education, Crewe Road, Crewe, Cheshire CW1 1DU (Tel. 0270 583 661)

Derbyshire College of Higher Education, Kedleston Road, Derby DE3 1GB (Tel. 0332 47181)

Exeter College of Art and Design, Earl Richards Road North, Exeter, Devon EX2 6AS (Tel. 0392 5 3530)

Falmouth School of Art, Woodland, Falmouth, Cornwall TR11 4RA (Tel. 0326 313269)

Gloucestershire College of Art and Technology, Pitville Campus, Cheltenham, Gloucestershire GL52 3DG (Tel. 0242 32501)

Goldsmiths' College, School of Art and Design, New Cross, London SE14 6NW (Tel. 01 692 7171)

Gwent College of Higher Education, Faculty of Art and Design, Clarence Place, Newport, Gwent NPT 0UW (Tel. 0633 59984)

Harrow College of Higher Education (in association with the Polytechnic of Central London), Northwick Park, Harrow, Middlesex HA1 3TP (Tel. 01 864 5422)

Huddersfield Polytechnic, Queensgate, Huddersfield HD1 3DH (Tel. 0484 22288)

Humberside College of Higher Education, Queen's Gardens, Hull HU1 3DH (Tel. 0482 224121)

Kidderminster College of Further Education, Hoo Road, Kidderminster, Worcs. DY10 1LX (Tel. 0562 66311)

Kingston Polytechnic, Knights Park, Kingston on Thames, Surrey KT1 2QJ (Tel. 01 549 6151)

Lancashire Polytechnic, Faculty of Art and Design, Preston PR1 2TQ (Tel. 0772 22141)

Leeds Polytechnic, Faculty of Art and Design, Calverley Street, Leeds LS1 3HE (Tel. 0532 462903)

Leicester Polytechnic, P.O. Box 143, Leicester LE1 9BH (Tel. 0533 551551)

Liverpool Polytechnic, Faculty of Art and Design, Hope Street, Liverpool L1 9EB (Tel. 051 709 9711)

City of London Polytechnic, 31 Jewry Street, London EC3N 2EY (Tel. 01 283 1030)

London College of Printing, Elephant and Castle, London SE1 6SB (Tel. 01 735 8484)

Loughborough College of Art and Design, Radmoor, Loughborough, Leicestershire LE11 3BT (Tel. 0509 261515)

Maidstone College of Art, Oakwood Park, Oakwood Road, Maidstone, Kent (Tel. 0622 57286/9)

Manchester Polytechnic, Faculty of Art and Design, Grosvenor Building, Cavendish Street, All Saints, Manchester M15 6BH (Tel. 061 228 6171)

Middlesex Polytechnic, Faculty of Art and Design, Cat Hill, Cockfosters, East Barnet, Hertfordshire EN4 8HU (Tel. 01 440 5181)

Newcastle upon Tyne Polytechnic, Faculty of Art and Design, Squires Building, Sandyford Road, Newcastle upon Tyne NE1 8ST (Tel. 0632 326002)

North East London Polytechnic, Faculty of Art and Design, Greengate House, Greengate Street, London E13 0BG (Tel. 01 590 7722)

North Staffordshire Polytechnic, Faculty of Art and Design, College Road, Stoke-on-Trent ST4 2DE (Tel. 0782 45531)

Norwich School of Art, St George Street, Norwich, Norfolk NR3 1BB (Tel. 0603 610561/5)

Plymouth Polytechnic, Drake Circus, Plymouth PL4 8AA (Tel. 0752 21312)

Polytechnic of North London, Holloway Road, London N7 8DB (Tel. 01 607 2789)

Portsmouth Polytechnic, Department of Fine Art, Lion Terrace, Portsmouth PO1 3HF (Tel. 0705 27681)

Ravensbourne College of Art and Design, Walden Road, Chislehurst, Kent BR7 5SN (Tel. 01 468 7071)

College of St Mark and St John, Derriford Road, Plymouth PL6 8BH (Tel. 0752 777188)

St Martin's School of Art, 107 Charing Cross Road, London WC2H 0DU (Tel. 01 437 0611)

Sheffield City Polytechnic, Faculty of Art and Design, Psalter Lane, Sheffield S11 8UZ (Tel. 0742 56101)

South Glamorgan, Institute of Higher Education, Faculty of Art and Design, Howard Gardens, Cardiff CF2 1SP (Tel. 0222 482202)

Stourbridge College of Technology and Art, Church Street, Stourbridge, Worcestershire DY8 1LY (Tel. 038 43 78531)

Sunderland Polytechnic, Faculty of Art and Design, Backhouse Park, Ryhope Road, Sunderland, Co. Durham SR2 7EF (Tel. 0783 41211)

Teesside Polytechnic, Borough Road, Middlesbrough, Teesside TS1 3BA (Tel. 0642 218121)

Trent Polytechnic, School of Art and Design, Burton Street, Nottingham NG1 4BU (Tel. 0602 48248)

West Surrey College of Art and Design, The Hart, Farnham, Surrey GU9 7DS (Tel. 0252 722441)

Wimbledon School of Art, Merton Hall Road, Wimbledon, London SW19 3QA (Tel. 01 540 0231)

Winchester School of Art, Park Avenue, Winchester, Hampshire SO23 8DL (Tel. 0962 61891)

The Polytechnic Wolverhampton, Faculty of Art and Design, Molineux Street, Wolverhampton WV1 1DT (Tel. 0902 29911)

University of Ulster, Art and Design Centre, York Street, Belfast BT15 1ED (Tel. 0232 228515)

Long-term residential colleges for adult students

Coleg Harlech, Harlech, Gwynedd LL46 2PU (Tel. 0766 780363)

Co-operative College, Stanford Hall, Loughborough, Leicestershire LE12 5QR (Tel. 050 982 2333)

Fircroft College, 1018 Bristol Road, Selly Oak, Birmingham B29 6LH (Tel. 021 472 0116)

Hillcroft College, South Bank, Surbiton, Surrey KT6 6DF (Tel. 01 399 2688)

Newbattle Abbey College, Dalkeith, Midlothian EH22 3LL (Tel. 031 663 1921)

The Northern College, Wentworth Castle, Stainborough, Barnsley, South Yorkshire (Tel. 0226 85426)

Plater College, Pullens Lane, Oxford OX3 ODT (Tel. 0865 67626)

Ruskin College, Oxford OX1 2HE (Tel. 0865 54331)

Correspondence colleges accredited by the Council for the Accreditation of Correspondence Colleges (CACC)

Enquiries to Mrs M H Lowe, BA, Secretary, CACC, 27 Marylebone Road, London NW1 5JS (Tel. 01 935 5391)

The Agricultural Correspondence College, Warborough, nr. Oxford OX9 8DQ (Tel. 086 732 8219)

The Association of Dispensing Opticians, 22 Nottingham Place, LONDON W1M 4AT (Tel. 01 935 7411/2)
Preliminary and Final Dispensing examinations courses. ADO Fellowship and Honours diplomas (leading to registration by General Optical Council)

British Careers Training College, Howard House, Esplanade, PO Box 253, JERSEY (Tel. 0534 79034)
Preparatory courses for careers offering good opportunities, particularly in developing countries, written especially for those whose mother tongue is not English.

British National Radio and Electronics School, PO Box 7, Teignmouth, DEVON TQ14 0HS (Tel. 062 67 6114)
Courses and training equipment in Radio, Electronics and Computer Technology.

Burleigh College of Concise Studies, College Road, HARROW, Middlesex (Tel. 01 863 2020)
Salesmanship

Business Training Ltd., Sevendale House, 7 Dale Street, MANCHESTER M1 1JB (Tel. 061 228 6735/6)
English for Business for those whose first language is not English.

The Canine Studies Institute (R.T.C. Associates), London Road, Lily Hill, BRACKNELL, Berks RG12 6QN (Tel. 0344 420898)
Courses leading to proficiency in canine breeding and judging; kennel management.

The Chartered Insurance Institute, Tuition Service, 31 Hillcrest Road, South Woodford, LONDON E18 2JP (Tel. 01 989 8464)
Insurance diploma and certificate courses.

Chart Foulks Lynch Ltd, Correspondence Courses, 53 Great Sutton Street, LONDON EC1V ODQ (Tel. 01 251 4981)
Accountancy

The Civil Service Correspondence School, Ware, Herts (Tel. 0920 5926)
Civil Service Examinations. GCE

College of Estate Management, University of Reading, Whiteknights, READING, Berks RG6 2AW (Tel. 0734 861101)
RCIS, ISVA, and other professional courses in land use, surveying, valuation, estate agency. External degree in estate management; Reading University. Certificate for technicians in quantity surveying.

The College of Law, Braboeuf Manor, St Catherines, GUILDFORD, Surrey GU3 1HA (Tel. 0483 576711)
Final Examination of The Law Society (Previous oral class attendance or Law Society exemption necessary).

College of Management Training Ltd, 30 Ferndale Road, Burgess Hill, West Sussex RH15 OHG (Tel. 044 46 43560)
Accountancy

Co-operative Union Limited, Postal Tuition Section, Stanford Hall, LOUGHBOROUGH, Leics LE12 5QR (Tel. 050 982 2333)
Courses relating to the Co-operative movement.

Ellis School of Surveying and Building, Albany House, WORCESTER WR1 3DZ (Tel. 0905 23706)
Professional and Trade examinations of the Building and Construction Industry.

The Institute of Grocery Distribution, Grange Lane, Letchmore Heath, WATFORD, Herts WD2 8DQ (Tel. 092 76 7141/6 (Radlett 7141)
Distributive Trades Certificates and Diplomas

Ilex Tutorial Services, Kempston Manor, Kempston, Bedford MK42 7AB (Tel. 0234 857711)
Law and Legal Practice for the Institute of Legal Executives, Common Professional Examination and Law Society Finals.

International Correspondence Schools, 312 High Street, SUTTON, Surrey SM1 1PR (Tel. 01 643 9568)
Technical, Professional, Commercial, General Education

London Montessori Centre – Correspondence Division, 18 Balderton Street, LONDON W1Y 1TG (Tel. 01 493 0165)
Courses leading to a teaching diploma in Nursery and Primary Education.

London School of Accountancy, 23–24 Old Bailey, LONDON EC4M 7PG (Tel. 01 248 0321)
Accountancy Courses.

London School of Journalism, 19 Hertford Street, Park Lane, LONDON W1Y 8BB (Tel. 01 499 8250)
Journalism, Short Story Writing, English.

279

May's Correspondence College, Cleveland Road, LONDON E18 2AF (Tel. 01 989 9726)
Institute of Bankers Part I and II

Mercers College, WARE, Herts (Tel. 0920 5926)
General Education. Full-time and Part-time Courses for children of School age.

Metropolitan College, OXFORD, OX2 6PR (Tel. 0865 52200)
Accountancy, Professional, Commercial

Metropolitan School of Machine Knitting-Correspondence Division, 139/141 Windham Road, BOURNEMOUTH BH1 4RQ (Tel. 0202 304581 – 24 Hour answering Service)
Tuition courses for single and double bed knitting machines.

The Methodist Study Centre, Room 70, 1 Central Buildings, Westminster, LONDON SW1H 9NH (Tel. 01 222 8010)
Biblical and Theological courses at basic, intermediary and advanced levels to equip lay and ordained Christians for work in the Church and Community.

NALGO Correspondence Institute, NALGO House, 1 Mabledon Place, LONDON WC1H 9AJ (Tel. 01 388 2366)
Professional and vocational qualifications; GCE subjects

National Extension College, 18 Brooklands Avenue, CAMBRIDGE CB2 2HN (Tel. 0223 316644)
Elementary courses; GCE 'O' and 'A'. Preparatory courses for Open University, Degree and Diploma, Professional, General Interest Courses.

National Marine Correspondence School, 28 Hamilton Street, BIRKENHEAD, Cheshire L41 1AL (Tel. 051 647 6777)
Courses for Yachtsmen (including Department of Trade and Industry Certificates)

The National School of Salesmanship Ltd, Sevendale House, 7 Dale Street, MANCHESTER M1 1JB (Tel. 061 228 6733/4)
Professional Diploma courses

New York Institute of Photography, 16–20 High Road, Wood Green, LONDON N22 6BX (Tel. 01 888 1242)
Photographic Studies

The Northern Institute of Massage/Northern College of Physical Therapies, 100 Waterloo Road, BLACKPOOL, Lancs FY4 1AW (Tel. 0253 403548)
Theoretical studies in massage plus practical work in approved centres.

Pitmans Correspondence College, Worcester Road, Wimbledon, LONDON SW19 7QQ (Tel. 01 947 6993)
Professional and Commercial courses. Secretarial and Secretarial Teachers courses. General Education.

The Rapid Results College, Tuition House, 27/37 St George's Road, LONDON SW19 4DS (Tel. 01 947 2211)
General Education. Professional courses, Commercial courses.

The School of Accountancy and Business Studies, Intertext House, 8 Elliot Place, Clydeway Centre, GLASGOW G3 8EF (Tel. 041 221 2926)

Professional examination courses. Other business and commercial courses.

The School of Herbal Medicine Phytotherapy – Correspondence Division, 148 Forest Road, TUNBRIDGE WELLS, Kent TN2 5EY (Tel. 0892 30400)
Courses in Herbal Medicine.

Transport Tutorial Association, PO Box 4UZ, London W1A 4UZ. (Tel. 01 631 3833)
Institute of Transport examination courses.

Trans-World Tutorial College, 9 The Esplanade, PO Box 42, JERSEY (Tel. 0534 76270)
Introductory courses especially designed in preparation for careers in Commerce and Industry principally in Developing Countries.

The Wheelhouse School of Navigation, Rudley Mill, nr. HAMBLEDON, Hants PO7 6QZ (Tel. 070132 467)
Course for Amateur Yachtsmen with special reference to RYA/DOT Certificate

Wolsey Hall, OXFORD OX2 6PR (Tel. 0865 52200)
General Education. GCE 'O' and 'A'. London University External Degrees. Diploma and Professional Courses. Preparatory Courses for the Open University.

The Writing School, 16–20 High Road, Wood Green, LONDON N22 6BX (Tel. 01 888 1242)
Courses in all forms of writing.

Workers' Educational Association district offices

Berks, Bucks and Oxon: 6 Brewer Street, Oxford OX1 1QP (Tel. 0865 246270)

Eastern: Botolph House, Botolph Lane, Cambridge CB2 3RE (Tel. 0223 350978)

East Midlands: 16 Shakespeare Street, Nottingham NG1 4GF (Tel. 0602 475162)

London: 32 Tavistock Square, London WC1H 9EZ (Tel. 01 387 8966)

Northern: 51 Grainger Street, Newcastle upon Tyne NE1 5JE (Tel. 0632 323957)

North Staffs: Cartwright House, Broad Street, Hanley, Stoke on Trent ST1 4EU (0782 24187)

North Western: 4th floor, Crawford House, Precinct Centre, Manchester M13 9GH (Tel. 061 273 7652)

Southern: 51 London Road, Southampton SO9 5UG (Tel. 0703 29810/29819)

South Eastern: 4 Castle Hill, Rochester, Kent (Tel. 0634 42140)

South Western: Martin's Gate Annexe, Bretonside, Plymouth PL4 0AT (Tel. 0752 664989)

Western: 17 Princess Victoria Street, Clifton, Bristol BS8 4BX (Tel. 0272 732630/732422)

West Lancs and Cheshire: 7/8 Bluecoat Chambers, School lane, Liverpool L1 3BX (Tel. 051 709 8023)

West Midlands: 9–11 Digbeth, Birmingham 5 (Tel. 021 643 0717/8)

Yorkshire North: 7 Woodhouse Square, Leeds LS3 1AD (Tel. 0532 453304/455944)

Yorkshire South: Chantry Building, Corporation Street, Rotherham S60 5GE (Tel. 0709 72121)

North Wales: 33 College Road, Bangor, Gwynedd, N Wales (Tel. 0248 353254)

South Wales: Tawney House, 11 Station Terrace, Conbridge Road West, Cardiff CF5 4AA (Tel. 0222 552277)

North of Scotland: 163 King Street, Aberdeen AB2 3AE (Tel. 0224 642725)

South East Scotland: Riddles Court, 322 Lawnmarket, Edinburgh EH1 2PG (Tel. 031 226 3556)

West of Scotland: 212 Bath Street, Glasgow G2 4HW (Tel. 041 332 0176/7)

Research Councils and sources of funding for postgraduate study

Agricultural and Food Research Council, 160 Great Portland Street, London W1N 6DT (Tel. 01 580 6655)

Department of Education and Science, Postgraduate Awards, Government Buildings, Honeypot Lane, Stanmore, Middlesex HA7 1AZ (Tel. 01 952 2366)

Economic and Social Research Council, Postgraduate Awards Division, 1 Temple Avenue, London EC4Y 0BD (Tel. 01 353 5252)

Medical Research Council, 20 Park Crescent, London W1N 4AL (Tel. 01 636 5422)

Natural Environment Research Council, Polaris House, Northstar Avenue, Swindon SN2 1EU (Tel. 0793 40101)

Science and Engineering Research Council, Polaris House, North Star Avenue, Swindon SN2 1ET (Tel. 0793 26222)

Training Opportunities (TOPS) Schemes. Enquire at Job Centres, Employment Offices or Training Services Division (MSC) District Offices.

Scottish Education Department Awards Branch, Haymarket House, Clifton Terrace, Edinburgh EH12 5DR (Tel. 031 337 2477)

Department of Education for Northern Ireland, Rathgael House, Balloo Road, Bangor, County Down, Northern Ireland BT19 2PR (Tel. 02247 66311)

Local Education Authorities in England, Wales, The Isle of Man and the Channel Islands

Full details about staff employed by LEAs, and addresses of schools and colleges are given in *The Education Authorities Directory*, which should be available for reference in libraries.

Avon County Council, Education Department, PO Box, 57 Avon House North, St James Barton, Bristol BS99 7EB (Tel. 0272 290777)

Barking and Dagenham, Town Hall, Barking, Essex IG11 7LU (Tel. 01 594 3880)

Barnet, Town Hall, Friern Barnet N11 3DL (Tel. 01 368 1255)

Barnsley, Education Department, Bernesial Close, Barnsley S70 2HS (Tel. 0226 87621)

Bedfordshire County Council, County Hall, Cauldwell Street, Bedford, MK42 9AP (Tel. 0234 63222)

Berkshire County Council, Shire Hall, Shinfield Park, Reading RG2 9XE (Tel. 0734 875444)

Bexley, Town Hall, Crayford, Dartford DA1 4EN (Tel. 01 303 7777)

Birmingham, Education Dept, Margaret Street, Birmingham B3 3BU (Tel. 021 235 2590)

Bolton, Education and Arts Department, PO Box 53, Paderborn House, Civic Centre, Bolton BL1 1JW (Tel. 0204 22311)

Bradford, Provincial House, Bradford BD1 1NP (Tel. 0274 752111)

Brent, Education Offices, PO Box 1, 9 Park Lane, Wembley, Middx HA9 7RW (Tel. 01 903 1400)

Bromley, Town Hall, Widmore Road, Bromley, Kent BR1 1SB (Tel. 01 464 3333)

Buckinghamshire County Council, County Hall, Aylesbury, Bucks HP20 1UZ (Tel. 0296 5000)

Bury, Athenaeum House, Market Street, Bury, Lancs BL9 0BN (Tel. 061 761 5121)

Calderdale, Northgate House, Northgate, Halifax HX1 1UN (Tel. 0422 57257)

Cambridgeshire County Council, Shire Hall, Castle Hill, Cambridge (Tel. 0223 317111)

Cheshire County Council, County Hall, Chester CH1 1SQ (Tel. 0244 602424)

Cleveland County Council, Education Offices, Woodlands Road, Middlesborough, Cleveland TS1 1BN (Tel. 0642 248155)

Clwyd County Council, Shire Hall, Mold, Clwyd CH7 6NB (Tel. 0352 2121)

Cornwall County Council, County Hall, Truro, Cornwall TR1 3BA (Tel. 0872 74282)

Coventry, Council Offices, Earl Street, Coventry CV1 5RS (Tel. 0203 25555)

Croydon, Education Department, Taberner House, Park Lane, Croydon CR9 1TP (Tel. 01 686 4433)

Cumbria County Council, Education Department, 5 Portland Square, Carlisle CA1 1PU (Tel. 0228 32161)

Derbyshire County Council, Education Department, County Offices, Matlock DE4 3AG (Tel. 0629 3411)

Devon County Council, County Education Offices, County Hall, Exeter EX2 4QG (Tel. 0392 77977)

Doncaster, Education Department, Princegate, Doncaster DN1 3EP (Tel. 0302 734444)

Dorset County Council, County Hall, Dorchester DT1 1XJ (Tel. 0305 63131)

Dudley, Education Dept, 2 St James's Road, Dudley (Tel. 0384 55433)

Durham County Council, PO Box, County Hall, Durham (Tel. 0385 64411)

Dyfed County Council, Carmarthen, Dyfed SA31 2NH (Tel. 267 234591)

Ealing, Hadley House, 79–81 Uxbridge Road, Ealing W5 5SU (Tel. 01 579 2424)

East Sussex County Council, Education Dept. PO Box 4, County Hall, St Anne's Crescent, Lewes, East Sussex BN7 1SG (Tel. 07916 5400)

Enfield, Civic Centre, Silver Street, Enfield EN1 3XQ (Tel. 01 366 6565)

Essex County Council, Education Dept, Threadneedle House, Market Road, Chelmsford CM1 1LD (Tel. 0245 267222)

Gateshead, Education Offices, Prince Consort Road, Gateshead NE8 4LP (Tel. 0632 783031)

Gloucestershire County Council, Shire Hall, Gloucester GL1 2T (Tel. 0452 21444)

Gwent County Council, County Hall, Croesyceiliog, Cwmbran (Tel. 06333 67711)

Gwynedd County Council, County Education Offices, Caernarfon LL55 1SD (Tel. 0286 5831)

Hampshire County Council, The Castle, Winchester SO23 8UG (Tel. 0962 54411)

Haringey, Education Offices, FE Division, 48–62 Station Road, Wood Green N22 4TY (Tel. 01 881 3000)

Harrow, Civic Centre, PO Box 22, Harrow, Middx HA1 2UW (Tel. 01 863 5611)

Havering, Education Dept, Mercury House, Mercury Gardens, Romford, Essex RM1 3DR (Tel. 0708 66999)

Hereford and Worcester County Council, County Education Office, Castle Street, Worcester (Tel. 0905 353366)

Hertfordshire County Council, County Hall, Hertford SG13 8DF (Tel. 0992 54242, Ext. 5543)

Hillingdon, Civic Centre, Uxbridge, Middx UB8 1UW (Tel. 0895 50529)

Hounslow, The Civic Centre, Lampton Road, Hounslow TW3 4DN (Tel. 01 570 7728)

Humberside County Council, County Hall, Beverley, Humberside HU17 9BA (Tel. 0482 867131)

Inner London Education Authority, The County Hall, London SE1 (Tel. 01 633 1066)

Isle of Man, Board of Education, Education Offices, Central Government Offices, Buck's Road, Douglas, Isle of Man (Tel. 0624 26262)

Isles of Scilly, Town Hall, St Mary's, Isles of Scilly, TR21 0LW (Tel. 0720 22537)

Isle of Wight County Council, Education Department, County Hall, Newport, Isle of Wight PO30 1UD (Tel. 0983 524031)

Kent County Council, Education Department, Springfield, Maidstone, Kent ME14 2LJ (Tel. 0622 671411)

Kingston upon Thames, Directorate of Education and Recreation, Guildhall, Kingston upon Thames K11 1EU (Tel. 01 546 2121 Ext. 2616)

Kirklees, Kirklees Educational Services, Oldgate House, Huddersfield HD1 6QW (Tel. 0484 37399)

Knowsley, Education Department, Huyton Hey Road L36 5YH (Tel. 051 480 5111)

Lancashire County Council, PO Box 61, County Hall, Preston PR1 8RJ (Tel. 0772 54868)

Leeds, 1 Great George Street, Leeds LS1 3AE (Tel. 0552 463000)

Leicestershire County Council, County Hall, Glenfield, Leicester LE3 8RF (Tel. 0533 871313)

Lincolnshire County Council, County Offices, Newland, Lincoln LN1 1YQ (Tel. 0522 29931)

Liverpool, 14 Sir Thomas St, Liverpool L1 6BJ (Tel. 051 236 5480)

Manchester, Education Offices, Crown Square, Manchester M60 3BB (Tel. 061 228 2191)

Merton, Station House, London Road, Morden SM4 5DR (Tel. 01 542 8101)

Mid Glamorgan County Council, Education Offices, County Hall, Cardiff CF1 3NF (Tel. 0222 28033)

Newcastle upon Tyne, Civic Centre, Barras Bridge, Newcastle upon Tyne NE1 8PU (Tel. 0632 328520)

Newham, 379–383 High Street, Stratford E15 4RD (Tel. 01 534 4545)

North Tyneside, Education Offices, The Chase, North Shields (Tel. 0632 576621)

Norfolk County Council, County Hall, Norwich NR1 2DL (Tel. 0603 611122)

Northamptonshire County Council, Northampton House, Northampton (Tel. 0604 34833)

Northumberland County Council, County Hall, Morpeth, Northumberland (Tel. 0670 514343)

North Yorkshire County Council, County Hall, Northallerton (Tel. 0609 3123)

Nottinghamshire County Council, County Hall, West Bridgford, Nottingham NG2 7QO (Tel. 0602 823823)

Oldham, Old Town Hall, Middleton Road, Chadderton, Oldham OL9 6PP (Tel. 061 624 0505)

Oxfordshire County Council, Macclesfield House, New Road, Oxford OX1 1NA (Tel. 0865 722422)

Powys County Council, County Hall, Llandrindod Wells, Powys (Tel. 0597 3711)

Redbridge, 255–259 High Road, Ilford, Essex IG1 1NN (Tel. 01 478 3020)

Richmond, Education Dept, Regal House, London Road, Twickenham, Middx TW1 3QB (Tel. 01 891 1433)

Rochdale, PO Box 70, Municipal Offices, Smith Street, Rochdale OL16 1YD (Tel. 0706 521100)

Rotherham, Education Department, Norfolk House, Walker Place, Rotherham S60 1QT (Tel. 0709 2121)

St Helens, Education Department, Century House, Hardshaw Street, St Helens WA10 1RN (Tel. 0744 24061)

Salford, Education Office, Chapel Street, Salford (Tel. 061 832 9751/ 8)

Sandwell, PO Box 41, Highfield High Street, West Bromwich, West Midlands B70 8RG (Tel. 021 525 7366)

Sefton, Education Department, Town Hall, Bootle, Merseyside L20 7AE (Tel. 051 933 6003)

Sheffield, Education Department, Leopold Street, Sheffield S1 1RJ (Tel. 0742 26341)

Shropshire County Council, The Shirehall, Abbey Foregate, Shrewsbury SY2 6ND (Tel. 0743 222100)

Solihull, PO Box 20, Council House, Solihull B91 3QU (Tel. 021 705 6789)

Somerset County Council, County Hall, Taunton, Somerset TA14 4DY (Tel. 0823 73451)

South Glamorgan County Council, Education Offices, Kingsway, Cardiff CF1 4JG (Tel. 0222 44291)

South Tyneside, Education Department, Town Hall, Jarrow NE32 3LE (Tel. 0914 891141)

Staffordshire County Council, Education Offices, Tipping Street, Stafford (Tel. 0785 3121)

States of Guernsey, States Education Council, Education Department, PO Box No 32, Guernsey (Tel. 0481 23535)

States of Jersey, Education Department, PO Box 142, Highlands, St Saviour, Jersey (Tel. 0534 71065)

Stockport, Education Division, Stopford House, Town Hall, Stockport SK1 3XE (Tel. 061 480 4949)

Suffolk County Council, Education Department, Grimwade Street, Ipswich, Suffolk IP4 1LJ (Tel. 0473 55801)

Sunderland, Town Hall, Civic Centre, Sunderland, Tyne and Wear (Tel. 0783 76161)

Surrey County Council, County Hall, Kingston-upon-Thames KT1 2DN (Tel. 01 546 1050)

Sutton, The Grove, Carshalton, Surrey (Tel. 01 661 5000)

Tameside, Education Dept, Council Offices, Wellington Road, Ashton-under-Lyne, Lancashire OL6 6DL (Tel. 061 330 8355)

Trafford, Education Dept, Council Offices, PO Box 19, Tatton Road, Sale, Cheshire M33 1YR (Tel. 061 973 2253)

Wakefield, Education Offices, 8 Bond Street, Wakefield WF1 2QL (Tel. 0924 370211)

Walsall, Civic Centre, Walsall WS1 1DQ (Tel. 0922 21244)

Waltham Forest, Municipal Offices, High Road, Leyton E10 5QJ (Tel. 01 539 3650)

Warwickshire County Council, Education Offices, 22 Northgate St, Warwick CV34 4SR (Tel. 0926 493431)

West Glamorgan County Council, Department of Education, County Hall, Swansea SA1 3SN (Tel. 0792 471111)

West Sussex County Council, County Hall, Chichester, Sussex PO19 1RF (Tel. 0243 777100)

Wigan, Gateway House, Standishgate, Wigan WN1 1XL (Tel. 0942 494929)

Wiltshire County Council, County Hall, Trowbridge, Wilts BA14 8JB (Tel. 02214 3641)

Wirral, Education Department, Municipal Offices, Cleveland Street, Birkenhead, Merseyside L41 6NH (Tel. 051 647 7000)

Wolverhampton, Civic Centre, Wolverhampton (Tel. 0902 27811)

Education Authorities in Scotland

Borders: Borders Regional Council, Regional Headquarters, Newtown St Boswells, Roxburghshire TD6 0SA (Tel. 08352 3301)

Central: Central Regional Council, Viewforth, Stirling FK8 2ET (Tel. 0786 3111)

Dumfries and Galloway: Education Offices, 30 Edinburgh Road, Dumfries DG1 1JQ (Tel. 0387 63822)

Fife: Regional Offices, Wemyssfield, Kirkcaldy, Fife KY1 1XS (Tel. 0592 262351)

Grampian: Grampian Regional Council, Woodhill House, Aberdeen AB9 2LU (Tel. 0224 682222)

Highland: Regional Buildings, Glenurquhart Road, Inverness IV3 5NX (Tel. 0463 234121)

Lothian: Education Department, 40 Torphichen Street, Edinburgh EH3 8SS (Tel. 031 229 9292)

Orkney, Council Offices, Albert Street, Kirkwall, Orkney KY15 1NY (Tel. 0856 3535)

Shetland: Education Offices, 1 Harbour Street, Lerwick, Shetland ZE1 0LS (Tel. 0595 3535)

Strathclyde: Strathclyde House, 6 India Street, Glasgow G2 6NR (Tel. 041 204 2900)

Tayside: Tayside House, 28 Crichton Street, Dundee DD1 3RA (Tel. 0382 23281)

Western Isles: Council Offices, Sandwick Road, Stornoway, Isle of Lewis PA87 2BW (Tel. 0851 3773)

Education and Library Boards in Northern Ireland

Belfast Area: 40 Academy Street, Belfast BT1 2NQ (Tel. 0232 229211)

North Eastern Area: County Hall, 182 Galgorm Road, Ballymena, County Antrim BT42 1HN (Tel. 0266 3333)

Southern Area: 3 Charlemont Place, The Mall, Armagh BT1 9BA (Tel. 076 252 3811)

South Eastern Area: 18 Windsor Avenue, Belfast BT9 6EF (Tel. 0232 661188)

Western Area: Education Office, 1 Hospital Road, Omagh BT79 0AW (Tel. 0662 44431–9)

Directory of Educational Guidance Services for Adults (1985)

Published by the Educational Counselling and Credit Transfer Information Service (ECCTIS) and the National Association of Educational Guidance Services for Adults (NAEGS)
The criteria used here for listing an EGSA is that each Service offers:

* Educational guidance independently of the interests of any supporting agency or institution.
* Educational guidance as its primary function.
* Educational guidance primarily for the general public.
* Educational guidance across the whole range of continuing education.
* Educational guidance free of charge.
* Educational guidance in most, if not all, of its elements: information, assessment, advice, counselling, implementation.

Projects and other activites doing work similar to EGSAs, but which may offer fewer of the elements of educational guidance, across a narrower range of education, or to more closely specified client groups, are marked★ and a brief description of their scope is given.

London and South East England

1. Aylesbury
Name: **Education Information Service for Adults**
Address: Youth and Community Department, County Hall, AYLESBURY HP20 1UZ
Telephone: 0296 5000 extn. 674
Contact: George Cook
Note: An occasional service, taking place at Amersham, Aylesbury, High Wycombe and Milton Keynes.

2. Camden
Name: **Camden Adult Learning Advice (CALA)**
Address: 58 Phoenix Road, LONDON NW1 1EU
Telephone: 01 388 4666
Contact: Val Forsyth or Anna Patterson

3. East Grinstead
Name: **Educational Advisory Service for Adults (EASA)**
Address: Open University, Wyvern House, 230–232 London Road, EAST GRINSTEAD RH19 1LA
Telephone: 0342 27821
Contact: Dick Darby

4. Fulham and South Kensington
Name: **Education and Training Advice for Adults**
Address: c/o Fulham and South Kensington Institute, Beaufort House, Lillie Road, LONDON SW6 1UF
Telephone: 01 381 0801 (direct) or 01 385 6167 (for messages)
Contact: Sue Thurston or any adviser

★ 5. Medway
One of four CET-funded projects focusing on non-formal learning opportunities and using a computerised database and interactive guidance program. This Service is aimed at unemployed adults.
Name: **Learning Links**
Address: Adult Education Centre, Green Street, GILLINGHAM, Kent.
Telephone: 0634 53429
Contact: Moira Henderson or Alan Deighton

6. Greenwich
Name: **Greenwich Education and Training Advice Centre (GRETA)**
Address: 12–14 Wellington Street, LONDON SE18 6PF
Telephone: 01 854 2993
Contact: Ruth Bird or Hansa Sehdev or Rob Imeson

7. Hackney
Name: **Hackney Education Advice Service**
Address: Advice Centre, 236 Mare Street, Hackney, LONDON E8 1HE
Telephone: 01 986 8446
Contact: Alison McGarry or Anne Short

8. Hatfield
Name: **Educational Guidance for Adults (EGA)**
Address: PO Box 109, HATFIELD AL10 9AB
Telephone: 07072 79499
Contact: Ruth Michaels

9. Islington

Name: **Education Advice Service for Islington Adults (EASIA)**
Address: c/o ILEA Learning Materials Service, Highbury Station Road, LONDON N1 1FB
Telephone: 01 226 9143 extn. 48
Contact: Jenny Clayton

10. Lambeth

Name: **Lambeth Education Opportunities (LEO)**
Address: Strand Centre, Elm Park, LONDON SW2 2EH
Telephone: 01 671 2961
Contact: Liz Smith

11. Lewisham

Name: **Lewisham Education Advice Project (LEAP)**
Address: Temporary premises, Deptford Library, Lewisham Way, LONDON SE14 6PP
Contact: Linda Byrne

12. London

Name: **Education Advice Line**
Address: BBC Radio London, 35a Marylebone High Street, LONDON W1A 4LG
Telephone: 01 486 7040 Thursdays only (3 pm to 5 pm)
Contact: Patsy Brown

13. North Kensington

Name: **Kensington and Chelsea Learning Advice for Adults**
Address: c/o HANKAEI, Wornington Road, LONDON W10 5QQ
Telephone: 01 968 8532
Contact: Mana McClew or Deborah Lowen (Co-ordinator)

14. Southwark

Name: **Information and Advice Network on Southwark Education and Training (INSET)**
Address: Education and Training Shop, 175 Rye Lane, Peckham, LONDON SE15 4TL
Telephone: 01 635 9111/9112
Contact: Any adviser

15. Sutton

Name: **Adult Education Advisory Service**
Address: Sutton College of Liberal Arts, St Nicholas Way, SUTTON SM1 1EA
Telephone: 01 661 5067
Contact: Paddy Powell

16. Tower Hamlets

Name: **The Education Shop (Tower Hamlets Education Advice)**
Address: 75 Roman Road, Bethnal Green, LONDON E2
Telephone: 01 981 3164
Contact: Kevin Burton or Francoise de Casparis

17. Wandsworth
Name: **Wandsworth Education Shop**
Address: 86 Battersea Rise, LONDON SW11
Telephone: 01 350 1790
Contact: Ros Gillham or Martin Oakeshott or Teri Riley

18. Westminster
Name: **Westminster Education Advice Project**
Address: Pimlico School, 17 Lupus Street, LONDON SW1
Telephone: 01 630 7298
Contact: John Brown or Caroline Fry

East Anglia

19. Cambridge
Name: **Cambridge Educational Guidance Service for Adults**
Address: Community Education, Shire Hall, Gloucester Street, CAMBRIDGE CB3 0AP
Telephone: 0223 317841
Contact: The Field Tutor for Community Education
Note: This Service available Mondays only (10 am to 1 pm), telephone 0223 64941.

20. Ipswich
Name: **Suffolk Educational Advisory Service for Adults**
Address: Education Department, Grimwade Street, IPSWICH IP4 1LJ
Telephone: 0473 55801 extn. 4414
Contact: Neil Williams

21. King's Lynn
Name: **Educational Guidance for Adults in Lynn (EGAL)**
Address: Orchard Hall, Norfolk College, Tennyson Avenue, KING'S LYNN
Telephone: 0553 61144 extn. 245
Contact: Paul Richards or Stephen Fish

22. Peterborough
Peterborough Educational Guidance Service (PEGS) is expected to be launched in 1985. Further information from:
Name: Jill Navid
Address: Community Education, Touthill Close, City Road, PETERBOROUGH PE1 1UJ
Telephone: 0733 52481 extn. 248

Midlands

23. Bedford
Name: **Educational Advice Centre**
Address: Bedford College of Higher Education, Adult Education Centre, 10 Rothsay Gardens, BEDFORD
Telephone: 0234 47914
Contact: Hilary Ferry

24. Luton

Name: **Educational Guidance for Adults Service**
Address: The Library, Luton College of Higher Education, Park Square, LUTON
Telephone: 0582 34111 extn. 293
Contact: Lee Hill
Note: A pilot service, currently available Mondays only (1.30 pm to 4.30 pm), though appointments may be made at any time.

25. Birmingham

Name: **Adult Learners' Enquiry Centre (ALEC)**
Address: Birmingham Central Library, Chamberlain Square, BIRMINGHAM B3 3HQ
Telephone: 021 233 2260
or
Address: Faculty of Education, City of Birmingham Polytechnic, Westbourne Road, Edgbaston, BIRMINGHAM B15 3TN
Telephone: 021 454 3550
Contact: Barrie Thompson

⋆ 26. Birmingham

This Service concentrates on educational assessment and vocational aptitude testing and analysis for the unemployed.
Name: **SCOT Vocational and Education Advice Centre**
Address: Solihull College of Technology, Chelmsley Annexe, Chapelhouse Road, BIRMINGHAM B37
Telephone: 021 770 2597 (Mondays to Wednesdays only)
Contact: Jane Macmillan

27. Cheltenham

Name: **Adult and Continuing Education Advisory Service**
Address: College of St Paul and St Mary, The Park, CHELTENHAM GL50 2RH
Telephone: 0242 528111 extn. 53
Contact: Peter Whiteley

⋆ 28. Northamptonshire

Name: **Educational Guidance for Adults in Northamptonshire (EGAN)**
Address: Delapre Middle School Annexe, Main Road, Far Cotton, NORTHAMPTON NN4 9EN
Telephone: 0604 66793
Contact: Gil Smith or Lüise Heron

⋆ 29. Nottingham

FEU-funded research project aimed at improving educational guidance and provision for unemployed adults in Nottingham. Further information from:
Name: Karen Beggs or Caroline Baker
Address: Basford Hall College, Stockhill Lane, NOTTINGHAM NG6 0NB
Telephone: 0602 704541

*30. Nottinghamshire
First phase of an ALBSU-funded country-wide Service focused on basic education operating from late 1985 at the Berridge Centre of Clarendon College. Further details from:
Name: Pat Green
Address: Berridge Centre, Stanley Road, Forest Field, Nottingham NJ7 6HW
Telephone: 0602 780942

31. Oxfordshire
Name: **Links in Adult Information Services on Education (LIAISE)**
Address: Open University, Foxcombe Hall, Boars Hill, OXFORD OX1 5HR
Telephone: 0865 730731
Contact: Stephanie Clennell

North East England

32. Bradford
Name: **Education Advice Service for Adults (EASA)**
Address: Central Library, Princes Way, BRADFORD BD1 1NN
Telephone: 0274 753658
Contact: Vivienne Rivis or Colin Neville

33. Halifax
Name: **The Education Shop**
Address: 2 Crossley Street, HALIFAX
Telephone: 0422 42106
Contact: Tony Lilley

34. Hull
Name: **Educational Guidance Service for Adults (EGSA)**
Address: c/o Careers Information Centre, Union Street, Albion Street, HULL HU2 8HB
Telephone: 0482 223081
Contact: Gwen Crozier

35. Leeds
Name: **Leeds Educational Guidance Service**
Address: Department of Education, Selectapost 18, Merrion House, 110 Merrion Centre, LEEDS LS2 8JN
Telephone: 0532 463829
Contact: Geoff Ford
or
Name: **Drop-In Education and Advice Centre**
Address: 54 The Corn Exchange, Vicar Lane, LEEDS LS1 7BR
Telephone: 0532 459816
Contact: Jane Riddell

36. Leeds

Name: **Education Advice for Adults**
Address: c/o Bramley Community Centre, Waterloo Lane, Bramley, LEEDS LS13 2JB
Telephone: 0532 556231
Contact: Reg Cliffe or Mary Myers
Note: Open Mondays and Wednesdays (9 am to 12 noon) and Thursdays (9 am to 2.45 pm). At other times contact Pam Thorne on (0532) 560664

37. Newcastle upon Tyne

Name: **Linked Educational Advisory Service for Adults (LEASA)**
Address: Room 10, 2 Ellison Place, NEWCASTLE UPON TYNE NE1 6EU
Telephone: 0632 329735
Contact: Margaret Locke

38. Rotherham

Name: **Live and Learn**
Address: Education Office, Norfolk House, Walker Place, ROTHERHAM S60 1QT
Telephone: 0709 2121 extn. 3197
Contact: Chris Morecroft

39. Sheffield

Name: **Sheffield Educational Information Service for Adults (SEISA)**
Address: Leader House, Surrey Street, SHEFFIELD S1 2LH
Telephone: 0742 755126
Contact: Frank Lipman

40. South Tyne and Wear

Name: **Linked Educational Advisory Service for Adults (LEASA), South Tyne and Wear**
Address: West Park Community Centre, Whitehall Street, SOUTH SHIELDS NE33 4SU
Telephone: 0632 568093 (Monday to Wednesday)
or
Address: Mowbray Villas, Ryhope Road, SUNDERLAND
Telephone: 0783 76474 (Thursday and Friday)
Contact: Eileen O'Connor or Clare Ambrose

41. Wakefield

Name: **Educational Counselling and Guidance for Adults**
Address: Wakefield Library Headquarters, Balne Lane, WAKEFIELD WF2 0DQ
Telephone: 0924 371231 extn. 24
Contact: Anna Salkeld or Mabel McGowan (Wednesdays only)

North West England

42. Bolton
Name: **Access Unit**
Address: Hilden Street Centre, Bolton Metropolitan College, BOLTON BL2 1JB
Telephone: 0204 31411 ext. 267
Contact: Melanie Tebbutt

43. Bury
Name: **Bury Educational and Training Advice (BETA)**
Address: Whitefield Centre, Higher Lane, Whitefield, MANCHESTER M25 7FX
Telephone: 061 766 6704
Contact: Sheila Morris or Susan Spencer

44. Lancaster
Name: **Educational Information and Counselling Service for Adults**
Address: Room D12, Lancaster College of Adult Education, St Leonard's House, St Leonardgate, LANCASTER LA1 1NN
Telephone: 0524 60141
Contact: Jeff Leonardi

45. Manchester
The Manchester Education Advice Service for Adults has three Information and Advisory Officers:

Central Area
Address: Central Area Community Education, 9 Anson Road, Victoria Park, MANCHESTER M14
Telephone: 061 224 8241
Contact: Letitia Opie (Service Co-ordinator, to whom general enquiries should be addressed)

North Area
Address: Miles Platting Community Education Centre, Holland Street, MANCHESTER M10 7AF
Telephone: 061 205 3594
Contact: Jane Barrett

South Area
Address: The Birtles Community Education Centre, Town Centre, Wythenshawe, MANCHESTER M22 5RF
Telephone: 061 499 1455 extn. 30
Contact: Ethne Freeman

46. Stockport
Name: **Stockport Education Advice Service for Adults SEASA**
Address: Stockport Job Centre, Merseyway, STOCKPORT
Telephone: 061 480 0351 extn. 144
Contact: Ann Rogerson

47. Tameside
Name: **Tameside Educational Advice Centre**
Address: Community Education Centre, Beeley Street, HYDE
Telephone: 061 368 1622
Contact: Norma Watkins or Liz Green

48. Warrington
Name: **Education Advice Centre**
Address: North Cheshire College, Faculty of Adult and
Community Studies, Museum Street, WARRINGTON
WA1 1HU
Telephone: 0925 52423
Contact: Judith Summers or Ken Kilbey

49. Wigan
Name: **Contact for Learning and Educational Opportunities
(CLEO)**
Address: Education Department, Gateway House, Standishgate,
WIGAN WN1 1XL
Telephone: 0942 827912
Contact: Bridget Fielding

Southern England

50. Portsmouth
One of four CET-funded projects focused on non-formal learning
opportunities and using a computerised database and interactive
guidance program.
Name: **Learning Links**
Address: John Pounds Centre, St. James Street, Portsea,
PORTSMOUTH PO1 3AP
Telephone: 0705 754287
Contact: Mary Barka or Jil Cuthberg

51. Reading
Name: **Reading Educational Guidance Service for Adults
(REGSA)**
Address: 18 Cross Street, READING
Telephone: 0734 581754
Contact: Stephen Pass or John Sykes

52. Southampton
Name: **Southampton Education Information Centre for
Adults**
Address: c/o The Argyle Centre, Argyle Road, SOUTHAMPTON
SO2 0BQ
Telephone: 0703 332676
Contact: Margaret Jones or Meg Ryves

South West England

53. Bath
Name: **Adult Advisory Service**
Address: City of Bath College, Avon Street, BATH BA1 1UP
Telephone: 0225 312191
Contact: John Manley

54. Devon and Cornwall
Name: **NETWORK (Advice Service for Adult Education)**
Address: Herondyke, West Charleton, KINGSBRIDGE TQ7 2AA
Telephone: 054853 289
Contact: Bob Pim
or
Address: Hayne Corfe, Dobbs Lane, TRURO TR1 3NA
Telephone: 0872 74503
Contact: John Hurst

55. Dorset
A Service for the county is under consideration. Two pilot schemes will be operating from 1986. Further information from:
Name: **Janet Roberts, Assistant County Co-ordinator for Adult Literacy and Numeracy**
Address: Commanders House, Constitution Hill Road, POOLE BH14 0QB
Telephone: 0202 682157

56. West Wiltshire
Name: **West Wiltshire Educational Advice for Adults**
Address: Trowbridge Technical College, College Road, TROWBRIDGE BA14 0ES
Telephone: 02214 66241 extn. 62
Contact: Keith Hopper
or
Address: Devizes Branch College, Southbroome, DEVIZES SN10 5AB
Telephone: 0380 3989
Contact: Marcus Toyne

57. Yeovil
Name: **Educational Guidance Service for Adults**
Address: Yeovil College, Ilchester Road, YEOVIL BA21 3BA
Telephone: 0935 23921 extn. 212
Contact: Mark Sutton or Allen Parrott

Northern Ireland

58. Belfast
Name: **Educational Guidance Service for Adults**
Address: Room 208, Bryson House, 28 Bedford Street, BELFAST BT2 7FE
Telephone: 0232 244274
Contact: Dorothy Eagleson

★59. Derry
One of four CET-funded projects focusing on non-formal learning opportunities and using a computerised database and interactive guidance program. This Service is aimed at unemployed people.

Name:	**Learning Links**
Address:	Centre for the Unemployed, 5/7 Antillery Street, DERRY
Telephone:	0504 260630
Contact:	Peter O'Hagan or Marguerite Enwright

Scotland

60. Scotland

Name:	**Network**
Address:	74 Victoria Crescent Road, GLASGOW G12 9JQ
Telephone:	041 357 1774
Contact:	Anne Docherty

★61. Dundee
MSC-funded information Service aiming for long-term status and full range of EGSA activities.

Name:	**Links to Learning**
Address:	Room 9, YMCA, 10 Constitution Road, DUNDEE
Telephone:	0382 26004
Contact:	John Lacy

★62. Edinburgh
Registered charity offering short courses and community projects.

Name:	**Edinburgh University Settlement**
Address:	Kirk O'Field College, 29 Guthrie St, EDINBURGH EH1 1JY
Telephone:	031 226 3801
Contact:	Bonnie Dudley or John Palmer

★63. Stornoway
Initially CET-funded projects focusing on non-formal learning opportunities and using a computerised database and interactive guidance program.

Name:	**Learning Links**
Address:	Public Library, Keith Street, STORNOWAY, Isle of Lewis, PA87 2QG
Telephone:	0851 3064
Contact:	Robert Eaves or Calum Hunter

Wales

64. Clwyd
EARS (Education for Adults Referral Service) is being re-formed. Enquiries in the first instance to:

Name:	**Gerson Davies**
Address:	Shire Hall, MOLD
Telephone:	0352 2121 extn. 2523
	or

Name: Maureen Polly
Address: Adult Education Office, Rhyl High School, Grange Road,
RHYL
Telephone: 0745 31609

Compiled by Linda Butler

Useful addresses

Adult Education Bursaries, The Awards Officer, c/o Ruskin College, Oxford OX1 2HE (Tel. 0865 54331) or, Welsh Office, Education Department, Cathays Park, Cardiff CF4 5PL (Tel. 0222 825111)

Advisory Centre for Education (ACE), 18 Victoria Park Square, London E2 9PB (Tel. 01 980 4596)

Agricultural and Food Research Council, 160 Great Portland Street, London W1N 6DT (Tel. 01 580 6655)

Art and Design Admissions Registry, Imperial Chambers, 24 Widemarsh Street, Hereford HR4 9EP (Tel. 0432 266653)

The Arts Council of Great Britain, 105 Piccadilly, London W1V 0AU (Tel. 01 629 9495) *and* 19 Charlotte Square, Edinburgh EH2 4DF (Tel. 031 226 6051) *and* Holst House, Museum Place, Cardiff CF1 3NX (Tel. 0222 394711) *and* 181A Stranmillis Road, Belfast BT9 5DU (Tel. 0232 663591)

Association of Commonwealth Universities, 36 Gordon Square, London WC1H 0PF (Tel. 01 387 8572)

Association of Graduate Careers Advisory Services (AGCAS), Central Services Unit, Crawford House, Precinct Centre, Manchester M13 9EP (Tel. 061 273 4233)

British Association for Commercial and Industrial Education (BACIE), 16 Park Crescent, London W1N 4AP (Tel. 01 636 5351)

British Computer Society, 13 Mansfield Street, London W1 (Tel. 01 637 0471)

The British Council, 10 Spring Gardens, London SW1A 2BN (Tel. 01 930 8466) *and* 1 Chlorine Gardens, Belfast BT9 5DJ (Tel. 0232 666611) *and* 3 Bruntsfield Crescent, Edinburgh EH10 4HD (Tel. 031 447 4716) *and* 6 Belmont Crescent, Glasgow G12 8ES (Tel. 041 339 8651)

British Institute of Management, Management House, Parker Street, London WC2B 5PT (Tel. 01 405 3456)

British Medical Association (BMA), BMA House, Tavistock Square, London WC1H 9JR (Tel. 01 387 4499)

Business and Technician Education Council (BTEC), Central House, Upper Woburn Place, London WC1H OHH (Tel. 01 388 3288)

Cambridge Intercollegiate Applications Office, Kellet Lodge, Tennis Court Road, Cambridge CB2 1QJ (Tel. 0223 355796)

Careers Consultants Ltd, 12–14 Hill Rise, Richmond, Surrey TW10 6UA (Tel. 01 940 5668)

Careers Information Unit, Fife, Albany House, Glenrothes, Fife KY7 5NZ (Tel. 0592 754411)

Careers and Occupational Information Centre (COIC), Manpower Services Commission, Moorfoot, Sheffield S1 4PQ (Tel. 0742 753275) *and* 5 Kirk Loan, Corstorphine, Edinburgh EH12 7HD (Tel. 031 334 9821)

Careers Research and Advisory Centre (CRAC), Hobsons Ltd, Bateman Street, Cambridge CB2 1LZ (Tel. 0223 354551)

Central Bureau for Educational Visits and Exchanges, Seymour Mews House, Seymour Mews, London WC1H 9PE (Tel. 01 486 5101) *and* 3 Bruntsfield Crescent, Edinburgh EH10 4DH (Tel. 031 447 8024) *and* Malone Road, Belfast BT9 5BN (Tel. 0232 664418)

Central Council for Education and Training in Social Work (CCETSW), Derbyshire House, St Chad's Street, London WC1H 8AD (Tel. 01 278 2455) *and* 9 South St David Street, Edinburgh EH2 2BY (Tel. 031 556 2953) *and* West Wing, St David's House, Wood Street, Cardiff CF1 1ES (Tel. 0222 26257) *and* 14 Malone Road, Belfast BT9 5BN (Tel. 0232 665 390)

The Central Register and Clearing House Ltd, 3 Crawford Place, London WC1H 2BN

Central Services Unit for Careers and Appointments Services (CSU), Crawford House, Precinct Centre, Manchester M13 9EP (Tel. 061 273 4233)

Channel Islands Education Authorities (see Appendix 11)

Charities Aid Foundation, 48 Pembury Road, Tonbridge, Kent TN9 2JD (Tel. 0732 356323)

Child Poverty Action Group, 1 Macklin Street, Drury Lane, London WC2 5NH (Tel. 01 242 3225)

The Clearing House for CQSW Courses, 4th floor, Myson House, Railway Terrace, Rugby CV21 3HT (Tel. 0788 75443)

The Clearing House for Postgraduate Courses in Art Education, Imperial Chambers, 24 Widemarsh St, Hereford HR4 9EP (Tel. 0432 266653)

Colleges of Art and Design (see Appendix 6)

Colleges of Education (Technical) (see Appendix 4)

Colleges and Institutes of Higher Education (see Appendix 3)

Commission for Racial Equality (CRE), Elliot House, 10/12 Allington Street, London SW1E 5EH (Tel. 01 828 7022)

Committee of Vice Chancellors and Principals (CVCP), 29 Tavistock Square, London WC1H 9EZ (Tel. 01 387 9231)

Correspondence Colleges (see Appendix 8)

Council for the Accreditation of Correspondence Colleges (CACC), 27 Marylebone Road, London NW1 5JS (Tel. 01 935 5391)

Council for National Academic Awards (CNAA), 344/345 Grays Inn Road, London WC1 8BP (Tel. 01 278 4411)

Department of Education for Northern Ireland (DENI), Rathgael House, Balloo Road, Bangor, County Down BT19 2PR (Tel. 0247 66311)

Department of Education and Science (DES), Elizabeth House, York Road, London SE1 7PH (Tel. 01 934 9000) and Government Buildings, Honeypot Lane, Stanmore, Middlesex HA7 1AZ (Publications Despatch)

Department of Health and Social Security (DHSS), Alexander Fleming House, Elephant and Castle, London SE1 (Tel. 01 407 5522)

Department of Health and Social Security, Students' Unit, Room 311, Government Buildings, Warbreck Hill, Blackpool, Lancs FY2 0XW (Tel. 0253 52311, ext. 462)

Disablement Income Group (DIG), Attlee House, Toynbee Hall, 28 Commercial Street, London E1 6LR (Tel. 01 247 2128/6877)

Economic and Social Research Council, 1 Temple Avenue, London EC4Y 0BD (Tel. 01 353 5252)

Educational Counselling and Credit Transfer Information Service (ECCTIS), Walton Hall, Milton Keynes (MK7 6AA) (Tel. 0908 368921)

Educational Grants' Advisory Service (EGAS), The Family Welfare Association, 501–505 Kingsland Road, London E8 4AU (Tel. 01 254 6251)

Educational Guidance Services for Adults (see Appendix 14)

Engineering Careers Information Service, Gresham House, 54 Clarendon Road, Watford, Herts WD1 1LB (Tel. 0923 38441)

Engineering Council, 2 Little Smith Street, Westminster, London SW1P 3DL (Tel. 01 222 3912)

Equal Opportunities Commission, Overseas House, Quay Street, Manchester M3 3HN (Tel. 061 833 9244) and Scottish Regional Office, 249 West George Street, Glasgow G2 4QE and Welsh Regional Office, Caerwys House, Windsor Place, Cardiff CF1 1LB

The Family Welfare Association, 501–505 Kingsland Road, London E8 4AU (Tel. 01 254 6251)

General Teaching Council for Scotland, 5 Royal Terrace, Edinburgh EH7 5AF (Tel. 031 556 0072)

Graduate Teacher Training Registry, 3 Crawford Place, London W1H 2BN

Health Education Council, 78 New Oxford Street, London WC1A 1AH (Tel. 01 637 1881)

Her Majesty's Stationery Office (HMSO), Government Bookshop, Brazennose House, Brazennose Street, Manchester 2 (Tel. 061 834 7201) *and* 13a Castle Street, Edinburgh EH2 3AR (Tel. 031 225 6333)

Hobsons Ltd, Bateman Street, Cambridge CB2 1LZ (Tel. 0223 354551)

Institute of Linguists Educational Trust, Mangold House, 24A Highbury Grove, London N5 2EA (Tel. 01 359 7445)

Isle of Man Board of Education, Government Offices, Buck's Road, Douglas, Isle of Man (Tel. 0624 26262)

Joint Matriculation Board (JMB), Manchester M15 6EU (Tel. 061 273 2565)

Local Education Authorities in England, Wales, The Isle of Man and the Channel Islands (see Appendix 11)

Long-term Residential Adult Colleges (see Appendix 7)

Manpower Services Commission, Moorfoot, Sheffield S1 4PQ (Tel. 0742 753275)

Medical Research Council, 20 Park Crescent, London W1N 4AL (Tel. 01 636 5422)

National Advisory Centre on Careers for Women (NACCW), Drayton House, 30 Gordon Street, London WC1H 0AX (Tel. 01 380 0117)

National Association of Educational Guidance Services (NAEGS), Chairman: Jonathan Brown, The Open University, Eldon House, Regent Centre, Newcastle upon Tyne NE3 3PW (Tel. 091 284 1611)

National Bureau for Handicapped Students (NBHS), Thomas Coram Foundation, 40 Brunswick Square, London WC1N 1AZ (Tel. 01 278 3459/3450)

National Consultative Committee for Agricultural Education, Shire Hall, Bury St Edmunds, Suffolk IP33 2AN

National Extension College (NEC), 18 Brooklands Avenue, Cambridge CB2 2HN (Tel. 0223 316644)

National Institute of Adult Continuing Education (NIACE), 19b de Montfort Street, Leicester LE1 7GE (Tel. 0533 551451)

National Institute for Careers Education and Counselling (NICEC), Balls Park, Hertford SG13 8QF (Tel. 0992 558451)

National Union of Students (NUS), 461 Holloway Road, London N7 6LZ (Tel. 01 272 8900)

National Environment Research Council, Polaris House, Northstar Avenue, Swindon SN2 1EU (Tel. 0793 40101)

Northern Ireland Adult Education Association, c/o 5 Hareshill Drive, Bangor, County Down

The Open University, Walton Hall, Milton Keynes MK7 6AA (Tel. 0908 74066)

The Open University Regional Centres (see Appendix 1.2)

Oxford Colleges Admissions Office, University Offices, Wellington Square, Oxford OX1 2JD (Tel. 0865 54501)

Polytechnics (see Appendix 2)

Polytechnics Central Admissions System (PCAS), PO Box 67, Cheltenham, Glos. GL50 3AP (Tel. 0242 526225)

Research Councils (see Appendix 10)

Residential Colleges Committee, c/o Ruskin College, Oxford OX1 2HE (Tel. 0865 54331)

Royal Association for Disability and Rehabilitation (RADAR), 25 Mortimer Street, London W1N 8AB (Tel. 01 637 5400)

Royal Academy of Music, 34 Marylebone Road, London NW1 5HT (Tel. 01 935 5461)

Royal College of Veterinary Surgeons, 32 Belgrave Square, London SW1X 8QP (Tel. 01 235 4971)

Royal Institute of British Architects (RIBA), Finsbury Mansions, Moreland Street, London EC1V 8VB (Tel. 01 580 5533)

Royal Society of Arts, John Adam Street, London WC2N 6EZ (Tel. 01 930 5115)

Science and Engineering Research Council, Polaris House, Northstar Avenue, Swindon SN2 1ET (Tel. 0793 26222)

Scottish Business Education Council (SCOTBEC), 22 Great King Street, Edinburgh EH3 6HQ (Tel. 031 557 4555)

Scottish Central Institutions (see Appendix 5). For the Scottish Central Institutions Handbook, write to the Assistant Registrar, Paisley College of Technology, High Street, Paisley PA1 2BE (Tel. 041 887 1241)

Scottish Community Education Department, Atholl House, 2 Canning Street, Edinburgh EH3 8EG (Tel. 031 229 2433)

Scottish Education Department, 43 Jeffrey Street, Edinburgh EH1 1DN (Tel. 031 556 9233)

Scottish Education Department, Awards Section, Haymarket House, Clifton Terrace, Edinburgh EH12 5DR (Tel. 031 337 2477)

Scottish Institute of Adult Education, 30 Rutland Square, Edinburgh EH1 2BW (Tel. 031 229 0331)

Scottish Technical Education Council (SCOTEC), 38 Queen Street, Glasgow G1 3DY (Tel. 041 204 2271)

Scottish Universities Council on Entrance (SUCE), Kinnessburn, Kennedy Gardens, St Andrews, Fife, KY16 9DR (0334 72406)

Secondary Heads Association, Gordon House, 29 Gordon Square, London WC1H 0PS (Tel. 01 359 9286)

Special Education Resource Information Service (SERIS), Anson Road, Manchester (Tel. 061 225 8319)

Standing Conference for the Advancement of Counselling (SCAC), 26 Bedford Square, London WC1B 3HU (Tel. 01 488 3555)

Standing Conference of Principals and Directors of Colleges and Institutes in Higher Education (SCOPDCIHE), Edge Hill College of Higher Education, St. Helens Rd, Ormskirk, Lancashire L39 4QP

Trades Union Congress (TUC), Congress House, Great Russell Street, London WC1B 3LS (Tel. 01 636 4030)

Unit for the Development of Adult Continuing Education (UDACE), 19b de Montfort Street, Leicester LE1 7GE (Tel. 0533 551451)

United Kingdom Council for Overseas Student Affairs (UKCOSA), 60 Westbourne Grove, London W2 5FG (Tel. 01 229 9268/9)

United States–United Kingdom Educational Commission, 6 Porter Street, London W1A 2LH (Tel. 01 486 7697)

Universities (see Appendix 1)

Universities Central Council on Admissions (UCCA), PO Box 28 Cheltenham, Glos. GL50 1HY (Tel. 0242 519091)

University of the Third Age (U3A), 6 Parkside Gardens, London SW19 5EY (Tel. 01 947 0401)

Welsh Office: Education Department, Crown Building, Cathays Park, Cardiff CF1 3NQ (Tel. 0222 825111)

Workers' Educational Association (WEA), Temple House, 9 Upper Berkeley Street, London W1H 8BY (Tel. 01 402 5608) *and* 1 Fitzwilliam Street, Belfast BT7 6AW (0232 229718) *and* (North of Scotland District), 163 King Street, Aberdeen AB2 3AE (Tel. 0224 642725) *and* (South West Scotland District), Riddles Court, 322 Lawnmarket, Edinburgh EH1 2PG (Tel. 031 226 3456) *and* (West of Scotland District), 212 Bath Street, Glasgow G2 4HW (Tel. 041 332 0176), *(see also Appendix 9)*

References

Hopper, E and Osborn, M (1975) *Adult Students: education, selection and social control*. Frances Pinter

Nisbet, J and Welsh, J (1972) 'The mature student', *Educational Research*, **14**, (3)

Roderick, G W and Bell, JM (1981) '"Unqualified" mature students at the University of Sheffield', *Studies in Higher Education*, **6**, (2)

Roderick, G W, Bell, J M and Hamilton, S (1982) 'Unqualified mature students in British universities', *Studies in Adult Education*

Walker, P (1975) 'The university performance of mature students', *Research in education*, No. 14, November

Ward, Peter and Lucas, Susan (1984) 'Mature students in higher education' (mimeo)

Woodley, Alan (1985) 'Taking account of mature students', in Jaques, David and Richardson, John, *The Future of Higher Education*, SRHE and NFER-Nelson

Index